Pistol Packin' Mama

Music in American Life

A list of books in the series appears at the end of this book.

Pistol Packin' Mama

Mama

AUNT MOLLY JACKSON AND
THE POLITICS OF FOLKSONG

Shelly Romalis

UNIVERSITY OF ILLINOIS PRESS

URBANA AND CHICAGO

Publication of this book was supported by a grant from
the L. J. and Mary C. Skaggs Folklore Fund.

1 2 3 4 5 C P 5 4 3 2 1

This book is printed on acid-free paper.

Library of Congress Cataloging-in-Publication Data

Romalis, Shelly, 1939–
Pistol packin' Mama : Aunt Molly Jackson and the politics of
folksong / Shelly Romalis.
p.   cm. — (Music in American life)
Includes bibliographical references (p.   ) and index.
ISBN 0-252-02421-4 (acid-free paper)
ISBN 0-252-06728-2 (pbk. : acid-free paper)
1. Jackson, Aunt Molly.
2. Singers—United States—Biography.
3. Protest songs—United States—History and criticism.
I. Title.
II. Series.
MS420.J15R66   1999
782.42'159'092—ddc21   [B]
98-19726
CIP   MN

Contents

PART 3: MUSIC, POLITICS, AND WOMEN'S RESISTANCE

Illustrations follow page 88

Acknowledgments

So many have talked to me, helped with research leads, listened to my papers, offered feedback and support since I started this journey in 1989 in Toronto. The beginnings were serendipitous: in one of Pete Seeger's writings, he referred to Aunt Molly in passing, noting that much had been written about Woody Guthrie—but nothing about Molly. Later, trying to locate this source, I called Pete to ask him about this. He couldn't recall writing it, but graciously shared some memories of Aunt Molly, and encouraged me to do the study. A few months later, in California, sitting at the Mill Valley dinner table of labor economist Dick Liebes and his wife Brun, I mentioned that I was trying to track down a book by the folklorist Archie Green. Dick allowed that he didn't know where to find the book . . . but he did know where to find Archie, who lived just across the Golden Gate Bridge in San Francisco! Shortly after, Bob Witmer, ethnomusicologist at York University, led me to Judith McCulloh, now an assistant director at the University of Illinois Press.

York University awarded me small research grants (SSHRC and Faculty of Arts); colleagues Marlene Kadar, Jane Couchman, Ann Shteir, Gus Thaiss, Margaret Rodman, and my administrative assistant in Interdisciplinary Studies, Agatha Campbell, showed special interest in the project; students in my graduate anthropology/women's studies course continue to inspire me. Terry Aihoshi's wonderfully organized tape transcriptions made tons of material visible that otherwise might have gone unnoticed. Archives and libraries like the Southern Folklife Collection at the University of North Carolina, particularly David Camp and Michael Taft, the

Schlesinger Library at Radcliffe College, the librarians at Southern California Library for Social Studies and Research, Gary Lundell at the University of Washington, Seattle, and the Archives of Folk Culture at the Library of Congress, especially Joe Hickerson, who I called many times to tap his encyclopedic knowledge—all were very helpful in my research.

In Seattle, Jim Garland's widow, Hazel Garland, and daughter, Margaret Garland Harrington, warmly opened their lives and photograph albums to me. Earl Robinson and Hazel Dickens spent hours talking with me about their encounters with Molly and Sarah. A memorable visit to Tillman Cadle, up a snaking, leaf-covered track to his cabin high in the Smokey Mountains, plunged me into the atmosphere and memorabilia of a mountain life long disappeared; with the exception of his taste for freshly ground coffee shipped to him by Margaret Harrington in Seattle, Tillman could have been living in 1930s Appalachia, surrounded by guns and dogs. Henrietta Yurchenco granted me two extensive interviews in person, telling me of her radio show and experiences with Molly, Sarah, Woody, Leadbelly, and the other musical transplants. Hedy West, Pete Seeger, Alan Lomax, and Alice McLerran spoke to me on the phone. Alice shared her colorful memories, recorded interview, and correspondence with Molly, while her brother Don Enderton dug up copies of obituaries and went searching in vain for Molly's Sacramento home. Mimi Pickering and Julia Ardery also were very helpful with information and support. Ellen Stekert graciously gave me permission to use quotes from her searching interviews with Sarah Gunning. The readers of my manuscript in draft versions—Deborah Vansau McCauley and an anonymous University of Illinois Press reader offered vital advice for improvements to the manuscript. Marlene Kadar's early feedback, Kate Dunlay's careful editing of one of the last drafts, and Jackie Esmond's source checking were invaluable. At the University of Illinois Press, Margo Chaney wore out her red pencil on my penultimate draft. Theresa Sears and my copy editor, Louis Simon, made it a better book. Judith McCulloh had faith before I did that the story would someday emerge and enthusiastically supported the entire process. Her advice to "write for the world" (presidential address to the American Folklore Society in 1987) continues to inspire me, along with other authors, to reach broader audiences. My deep thanks to all of them.

I owe a great debt to my son, Liam, and daughter, Milena, and my music friends for essential soul nurturing during the research and writing years: in Toronto, my fiddle teacher and friend, David; Celtic musicians Kate, Jean, and Karen; my "Woods" colleagues and friends, especially Sue, Grit, Ken; the San Francisco Scottish Fiddlers, especially Alasdair, Duncan, Margaret, Pate, Judy, Andrea, Terry, Kathy, and Howard. Louanne Green suggested the great term "amanuensis," and showed heroic patience while I perched in her kitchen and living room endlessly chattering, laughing, arguing with Archie.

And the two men who changed my life: Archie Green permeates these pages with tireless passion for debate and energy for labor lore archaeology. His contribution to the fields of folklore and ethnomusicology, and generous help to students and colleagues, are inestimable. Coleman Romalis, my life partner, whose amazing critical eye, joy for learning, and editorial skill I constantly rely on, helps me daily to find the path. To them I dedicate this book and a thousand flowers.

A Note on Available Recordings

If you would like to hear Aunt Molly Jackson's and Sarah Gunning's songs, excellent discographies exist in Jim Garland's book *Welcome the Traveler Home*. Aunt Molly's only available commercial recording is vinyl: *Aunt Molly Jackson,* Rounder 1002, Library of Congress. John Greenway sings Molly's songs accompanied by her voice telling the stories on *The Songs and Stories of Aunt Molly Jackson,* Folkways FH 5457. Sarah's two commercial (also vinyl) recordings are *Girl of Constant Sorrow,* Folk Legacy FSA 26, 1965, and *The Silver Dagger,* Rounder 0051. Mimi Pickering's documentary *Dreadful Memories* (Appalshop Films) contains live footage of Sarah. Both women's songs were recorded by others, e.g., Pete Seeger's *American Industrial Ballads* includes Molly's "Fare Ye Well, Old Ely Branch," and Mike Seeger included Sarah's "Come All You Coal Miners," on *Tipple, Loom & Rail,* Folkways FH 5273. Jim sings "The Ballad of Harry Simms" and "I Don't Want Your Millions, Mister" on *Newport Broadside: Topical Songs at the Newport Folk Festival, 1963,* Vanguard VRS 9144. Pete Seeger recorded a number of Jim's songs on *Songs of Struggle and Protest, 1930–1950,* Folkways FH 5233.

Ronald Cohen and Dave Samuelson have co-produced a ten-CD compilation set with accompanying book: "Songs for Political Action: Folk music, Topical Songs and the American Left, 1926–1953," Bear Family Records BCD 15720, 1996. They include Aunt Molly's original Columbia recording "Ragged Hungry Blues," parts 1 and 2, and Sarah Gunning's "I'm Going to Organize Baby Mine," from the original Library of Congress recording, 1937.

Pistol Packin' Mama

Introduction: "Hungry Ragged Blues"

November 1931. The self-styled "people's" team of inquiry into labor and living conditions in the coalfields of Appalachia finally arrive in Harlan County, Kentucky, for a two-day visit. Coal miners and their wives wait, nervously preparing testimonies. Haggard faces in the Arjay Baptist Church hall on this frosty winter day betray immeasurable demoralization from months of striking, food deprivation, and mine accidents. A graying midwife in a faded muslin dress sits in front of the panel to attest to the tyranny of the mine operators. Defiance and passion in her voice, she alerts the northern delegation: this is no ordinary witness. But when she sings her own "Ragged Hungry Blues," the harsh nasal tones mesmerize them, penetrating to the bottom of their souls, capturing in starkly poetic phrases months of desperation in Harlan and Bell Counties. Theodore Dreiser's committee of distinguished writers quickly discern the enormous symbolic potential of this miner's wife, metaphor for Appalachia—forgotten backwater, dominated, ravaged, and imprisoned by coal operators and their gun thugs, yet resonant with a fiercely independent spirit of resistance. New York intellectual radicals "discover" Aunt Molly Jackson at fifty years of age. Her life will change so dramatically that even she, blessed with a most fertile imagination, cannot prophesy it.

Mary Magdalene Garland (Mills?) Stewart Jackson Stamos, born in 1880 in the Kentucky mountains, became one of the most intriguing figures on the American folk-music stage. She brought a distinctive singing style to radical political activism and labor organizing, leaving an imprint on such icons of American folk culture as Pete Seeger, Woody Guthrie,

Alan Lomax, and members of the musical and intellectual elite, Elie Siegmeister, Earl Robinson, and John Dos Passos. Her songs, fusing life experience with rich Appalachian musical tradition, conveyed a deep awareness of social injustice. They became her weapons of struggle—narratives of resistance.

Molly's extraordinary journey took her three thousand miles from Kentucky to Sacramento, California. When death arrived in 1960, her prominent role in the "bloody Harlan" strike, and the attention she garnered through Dos Passos's published writings, had long been forgotten. Only a handful of family and friends paid respects at her funeral on September 10; her grave in the Odd Fellows Lawn Cemetery next to her last husband, Tom, remains to this day, unmarked. Lula, her niece and only neighboring relative, quickly disposed of Molly's few tattered belongings in the little house on Fourth Street. Scraps of paper on which she penciled her songs were tossed out with the trash.

The northern investigators' trip to Harlan is an apt place to begin Aunt Molly's story because it marks, too, the beginning of her public fashioning. In December 1931, sponsored by the visiting delegation, Molly left Kentucky for New York City. She and younger brother Jim Garland, who followed shortly afterward, had an explicit mandate: to be firsthand emissaries and fundraisers for the striking miners. The northern radicals knew that the Garlands' song compositions, their own words written to old Appalachian hymns and ballads, depicted conditions more graphically than any journalist's pen.

Molly spent the next year traveling and appealing to audiences in various northern cities until an incapacitating bus accident in Ohio confined her to a flat on New York's Lower East Side. Sarah, Jim's sister and half-sister to Molly, joined them in 1936, and with sporadic visits home to Appalachia, the Kentuckians remained on the Lower East Side for another six years. Their community of neighbors and associates included other "real folk" such as Huddie Ledbetter (Leadbelly) and Woody Guthrie, and young urban radicals—Pete Seeger, Alan Lomax, Earl Robinson, Lee Hays. Shared interests and creative sparks among these unlikely cohorts during the 1930s inspired sociologist Serge Denisoff's term "proletarian renaissance" for the mini-folk revival culminating at the end of the decade, merging music with working class consciousness and progressive intellectual values.[1]

The Garlands (and I would argue, especially Molly) defined Southern Appalachia for their urban political allies. As "cultural brokers," they forged a symbolic bridge between working-class rural Appalachian coal-mining life and sophisticated big-city political activism. With one physical journey from Kentucky to New York City, they crossed several social boundaries: from rural to urban, working to middle class, traditional to modern, periphery to center. But in the political structure built by the urban activists, including Aunt Molly and the Garland family, ideological commitment and similarity of perspective transcended disparities of class, culture, and experience.

Molly, Jim, and Sarah were not only living, breathing exemplars of Appalachian mountain culture, but models of working people's courage and resistance, writing and singing songs that articulated class consciousness. Although a mere fraction of these songs appeared on commercial sound recordings and even fewer have lingered longer than their historical moment, the real Garland legacy extends beyond their musical repertoires.

I approach the Garlands as an anthropologist with an interdisciplinary bent. Their lives inform popular history and illuminate relationships among region, class, gender, music, and politics. Of the three Garlands, Molly interests me the most for some of the same reasons that gripped Dreiser and Dos Passos on their visit to Kentucky. How well her "authentic" representation fit with their preconceptions of Appalachia! The poetry of her song texts, raw and unschooled, contrasted with the elegant phrases of the literary set. Moreover, her identity as a woman became a cluster point for acquired meaning: she spoke with passion from the heart, from experience. The northerners could not have found a more credible model for espousing the cause. Aunt Molly Jackson was the perfect miners' voice.

Compared to Jim and Sarah, Molly's character remains complex and contested. Proud, self-involved, she grabbed opportunities for public attention. She loved to embarrass, offend, goad, threaten those she saw as adversaries, delighting in their discomfort. Molly assured journalists that she was the "real" "Pistol Packin' Mama," in the Tin Pan Alley song. Her husband's cousin wrote it to commemorate Molly's gun-toting exploits, she claimed—and not, as everyone believed, popular songwriter Al Dexter. With chameleon ease, she shifted from charming and generous one moment to belligerent, acerbic, crassly sexual the next. If potential sources of admiration or money came along, Molly would use any ploys at her disposal: fawning and groveling were in her strategic grab bag. Her relationships—volatile, unpredictable, and uneasy—often disintegrated into mutual disillusionment. Acquaintances comparing notes found glaring inconsistencies in her stories, ultimately agreeing that she was not a reliable source.

Still, many found Molly Jackson fascinating. In the early 1930s, New York University English professor Mary Elizabeth Barnicle considered the mountain woman a treasure trove of Appalachian cultural lore and intended to base a scholarly book on her extensive interview notes. When she eventually became suspicious of the veracity of Molly's stories, Barnicle shelved the project. (Molly told it differently: she didn't want Barnicle to write her life story because the professor used fancy, high falootin' talk). Folklorist Alan Lomax, regarding Molly as a quintessential source of traditional song style, befriended the miner's wife, and recorded her songs for the Library of Congress—despite Molly's pleadings, cajolings, and reproaches in her correspondence to Lomax (who she claimed never told her what the recordings were for). According to Molly, Lomax failed to pay for her songs or help publish her writings. John Greenway, another folklorist, clearly enamored of Molly, used her as a key informant for his doctoral thesis and subsequent 1953 book, *American Folksongs of Protest.* When her voice became too enfeebled by illness and age, Greenway himself sang her ballad versions and compositions for a commercial recording, prefaced by Molly's own narrations. But Greenway, too, would subsequently denounce her as an unreliable source, even though he called her a "great woman as well as a truly great informant."[2] Folklorist Archie Green, ferreting out song origins while researching *Only a Miner,* tried to uncover the sources and paths of Molly's versions. Green's lengthy, probing interviews, taped in Molly's Sacramento living room during her final years in the late 1950s, reveal his frustration with her elastic responses. Her elaborations, flexible dates, imperious claims to song authorship, and centrality in events were often inconsistent with those of others. She might even contradict her own prior accounts. When challenges or discrepancies were pointed out, Molly remained unfazed.

The contrasts between Molly and her younger half sister, Sarah Ogan Gunning, are striking. All who had encountered both women, either in person or by reputation, noted and underscored their differences. Their personalities couldn't have been more antithetical, one wily, boisterous, and a braggart, the other, direct, modest, and even-tempered. Molly's can-tankerousness grated on people while Sarah's gentle, dignified manner won them. Molly claimed to have written songs since she was a child, whereas Sarah wasn't inspired to compose until she moved to New York City. Molly saw herself as a communicator, a leader, and radical defender of the oppressed; Sarah's primary identity was wife and mother, and a tru-er bearer (than Molly) of Appalachian tradition.

Molly, extremely smart, flaunted her extraordinary memory, and confidently filled its gaps with her own creative versions of the truth. In-furiated when she thought that another had "mommicked" (messed up) her songs, Molly insisted that her versions held priority. The older Appa-lachian woman's detracters deemed her an opportunist with an inflated sense of self-importance, given to "stretching her blanket" (a kind south-ern mountain term for exaggeration). Sarah, equally quick-minded but self-effacing, drew others to her solidity, honesty, and "authenticity." Regarded as a trusted friend who put others' needs above her own, Sarah emerged as "the real singer" in the Garland family. She was lukewarm, even resentful, toward her older sister Molly, and if not for the overlapping years in New York City, the parties and benefit events that threw them together, probably would have avoided Molly's company entirely. Sarah consciously and doggedly constructed herself as an "opposite" to her old-er, dominant, half-sister.

The time periods framing each sister's life afford the most obvious comparison. Molly was born in 1880, thirty years earlier than Sarah, and died in 1960, twenty-three years before Sarah. Their shared father, Oliver Perry Garland, remarried after his first wife Deborah died, leaving two liv-ing (of four) children, Molly and her brother, John. Oliver sired eleven more (including Jim and Sarah) with his second wife, Elizabeth. Sarah's story then begins when Molly's ended, with some overlap in the middle. Sarah "came into her own" when organizers invited her to perform at northern folk music festivals during the commercial revival in the 1960s and although never a darling of the media, she gained a modicum of at-tention. Molly never lived to see this wider appreciation of traditional music.

The sisters' lives bridged more than a century, paralleling the transfor-mation of American culture and politics. In more geographically specific terms, Molly grew to adulthood before coal mining came to Appalachia, while during Sarah's early years it was becoming an established part of the regional culture and economy. The decades between Molly's birth in 1880 and Sarah's death in 1983 thus provide a screen interweaving various issues relating to music, politics, and gender.

Contrasts between the women, their relationships, and cultural historical events that contextualize their lives, all pique my interest. Jim Garland's autobiography, *Welcome the Traveler Home,* edited by Julia Ardery while Jim was still alive, was published in 1983, several years after his death (in 1978). Although he was apparently disappointed that the Appalachian material he spent years collecting could not be included in the final book, its publication constituted an enormous achievement that would have made Molly envious. A number of scholars interviewed and wrote about Sarah, but as far as I know, song texts were her only autobiographical outlets. Molly, motivated by an intense desire to communicate her specialness, and possibly because she knew of Jim's plans to write a book, yearned to publish an autobiography. She regaled interviewers and acquaintances with exploits, dramatically embellishing them with dialogue and shifting voices. A gifted performer, Molly played her audience, whether one or hundreds, scrutinizing faces for reactions, hoping someone would record and publish her dictation or penciled notes. Although the occasional typist turned up who fine-tuned her colorful prose, Molly's attempt to recruit potential collaborators for a joint book-writing endeavor met with little success. Molly's passionate unfinished business became one motivation for my story here.

It might be useful at this point to consider some issues that inspire anthropological debate regarding truth telling and authenticity. Was Molly's sense of self-worth exaggerated, as so many claimed? Did her particular lens cloud any possibility of reliable historic reconstruction? And if so, does it mean we discount or dismiss her tellings in favor of others' versions?

Some would argue that "subjective truth," although a valid part of identity production, distinguishes itself from "historical truth."[3] But how do we search for truth when scholars now challenge the very nature of data collection and text construction? In these postmodern times, the ethnographic canon—born out of the notion of "objective" fieldwork—trembles to its very core. Some regard it as a body of masked reflections, fictionalized creations by a variety of authors whose class, gender, age, ethnicity, and personality locate and represent the subject.[4] Others remind us that discourses cannot be decontextualized, researchers politically shape their findings, disciplinary or departmental politics influence studies, scholarly perspectives, and grant applications.[5] ⊃

Alessandro Portelli, with an illuminating methodological approach to oral history, argues that "historical, poetical and legendary narratives often become inextricably mixed up."[6] For him, the very subjectivity of the speaker forms the "unique and precious" part of a narrative. This subjectivity enables us to see how people order, make sense of, contextualize their pasts. He notes the irony in the historian's favoring of written rather than oral sources. The former, which often rely on the "uncontrolled transmission of unidentified oral sources,"[7] may be even more removed from so-called historical truth. Historians, he argues, shaping discourse and grammar, ultimately control their sources. The true radical historian not only becomes a character in the life drama, but acknowledges her/his role.

Paralleling scholarly reconsideration of ethnographic and historical "truths," feminist theory and method poses epistemological challenges to taken-for-granted masculinist assumptions. Gender, for Henrietta Moore a fundamental principle of social organization, "can no more be marginalized in the study of human societies than can the concept of 'human action,' or the concept of society."[8] Aunt Molly Jackson, Sarah Ogan Gunning, and Jim Garland, were not just Appalachians or Kentuckians, but women and men with gendered identities. Feminist inquiry, drawing its problematics from women's experience, understands knowledge as politically constituted and never disinterested, challenging notions of scientific objectivity. It demands, too, a reflexive stance: How do we, as researchers, choose subjects? How do our gendered perceptions, experiences, guide analyses? As a feminist anthropologist, I am especially interested in how gender differences are produced and negotiated by informants and scholars.[9] Writings about women by anthropologists like Ruth Behar and Marjorie Wolf bulge with reflections on their own perspectives and authorings.[10] They render story collaboration and production visible, integral to the tellings. Not only do women, as agents of change, have to be reclaimed historically; gender difference is inextricably bound up with the way people think about power—a gendered history is by definition, a fuller history.[11]

All but the most conservative scholars, whether feminist or not, now question the notion of a single historical "truth." Without swinging over to an extreme relativist position—"no truth" only "text"; or everything as "equally true"—we can recognize that multiple historical accounts depend on one's vantage point. The perspectives of the hitherto unrecorded also lie in wait. Despite Molly's contradictory testimonies, her insistence on being at the center of every struggle, her stories clearly have "historical validity." Even if she made what others perceived as untrue statements, they nevertheless would be "psychologically true," since I agree with Portelli's view that "there are no 'false' oral sources."[12] This echoes the idea that all oral history (and, of course, written history) is imaginative re-creation or "structured remembrance" that reflects social, political, and ideological intervention.[13]

In her autobiographical fragments, Molly did not simply keep a diary of events as they happened. Journalists, scholars, acquaintances, for whom this Appalachian mountain woman served as a symbol of a disappearing culture, contoured, in large part, her "structured remembrances." Molly's Communist and left-wing associates inspired her to continually reinvent herself as a radical, a resistance fighter, a voice against the injustices of a capitalist system.

Fierce inner forces drove Molly to make her mark on history, to offer her personal vision, the benefits of her experience to younger generations. Langness and Frank see autobiography as a process of self-creation, a struggle for personal freedom, and a revolutionary act. "Through this medium, people who exist somehow on the margins of mainstream America . . . have shaped self-images of their own design. . . . And their lives become available by the autobiographer's own intent, or simply by the act of publication, as models for other human beings who share certain conditions with the writer."[14]

Although Molly failed to have her story published or make her life "available," the very act of writing as a middle-aged woman must have offered her a sense of order and control. She understood impotence but pugnaciously pushed on, believing that writing songs and telling stories would make a difference. They would open people's eyes to oppression: class, religious dogmatism, racism, bureaucracy, intellectual arrogance, rigid sexual inhibitions.

I would argue that Molly also understood the consequences and constraints of gender. Although she tended to use the language of class rather than sexual politics and had no access to an articulated feminist discourse, women's particular struggles as wives and mothers captured her: she knew how to engage others by writing and singing about these. Perceiving the world through an Appalachian woman's eyes, from the stance of a midwife, she professed special interest, a deliberate role in the creation of life. Molly's outrage at miners' mangled bodies, at children's hunger, came from one who claimed responsibility for life's beginnings. Her songs became narratives, strategies of resistance.

The "facts" or details of Molly's story remain, for me, less important than her mission to be heard. She chose, of course, between different personal and historical truths, but actively processed and produced a popular history, which can potentially transform and shape larger consciousness.

Molly's life is particularly fascinating when contrasted to Sarah's, and placed within family and community. Several key settings bracket her story: coal-mining Kentucky during the first decades of this century; New York City during the Depression years; diverse intellectual and political frameworks of the folk music "revivals"; women's resistance in historical and cross-cultural contexts. Molly and Sarah become paradigms, thrown into relief by cultural and political factors that condition individual experience. Their lives and songs are inseparable from the relationships and circumstances that inspired them, the routes they traveled, and the huge boundaries they crossed.

The Southern Appalachian mountains, where the Garlands' stories begin, pulled journalists and scholars for over a century. The "isolated," largely fundamentalist Baptist mountain region set an ideal stage for contemplating cultural survivals, tradition, internal colonialism, and cultural hegemony. Notions of a backward population arrested in a time warp attracted a variety of saviors: benevolent workers, educators, song collectors.[15]

Appalachia's complex symbolic construction overlay a rather straightforward case of political and economic exploitation. At the turn of the century, abundant timber and coal resources lured outside business interests to whom farmers sold their land. Developers built railroad networks to accommodate resource extraction, connecting the region to national and international markets. Bituminous coal-mining companies forged the final and most wholesale link with a world economy. During the first two decades of this century, industrial fuel needs swelled Appalachian production. Competition from European mines after the First World War, however, as well as from other sources of fuel and rising shipping costs, caused a decline in the demand for coal. Lower market prices and plummeting wages threw the once relatively prosperous coal communities into depression.[16]

By the end of the 1920s, Southern Appalachian miners' conditions worsened. They were hungry, indebted to company stores, exposed to constant danger of mine explosions, sickness, and accidental death. In

1931, in desperation, some miners turned away from the conciliatory stance of John L. Lewis's United Mine Workers Union (and his autocratic leadership) toward the alternative Communist-led National Miners Union (NMU). The NMU organizers sent to Harlan provided the miners with a class-based model and some hope for resisting the mine bosses. The "Bloody Harlan" strike of 1931–32, despite its disastrous failure, became (and many argue it still is) emblematic of working-class struggle and courageous labor defiance. Tracked closely on the front pages of the New York Communist paper, the *Daily Worker,* as well as the less partisan *New York Times,* the Harlan strike thrust the coal miners into a world arena and, irrevocably, altered worker consciousness.

In organizing resistance, miners drew upon a thriving traditional musical heritage. Mountain people accustomed to singing about events, amusing experiences, love and work, enjoyed invoking and sharing family versions of ballads. Songs communicated life, reflected and crafted a people's history. When mining companies industrialized the region, singers reached into their repertoires for familiar tunes, and composed songs of resistance. New texts matched with old gospel or ballad melodies not only expressed frustration or despair, but hopes for decent wages and working conditions, articulating an emerging proletarian class consciousness.

Women didn't go down in the mines during the first half of the century but were, nevertheless, integral to mining economy. Some women worked for wages as mine operators' domestics, others took in boarders and washing, but all directly and perpetually suffered the consequences of dangerous work conditions, paltry mine wages, and debt relationships with the company store. Coal camp women rose before dawn to pack miners' lunch pails, trekked long distances for water, food, and wood, children clinging to their dresses. Frequent mining accidents confined women, themselves barely out of childhood, to continuous caretaking of maimed husbands, or to widowhood. But women, too, died from disease or in childbirth. As Jim Garland tells us, "Many a mountain man outlived both his first wife and a second."[17] In mining communities, women conveyed their experiences singing at the kitchen table, at the creek while washing, or to their children at bedtime. Some would personalize family ballads or blend new stories with old tunes, incorporating, during labor strife, themes of protest and resistance. In 1931, mine operators' hired gun thugs forced their way into Florence Reece's log cabin in Straight Creek to search for her husband, Sam. After they left, Florence scribbled her outrage in the form of a song on her kitchen wall calendar, to the tune of a familiar broadside ballad, *Jackie Frazier*. "Which Side Are You On" would become one of the most poignantly familiar and lasting statements of class conflict. Women in Piedmont textile communities also wrote songs of resistance. Ella May Wiggins's "Mill Mother's Lament" gave voice to the hardships of balancing child care with meager wages and night shift work. After gun thugs hired by mill owners murdered the young working mother in 1929 during the Gastonia, North Carolina, strike, mourners sang her heart-wrenching ballad at the graveside.

Women's stories are more apt than those of men to focus on everyday events, life-cycle turning points, relationships, marriage, childrearing, aging. In this way women's writing often reveals an "embeddedness" that seems to transcend cultural or class difference.[18] Since documented incidents of women's resistance commonly focus on home and family, they appear geared to preserving traditional (male) dominance hierarchies. But domestic radicalism can also lead to revolutionary consequences. Women's strikes and riots initially inspired by food deprivation, rising prices, perceived threats to reproductive and family welfare, inevitably draw participants into regional, national, even international arenas. Women camping at the perimeter American airbase in Britain, Greenham Common, as a simple statement about creating a peaceful world for their offspring, soon become aware of the links among militarism, poverty, and women's abuse.[19] In Argentina, the Madres de La Plaza de Mayo translate the despair of personal searches for lost children into a profoundly radical understanding of the politics of terrorism. In much the same way, symbolic actions of resistance serve to empower individuals and solidify groups. Union activist Mother Jones's army of women wielding kitchen pots and pans, Greenham Common women weaving spider webs on the stark green wire fence around the perimeter of the base—both invoke potent symbols, dramatizing connections among the domestic, women's collective visions, and large political concerns. The women's actions in all of these cases are strategic and instrumental expressions of maternalist political discourses, rather than simply reflections of "essential" womanhood.

Although women in Appalachia sang songs of all kinds, many reflected a gender subtext: family or domestic concerns, responsibility, or relationship to others, the particular effect of poverty and powerlessness on them as women, and on their men, marriages, and children. Whether particular compositions entered tradition (as in Florence Reece's case), and/or were contextualized by a particular historical period (Molly Jackson, Sarah Gunning, Ella May Wiggins), the songs form part of a less visible dimension of regional and class memory. Through these women's songs we know not only of the difficult and tragic lives of coal miners and textile workers but of wives, mothers, and women workers. Through them we unearth an expanded people's history.

Although Molly and Sarah quarried their personal ordeals and tragedies for their song texts, they intended to, and indeed expressed, communal sentiments. They incorporated, created, and configured popular memory. As poignant documents of ordinary Appalachian women's and men's lives, they universalized experience. Searching for compelling common ground, particularly responsibility for children, Molly and Sarah attempted to engage others in collective struggle for political change. A vehicle for mobilizing class and gender consciousness, their songs served as what James C. Scott would call "weapons of the weak," and the "stuff of revolution."[20]

I've not yet considered the cultural politics surrounding Molly's life and times, integral to comprehending her reality as well as my own perspective. Several issues keep surfacing throughout this research: one relates to radical and Communist shaping of traditional music; the other to the slippery and problematic notion of authenticity.

Folklorist Archie Green maintains that if not for Communist and left-wing romanticization and co-optation of traditional music and regional archetypes in service of their ideological cause, the Garlands would have remained mute in their communities, unheard of and unknown to us.[21] In my view, while there is no question that radical interests have influenced, even determined, the Garlands' historical paths, we have to look more closely at the dynamics—actors, relationships, places—in this social drama.

"People's music" resonates with meaning that extends beyond its revolutionary marching referents. A music from and of the folk contrasted with a refined, elite, educated music, has served as a critical cultural bridge between classes, regions, and genders. It communicated class difference and struggles in the 1930s, functioned to bond culturally diverse rural people and urban scholars and radicals during the 1930s and 1940s, and reached large audiences during the revival or "folk boom" from the late 1950s through the early 1970s.

Molly died in 1960, too early for the great boom in folk music's popularity. But, it burrowed its way soon afterward into Sarah's basement apartment in Detroit, Michigan, giving her a newfound celebrity. Sarah came into her own after Molly's death. In 1964, she performed at the Newport Folk Festival, and in the following years until her death in 1983, appeared at a number of other festivals and concerts around North America. In a way, the Newport experience for Sarah in the 1960s was like the Dreiser inquiry for Molly in the 1930s—a discovery, a chance for a new beginning, an appreciation of her Appalachian traditional ballads and style as well as her own compositions. Molly would have whirled in her grave if she knew her younger sister stood in the spotlight on a festival stage. A pact with the devil wouldn't have been too great a price for such a golden opportunity!

Sarah's role in the 1960s folk revival in contrast to Molly's place in the earlier folk renaissance also highlights issues relating to definitions of folk music, as well as to the uses of authenticity and tradition. The term "folk music" has been subject to much debate, but many associate it with recently composed, folk-like, protest song—products of the urban revival rather than with a resurgence of traditional music. Some insist that "folk music" should not share the category with "traditional music," since the former's reputation has been somewhat tarnished by its political (and/or popular) associations. Hair splitting aside, folk-music scholars generally agree that although all songs have been authored, a "real" folksong must be appropriated or adopted by others in the community. The origin of the song, might, but not necessarily, be forgotten as it enters tradition. Although few would argue that songs are merely transmitted as learned or deny that singers innovate, most emphasize the integrity and continuity of style and content. John Greenway quotes Molly's unambiguous definition of folksong: "'This is what a folk song realy is the folks composes there own songs about there own lifes an there home folks that live around them.'"[22]

When Aunt Molly—one of the real folk—wrote about or adapted songs about her life and times, they qualified as folksong. I suspect, though, that she wasn't concerned if others didn't sing them. In fact, if they did, Molly's claim to authorship might be (as it often was) called into question. Moreover, others might have "mommicked them" or messed them up. Sarah perceived and presented herself as more of a channeler, a communicator of old songs. She told Archie Green that she never heard the term "folksong" until she went to New York, that they just called them "songs." Sarah emphasized (probably to counterpoint Molly's claims) that she wrote her own songs only after coming north.

The shaping of tradition and authenticity is of special interest in the Appalachian context. Legendary British song collector Cecil Sharp imprinted his own notion of real folksong on our legacy (and that of the Appalachians) as he uncovered survivals of the pure English ballad in what he perceived as an isolated, anachronistic pocket of the new world. Representations of an authentic musical tradition through selective collection, sound recording, and commercial distribution continued to define Appalachian regional repertoire in the early twentieth century. We have thus a rather skewed legacy as well as a prime example of how dominant class interests can selectively shape the past. Scholars are exploring how Western market interests influence, sometimes even determine, traditional artists' production.[23] Whether these interests are academic or commercial, they define the nature of "desirable material." Informant and researcher become engaged in an interactive process of reflection and memory alteration. The questions—Whose song is it? Where did you learn it?—develop into ideological clashes over identity, right, privilege. With economic or social status advantages accruing to the composer/ writer, the authorship of specific versions of songs and tunes matters greatly. Folklorists' interests, song collectors, commercial radio or record producers, and copyright laws all contribute to claims for the "most" traditional or authentic, to "structured remembrances."[24] At the very least, tradition is pliant and dynamic, and even those who perceive themselves as "true bearers," genuinely concerned with continuity and integrity of style, actively interpret history.[25] Molly probably would agree with this analysis: she saw no conflict between her sense of tradition and her own creativity. Although she was undoubtedly a more active interpreter than Sarah, neither functioned simply as a bearer of tradition.

To return to Archie Green's assertion concerning radical influences on traditional music: there is no doubt that left-wing and Communists' use of traditional music influenced many of Molly's songs. But if Molly had not been marginal in her community, already writing songs that reflected a consciousness of her personal, as well as her class and gender oppression, and had she not had the ardent desire to communicate this to outsiders, the Left would never have discovered her. Molly actively invented herself for others, but in terms that suited her interests.

I am an unlikely amanuensis for Aunt Molly Jackson. A middle-class Jewish academic woman living in Toronto, Canada, doesn't have much in common with an Appalachian midwife and radical songwriter. Yet, my curiousity about her, kindled some years ago, developed into a full-blown desire to tell Molly's story. Surely, scholarly rationales exist for the project: as a portrait of an Appalachian woman, a songwriter and political activist, Molly's story is an extraordinary vehicle for exploring issues of class and gender identity, cultural hegemony, appropriation, and the construction/invention of tradition. Her life also suggests intriguing relationships among music, ideology, and women's resistance. A good portion of my academic interest has focused on women's domestic radicalism, a framework into which Molly easily fits. But in these politically sensitive times, I, as others, am compelled to scrutinize my choice of subject. How can I (dare to) understand, represent, give voice to, a woman whom I've never met and who comes from another culture, class, historical time—a very different other?

Twenty years ago, this problem would not have generated such soul searching. As anthropology graduate students in the 1960s our teachers urged us to study remote sites and subjects (easier to maintain distance and thus, objectivity) and to produce seamless ethnographies. My student trajectory included a master's thesis on South American Indian warfare patterns, and a doctoral thesis on the economics of banana growing in St. Lucia. Our mentors considered studies of women's lives or those that referred to personal issues, both self-indulgent and professional smooches of death. In the 1970s, a burgeoning feminist scholarship and consciousness with a mandate to deconstruct (male) notions of "scientific objectivity," dramatically changed my intellectual world. Engendered subjectivity, rather than something to be apologized for, rationalized, or simply tacked on to a text, became essential to its production. The personal, merged with the political and scholarly, informed an ongoing critical narrative.

As for my differences from Aunt Molly Jackson: I was born in 1939 in Brooklyn into a staunchly Roosevelt Democrat family. By the time my political consciousness emerged as an adolescent in the mid-1950s, my parents and their friends led optimistic middle-class lives and encouraged me to pursue professional interests. The late 1950s was a fascinating time to be around New York City. Sporting sandals and guitars, we made frequent subway pilgrimages to Greenwich Village's Washington Square Park, convening and singing with our cohort of fellow "bohemians." Our idols were "international" singers: Cynthia Gooding, Theodore Bikel, Richard Dyer-Bennet, the Clancy Brothers. Pete Seeger was too "American," too "unsophisticated." But graduate school, career, marriage, children, and moving around (although always with boxes of well-worn vinyl LPs) relegated my folk-music involvements to the past—part of another, freer, era.

Dormant for two decades, my musical interests recharged in the early 1980s after a serendipitous weekend at a folk-music and dance camp (which I would later organize and direct). Pete Seeger's writings drew me; in one I came across a passing remark (which I have yet to find again): something about Aunt Molly Jackson being little known or studied compared to Woody Guthrie. I knew Aunt Molly as an Appalachian protest singer who wrote "I Am a Union Woman," but little else about her. For some unexplainable reason, Seeger's comment leapt from its page, investing Molly with great meaning. I began to hunt for published writings about her.

My search for Molly Jackson led me early on and, inevitably, to Archie Green's classic source on occupational and labor music, *Only a Miner.* When I wrote to Green in the fall of 1989 with the first of many naive inquiries, I had no way of anticipating how central a role he would play in the unfolding of Molly's story. He had known and interviewed both Molly and her half-sister, Sarah Ogan Gunning, and suggested where I could find other potential sources, including a copious, interdisciplinary literature in labor, social history, Appalachia, music, and folklore. Green kept urging me to consider the contrast between the two women: Why are Molly (and Sarah) important today? How can we understand them from the perspective of the 1990s? Although our interests and conclusions differ, his queries became part of my internal dialogue, inspirations for the story I craft and tell.

I rely on written and oral sources, libraries, archives, audio tapes, interviews, Molly and Sarah's songs and stories. Recorded interviews of Aunt Molly by Archie Green and other researchers, of Sarah by Green and Ellen Stekert, yield wonderful insights regarding the women's perceptions, relationship to others and to each other, views of scholarship and politics. John Greenway's profile of Molly in *American Folksongs of Protest,* Mary Elizabeth Barnicle's detailed interview notes, and dictations of Molly's autobiography, and Molly's handwritten (and proxy-typed) letters to folklorist Alan Lomax, composer Earl Robinson, and writer Alice McLerran, Archie Green's *Bio-Bibliography* of Aunt Molly, provide priceless information. My own visits and interviews with Jim Garland's widow, Hazel, and daughter, Margaret Garland, collector Tillman Cadle, singer Hazel Dickens, and others who knew Molly and Sarah—scholars, collectors, singers—and continue to appreciate the women's contributions, contribute vital pieces of the puzzle. Jim Garland's posthumous autobiography edited by Julia Ardery and other published material on the women's social milieus offer invaluable keys to their lives.

These sources laid the foundation for my own impressions, text, portraits. Aunt Molly Jackson and Sarah Ogan Gunning have become for me exemplars of courageous women—actors as well as symbols. Their stories magnify our understandings of how ordinary people's lives, women's experience, history, and ideology merge.

The following pages divide into three sections: "The Appalachian Context," "Aunt Molly's (and Sarah's) Life," and "Music, Politics, and Women's Resistance." The first chapter will be useful for readers who aren't familiar with the history and evolution of coal mining in Appalachia. I go on to discuss the arrival of the Communist-led National Miners Union. Aunt Molly's story follows: her early life, later years in New York, decline and death in Sacramento. A chapter on Sarah's experiences shows how they contrasted to Molly's, and finally, the larger cultural-political contexts of music, politics, and resistant women.

A few further reflections before we begin. Writing about Molly's life and times has both academic and emotional facets. As a feminist anthropologist, I am comfortable with the gender of my subject. Without romantic notions about an essential woman or sisterhood, I feel more of an affinity to other women, sometimes despite considerable cultural differences, than I do to men of my own class and culture. Molly's songwriting and political activism certainly fit with my academic interests in domestic resistance and radicalism. But Molly herself, as you know by now, intrigues me. Although I was not initially attracted to her voice on aesthetic grounds, I now find it extremely moving. I admire her boldness, defiance, creativity. She continually reinvented Appalachia as well as herself. Molly produced, "wrote" her culture, placed herself within her narratives. She yearned to change the world, to make a difference, and to let everybody know just how she was doing this.

Molly's ability to cross multiple boundaries—class, gender, place—impresses me. In some way, her marginality has a deep resonance with my own: as a female who became an academic at a time when the university world was heavily masculine; as a native of Brooklyn transplanted to Toronto; as an academic heavily involved in a folk music community that spurns scholarly detachment and cerebralism; as a folkie in a scholarly community that spurns popular culture. In a small way, I, too, cross boundaries by singing Molly's songs in academic settings.

On some level my central question—Why Molly Jackson?—can never be answered. This exploration, though, is not intended as a personal exercise, but as a social and political problematic, forcing the confrontation of issues of identity that shape and frame the construction of subjects. My dialogue with Molly continues as it will long after this book appears. I'm always negotiating with her. She would, I'm sure, resent me for "messing up" her songs, for not reproducing Appalachian style, for critically examining her motives. But she would, I hope, also be pleased: someone finally will tell her story.

PART 1

The Appalachian Context

1

"Hard Times in Coleman's Mines":
Coal and Community in the Kentucky Mountains

Aunt Molly Jackson was fifty years old when she first set foot outside the South. Apart from one short visit to Florida, her entire world consisted of the mountain country deep in Appalachia. When she did finally leave for the North, Molly was to begin a second life in the most diverse city in the world: New York.

Although she left Kentucky behind, and only returned for brief periods, the southern mountains continued to define Molly for the rest of her days. Images of coal and dying children, which she sang about, haunted her, invaded her dreams. I start my story of Molly with the earliest and most elemental of her contexts: the rock hard country of Appalachia. The voices that gather—Jim Garland's, Mary Elizabeth Barnicle's, regional scholars', and of course, Molly's own—help paint my portrait of this "other" locale and historical period.

What was the region that formed Molly, forever gripping her imagination? An extensive geographic area, Appalachia consists of three separate mountain ranges (Blue Ridge, Allegheny, the Cumberland Plateau) cutting across nine states—Maryland, Kentucky, Virginia, West Virginia, Tennessee, North Carolina, South Carolina, Georgia, Alabama. Populated mainly by whites of German, Scots-Irish, and English descent, the "upland" South, divides culturally, as well as physiographically, from the lowlands.[1]

In its narrowest definition, Appalachia usually refers to the delineated area of central Eastern Kentucky and Southwest Virginia (or Central Appalachia), summoning graphic images of an exploited economic and cultural backwater, a colonial outpost. Robert Coles's dramatic words invoke strip mining's ravages:

> . . . large stretches of hilly land being worked over, dug into, eviscerated by incredibly powerful and merciless machines that claw and carve and scrape and scoop and gouge—until coal is reached, until the land is made to yield that coal, yield it in abundance. And when the coal is gone, the opened, wounded, bleeding land is abandoned. The wounds are simply left to weaken the rest of the region's body: acid trickles out of enormous craters; landslides come roaring down after rain upon farms and homes and trees and streams and roads, dumping rocks and boulders and thick unfertile mud upon everything and anyone. Innocent people living up a hollow all of a sudden become refugees, forced to leave or be killed, forced to leave because their land is literally overwhelmed.[2]

While Appalachia's rich coal seams tempted some outsiders, others became curious about its impoverished people strung along mountain roads and nestled in valleys. Literary and symbolic mining of the mountain culture paralleled its mineral extraction. Some are old enough to remember laughing at the daily comic strip idiocies of Mammy and Pappy Yokum, Little Abner and Daisy Mae, in Al Capp's Dogpatch. Feuding cousins, fools, and moonshiners populated the Appalachia of relatively recent popular consciousness, blending together into a portrayal of quaint retardation. Most scholars explain these archetypal cultural images by looking to nineteenth- and early-twentieth-century metropolitan and political interests that shaped them. Nineteenth-century American fiction and travel writers represented the southern mountains as prototype of an ancestral age—in, but not of America.[3] Toward the end of the century, the primitive "they"—antithetical to the modern "we"—lured cosmopolitan benefactors whose schools and churches imported civilization for the deprived natives. Do-gooders not only disseminated northern values, but, in doing so, deflected concern from political issues of class and resource exploitation.[4]

Appalachia's regional isolation and cultural motherlode drew English folklorist Cecil Sharp, who, during the summer of 1916 collected old ballads from the mountaineers. Sharp thus defined and rescued traditional song for scholars and Appalachians alike. His extraordinary influence established the idea of Appalachia as an outpost of English folk culture. Pure forms of folksongs and tales, locked in with their own peculiar modifications were there to be discovered. Sharp, in his 1932 book *English Folk Songs from the Southern Appalachians,* set into motion the study of Appalachia as an undisturbed fount of authenticity.[5] For some, text and performance continues to culturally produce or "invent" Appalachia, perpetuating the area's exploitation and political subservience.[6] For others, the roots of Appalachian identity begin as far back as the twelfth and thirteenth centuries, with a process of peripherization in Britain. "Appalachianality" thus predates and sets the stage for more recent "inventions," or versions of what constitutes Appalachia.[7]

Theories of identity aside, scholars largely agree about Appalachia's economic and social evolution. Cherokee Indians populated the territory for some four thousand years before European settlement. In the early eighteenth century, Scots-Irish, Welsh, German, and English settlers moved into the southern mountains. The egalitarian, independent, religious pioneers—as writers liked to characterize them—cleared the forested valleys and hillsides for farms. Families worked the land together, men, women, young children sharing tasks. Although farming provided subsistence essentials, men were quite mobile, supplementing farming income with sharecropping, sawmilling, livestock driving, and whiskey making.[8] Autonomous households gathered with kin and neighbors into larger communities—for dances, harvests, weddings, funerals, and church services (principally Baptist and Methodist). Appalachian mountain religions incorporated a variety of religious experience—revivalism, pietism, camp meetings.[9] Mary Barnicle recorded Aunt Molly's belief in ghosts, signs, tokens, and charms, regarding them as remnants of European paganism.[10] Fighting and feuding, in its own way, cemented family alliances, marking off clearly who could be trusted from who couldn't. Molly tells us: "The mountain parts of Kentucky has always been to my knowin' a bad place for waylaying and killin up each other over some old grudge or quarrel that has occurred ages ago."[11]

Hollows and valleys impaired easy access and communication, but inhabitants' isolation from one another, and that of the region from the outside world, remained more fiction than fact. Since the beginning of the twentieth century, salesmen, medicine hawkers, preachers, and politicians, traipsed all over the mountains. Mail deliveries, newspapers, traveling shows, and trains connected pockets of population and thrust them into a larger society.

Nevertheless, mountain people themselves shared outsiders' perceptions of insularity that sculpted their self-image. Molly heard this anecdote from a preacher in 1922:

> The preacher . . . he went up one of these long branches to sell a bible to a family . . . settled up in the head of Buzzards Nest Branch five miles from the main highway. He rode up to the fence and said, "Sister, can I sell you a bible?" and she said, "Man, what is a Bible?" He said he told her it was a book that told all about the death and burial and the resurrection of Jesus Christ, and she said, "Well, well, is he dead? I have lived up this branch fer so long, I never hear who dies and who lives." Then the preacher said to her, "Sister, you're in the dark." Then she said to him "Yes I am, I've tried to git John to saw out a winder in this log cabin, but he keeps a puttin' me off from time to time."[12]

Appalachia's wholesale transformation from primarily agrarian to industrial coal mining occurred between 1880 and 1930—the very half century that bracketed Molly's Kentucky years. Mining, in the earlier days, remained small-scale and local. Entrepreneurs needed little capital to build a tipple (for weighing raw coal), buy some mules, and hire a few hands. Near the end of the century, with potential prodigious timber and mineral deposits driving up land values, developers with offers in hand started to knock at farmers' doors. Unable to foresee the disastrous consequences of these "opportunities," many sold mineral rights under their land to outsiders.[13]

Flourishing companies built rail networks to bring labor—Italians, Hungarians, Poles, blacks—from the rural South to the mining areas and haul coal back to northern cities. By the end of the nineteenth century, non-Appalachians owned most of the mineral lands in the Kentucky coal counties—Bell, Harlan, Leslie, Letcher, Rowan.[14] The industrializing North's voracious appetite for coal and lumber—to feed factories, electric power plants, heat homes—continued to draw absentee investors and fostered precipitous, often damaging, methods of extraction.

Harlan County, the site of Molly's discovery, is of particular interest to this story. Lying in a narrow valley north of the Cumberland Gap where Kentucky adjoins Virginia and Tennessee, Harlan did not see trains, highways, or newspapers before the second decade of this century. Malcolm Ross, writing in the early 1930s, captures the pre-coal feeling: "In 1910, Harlan . . . was a backwoods community, dotted with log cabins, roadless, and content with such social life as suns itself in Kentucky courthouse squares, swapping news and squirting ruminative tobacco juice on the steps of justice."[15] But its horizontal mines, less prone to explosion, and packed with choice coal, soon enticed developers. Within a few years, the county blossomed into relative affluence. Harlanites, overwhelmed by their newfound prosperity, rushed into the twentieth century, buying new automobiles, silk shirts, radios, and washing machines.

Coal companies gravitated toward Harlan's bituminous and other Kentucky coal sources. Mining camps and towns sprouted, first for single mineworkers, then for families, gradually replacing farmsteads. Secluded in hollows interrupted by ridges, or strung along roads, the new settlements housed from one to several hundred inhabitants. The mine tipple, company time office, boiler house, repair sheds, washery, coke oven, all defined the coal town's built landscape. Miners bought food and supplies for cash or scrip at the company store, the heart of town life. Depending on size, coal towns likely comprised union halls, chapels, libraries, saloons, and schoolhouses. To attract workers in boom times, operators added recreation areas, pool halls, and movie theaters, and offered such perks as house maintenance and sanitation.

Most descriptions of coal towns depict a bleak physical and social environment affording little more than basic survival—images of squalid housing, air noxious with sulphur fumes and coal dust. The "typical village [is] in the country, but not of it. Grass and flowers . . . were missing. . . . The streets were unpaved. . . . Dirty [animals] wandered everywhere."[16] Another scenario of company control and worker entrapment is equally dismal, with rent, groceries, doctor bills, and light bulbs deducted from wages. Coal companies discouraged home gardens in order to insure that miners purchased commercial canned goods. The five-mile walk to the nearest town and interception of mail order catalogs at the post office, bound miners and families to the company store.[17] Without voice in community affairs or working conditions, miners and their families depended on employers' benevolence. At the height of the coal boom, more than two thirds of miners lived as captive town populations—unable to return to the land and without resources to move to the city.[18]

Coal towns, as unincorporated political and social entities created by the mine owners, maintained no elected officials. Segregated by race and ethnicity, miners' housing perpetuated cleavages and undermined possibilities of worker solidarity. Class and ethnicity also determined house quality, a descending ladder from local whites, to immigrants, to blacks at the bottom. Rural southern blacks bathed, prayed, and lived in their own camps, apart from the others. Worker and owner, however, remained the most critical divide. Substantial, often luxurious structures, housing coal operators, looked down impassively at miners from their hilltop lots, casting income and status difference into further relief. Even the most resigned miners couldn't help comparing their hovels to grand houses, their women's threadbare clothing to operators' wives' fancy dress.

In a pamphlet produced by the Cabin Creek Consolidated Coal Company in West Virginia, a mining administrator cautions coal operators' wives against openly flaunting their finery. "When the miner comes to town he expects to see fine houses—that is what a town is for. But richly dressed women parading through a mining camp have about the same effect as a bird of gorgeous plumage feeding among sparrows—they all want to peck at it."[19]

Mining was extremely arduous—hand coal extraction demanded concentration and physical stamina. At three or four in the morning, men, groggy with sleep, donned overalls and lamps, lugged picks, shovels, pry bars, saws, axes, and explosives to their work site. They spent the next twelve hours blasting, boring, digging, often knee-deep in water, in confined spaces or "rooms." A clear hierarchy defined their tasks. Digging and loading, compensated by tonnage, exacted more skill than hauling; tracklaying, smithing, jobs paid on a daily basis, demanded less. Boys as young as six years became helpers, graduating to apprenticeships in their late teens. Like other crafts, mining skills passed (often with considerable pride) from father to son. With the evolution from farming to mining, radical changes occurred in one's relationship to work. Dark cramped spaces, insecurity, time pressure, and supervision replaced fresh air and light, relaxed production, and independence.[20] Mining necessitated, as farming did not, finely honed coordination and mutual support on the job. But while experience and cooperation helped, the volatile combination of fatigued workers and hazardous conditions produced frequent disasters: falling slate, oxygen deprivation, and explosions commonly occurred in underground mines.

A gendered division of labor, another cleavage in coal town society, occurred within, as well as across, class and ethnic lines. Since miners considered a woman's presence underground both unlucky and dangerous, strict work separation prevailed: men mined and women kept house. Coal-mining women, likely married with children by their early to middle teenage years, faced domestic responsibilities. They fed and clothed their households, tended vegetable gardens and livestock, made butter and soap. Taking in boarders or clothes to launder, and cleaning mine owners' homes frequently supplemented mining wages.

Jim Garland felt a mining wife's working life was often more arduous than her husband's, with less time for recreation. Rising first in the chilly darkness, she cooked breakfast, then packed her man's "dinner" bucket. After her husband trudged off to the mines, she cleaned up the dishes, made beds, and washed the cabin's wood-planked floors with caustic lye. Hoisting the pile of gray laundry onto her back, she walked down to the river to scrub it out. Finally completing house chores, the wife counted out the scrip to take it to the company store and bought the day's food, returning in time to prepare and serve it at five o'clock, when her husband finished his bath.

A mountain woman would haul water from a distant pump, split kindling, find coal for the stove, often with "two or three children hanging to her dress tail." Miners didn't consider helping with housework because, in Garland's words, "a man who has worked on his knees all day in thirty to thirty-six inch coal is about pooped out."[21] Magazine writer Freda Kirchwey poignantly captured West Virginia coal women's depressing and impotent lives: "If the miners are the slaves of coal, the women are the slaves of slaves."[22] One gender-conscious woman, Mrs. Rathom of West Virginia, says:

"I married him when I was seventeen; my mother got me into it. I wanted another man, but she put me off on this one. Perhaps it wouldn't of made no difference. Marriage . . ." She stopped again. Then she said in a flat, lifeless voice that denied the smoldering malice in her eyes: "He's no more nor less than a snake. I hated him when I married him an' I've hated him every minute since. I've always been sick like ever since I married. He's always well an' hearty; never a sick day. I've had twelve children that lived. I don't rightly know just how many others. He don't care; men don't."[23]

Here's one of Molly's cynical songs about male-female relationships:

These Lost Creek miners
Claim they love their wives so dear
That they can't help giving them
A baby or two every year[24]

Barnicle collected material from Molly on early marriage and child-rearing. The mountain woman described women's limited possibilities—wife and mother. Some became, like herself, midwives and herbalists. With little opportunity for education, girls married and bore children early.[25] Hard work, low returns, and too many children, were only part of the problem. The spectre of dangerous conditions and low safety standards hung over the whole community. Miners' wives lived in fear of the inevitable. Tragedies were weekly, even daily occurrences.

While the damages of coal mining, especially in a depressed market, are sharply etched, towns offered inhabitants a community life. Crandall Shifflett, cautioning against either wholly negative constructions or romanticizing the independence of a pre-coal farming period, sketches a series of overlapping stages through which coal towns evolved. The first, or "pioneer" phase, spanned from the 1880s until the First World War; it was followed by a second "paternalistic" phase, from the war until the Great Depression, and a third, "decaying" phase, from the middle 1930s until the middle 1950s. In paternalist times, operators with business acumen in a tight market, guided by policies of "contentment sociology," supplied medical and sanitary facilities.[26] Even in hard times, miners chose where they shopped: the company store, independent merchants, or at outlets in other towns where they managed to get around the scrip system. Miners, who used their own tools, were a largely unsupervised work force, relying on their skills, networks, and mobility.[27]

Paternalism modified many worker/management relationships, making it possible to endure the down sides, while at the same time cementing power relationships. The mine owner or operator, who resided in town, might offer workers a clean camp, electricity and running water, prizes for pretty gardens, or money if needed. He might live as neighbor, attend church and show genuine care for workers, be considered "a good feller." The relative conditions in a particular camp became a yardstick, a source of pride for its residents. Alessandro Portelli tells how Hazel King, from Louellen, Harlan County, appreciated her coal operator. "The Mr. Lawson I knew was a very likeable person. He was very fatherly like, I would call it, and he knew every one, and all the children. He was always willing to assist 'em, you know, especially in their interests of having flowers and everything there, neat and . . . I liked Mr. Lawson."[28]

Verbal strategies by coal town residents negotiated and managed some of the contradictions. When the company cut wages, the impersonal "they" did it; but "he" was good to his workers. "The combined picture is the essence of paternalism: a personal bond beween the oppressors and the oppressed, which obscures under a veil of human relations, even of affection and friendship, the nakedness of exploitation and the totality of power."[29]

Somehow, great imbalances remained muted in everyday coal town life. The company store pulsed with activity: miners and families shopped, congregated, shared the latest gossip. As in any community, they watched movies together, read magazines, met trains. Neighbors idled, hunted foxes, enjoyed corn shuckings, apple pickings, hog killings, chicken fights, baseball, relished a good tale or a spirited Holiness church service. Women gathered to quilt and can fruit; if family members or friends took sick, they helped care for extra children and prepare food. Some, like Molly, with special healing talents, treated sprains, cured coughs, attended births.

As in pre-coal days, music remained a vital glue for community life, men and women often gathering to sing and play. Families passed down their favorite renditions of tunes and ballads—of work, sex, love, tragedy. Friends shared and compared variants, told how they learned their version from their granddads and aunts. Celebrations or misfortunes would inspire new lyrics, adapted to traditional hymn or ballad melodies. Jim Garland's porch would bulge with thirty or forty people playing fiddles, guitars, banjos, and Jew's harps.[30] Songs conveyed experiences, offered moral guidance, expressed religious faith, ignited or spurned ardors, triumphs, and tragedies. Molly, who thought of all ballads as love songs, described how they nurtured romance and reflected its risks. Mary Barnicle noted the following based on her conversations with the mountain woman.

> The evening and weekend parties at which they were sung gave an opportunity for love-making that other occasions did not furnish. Perhaps neither the listeners nor the singers paid much attention to the ballads. . . . Certainly the pleasures in these was much . . . because their singing provided an occasion for courting. When these sad tragedies of love were sung, a glance or an attitude could carry feeling. Certainly the ballads made clear both in melody and text what a dangerous and tragic thing love must be in the mountains and what a dreary thing it usually was with its early marriages, Puritan conventions, and harsh and violent double standards.[31]

Coal operators supported musical gatherings, even if for their own purposes. Recognizing music's social control functions, they subsidized local bands and established singing schools.[32] In the 1920s, radio and phonograph records entered coal town homes, and miners, with ever flexible musical tastes, sang and played commercial hits.[33] Coal camp life, despite the work, the anxieties, the internal divisions, was, for Jim Garland, a close-knit community and "never dull." "If the people who ran the mines had cared about the local families as much as they did about profit (and everything else was secondary to that profit), if the miner had made a large enough wage to give his family a decent diet, if the houses had been sturdier—even if that had meant charging more rent—and if living conditions had been more sanitary, the coal mining camp would have been as fine a place to live as one might have hoped for."[34]

But the Depression arrived and the miner earned little: his family ate poorly, inhaled the coal dust that settled in every pore and member of their bodies, endured bitter winds screeching through gaping holes in the walls of their shacks. Relentless in his criticism of the mine bosses, Jim Garland wrote of minimal safety standards, accidents, and cynicism of the companies epitomized in the popular saying, "Kill a mule, we'll buy another. Kill a man, hire another."[35] One pithy quote exposes the miners' hatred for the coal operators: "'They worked their men for a song—*and the men sung it themselves.*'"[36]

In the early 1920s, suffering from competition from other fuel sources and sagging demand, the coal industry began to retrench. Some mines operated only a few days a week, while workers' wages plummeted. Harlan miners and their families, who, in good times, overlooked the strains and divisions of coal town life, now found them intolerable. Company policies of deducting supply and food expenses from miners' now-meager pay strengthened debt relationships, shackling workers. If a miner joined the union, credit at the company store, so easily obtained in boom times, slowed to a trickle or stopped. With several members of one family working for single employers, pressures to conform intensified. Hungry and desperate, miners vented frustrations by stopping work, walking out, wildcatting, while mine operators replaced them with scabs and gun thugs. These conditions set the stage for deepening labor conflict and brutality, the entry of the Communist National Miners Union, and "bloody Harlan coal struggles," a story that continues in the next chapter.

2

"I Am a Union Woman": The Communist National Miners Union Comes to Harlan County, Kentucky

"Bloody Harlan" conjures up one of the most graphic models of worker/ boss struggles in our century. Those who know little about labor history, less of the details of specific strikes, and nothing at all of Aunt Molly Jackson, perk up their ears when I mention Harlan County. This chapter will tell the story of how and why it happened, the political and economic underpinnings of the downfall of coal, the opportunity that arrived with the outside union organizers, and the hopes that were dashed when it failed. In the Harlan County story we encounter the strangest of bedfellows—miners, radical writers, and outside organizers. Violent physical and ideological confrontations between bosses and miners, gun thugs and the union, religious and secular interests, resulted on one hand in demoralization and death, and on the other, in new paths for Molly Jackson, Jim Garland, and Sarah Gunning.

During the 1920s, Central and Southern Appalachian mines rumbled with overproduction. Capitalists hauled out increasing amounts of coal with reduced returns. Profits sagged for several reasons: freight costs skyrocketed and European coal and other fuel substitutes, like oil and electricity, competed with North American resources, driving coal's marketability into the ground. Harlan County, particularly prosperous during boom times, felt declining interest in its once-precious bituminous. Toward the end of the decade, mines either shut down completely or severely slashed operating hours, cutting wages and tonnage pay. Miners recalled chunks of 1930 and 1931 replete with layoffs, lockouts, and wildcat strikes, as the bottom of a pit. John dos Passos described the situation: "The race for riches went to the heads of the operators. The fact of having a little cash every two weeks went to the heads of the miners. The union turned into a racket and lapsed. Financiers skimmed the cream off the coal companies and left them overcapitalized and bankrupt. . . . Headlong deflation left the coal operators broke and the miners starving."[1]

Evarts, Kentucky, became the first battlefield of the Harlan mine war. On May 5, 1931, heavily armed deputies accompanied Peabody Company scabs as they trucked into Black Mountain. When a mine operator's gun thug harassed one of the pickets, miners, lying in ambush, opened fire. The miners killed the three deputies (one miner was killed) and temporarily seized the upper hand. The state militia, which promptly appeared to "keep the peace," confiscated weapons and arrested the leaders. The unjust trial "returned thirty triple-murder indictments and thirty indictments for banding and confederating." Mine guards and deputy sheriffs were immune.[2] One line from Florence Reece's song "Which Side Are You On" tells it all: "There are no neutrals there."

Local officials depended on the "criminal syndicalism" law, relating violence to politics, to punish the Evarts rebels and other designated resistors:

> Any person who, by word of mouth or writing, advocates the propriety of doing any act of violence as a means of establishing any political ends, change or revolution; or who publicly displays any printed matter suggesting the doing of any act of physical violence, the destruction or damage to any property as a means of bringing about any political revolution, or who shall attempt to justify by word of mouth, or voluntarily assembles with any society which advocates physical violence as a means of accomplishing any political ends is guilty of a felony and upon conviction thereof shall be punished by imprisonment in the state penitentiary for a term or not more than twenty-one years, or by a fine or not more than $10,000 or both.[3]

When Evarts coal operators blacklisted thousands of miners, the United Mine Workers Union of America (UMWA) abandoned ship. John L. Lewis, the union's dictatorial president, plagued with his organization's internal schisms, squandered the miners' confidence. Jim Garland maintained that the "pantywaisted" leaders of UMWA deserted thousands of miners, leaving a lacunae ripe for an alternative—the Communist National Miners Union.[4]

In "Communists and Miners 1928–1933," Theodore Draper grounds the National Miners Union's arrival in Kentucky. During the 1920s the mainstream American Federation of Labor suffered dramatically declining membership, especially in mass production industries—iron and steel, autos, food production. Supporting white skilled craft workers, they offered little to the swelling numbers of immigrants and unskilled workers flooding the labor force.

The Communists, to sway a lethargic union movement, founded the Trade Union Educational League (TUEL) in 1920. Eight years later, with Stalin's Third Period, they shifted away from policies of infiltration toward creating parallel, dual unions. The Communist Trade Union Unity League (TUUL), formed in 1929 as an offshoot of the original TUEL, resolved to fill the vacuum left by the American Federation of Labor's United Mine Workers of America union with one of its constituents, the National Miners Union—an organization for the real people: unskilled, immigrant, black, and women workers.

In September 1928, despite the party's flimsy base in mining, the NMU pledged to "'break completely with the John L. Lewis machine,' and 'fight to the last to remove every obstacle to build an organization to comprise the whole of the rank and file coal miners . . . its eventual aim the complete emancipation from capitalist exploitation.'"[5]

Deeply alienated, hungry and agitated, furious at profit mongering bosses, miners wildcatted throughout Appalachia. The Depression sapped every mountain hollow as picks and shovels gathered dust in corners of drafty shacks. In one instance, ten thousand miners, scattered through western Pennsylvania, eastern Ohio, and northern West Virginia, walked out. Communist union organizers materialized in several of these coalfields, claiming responsibility for the massive strike. But when the Pittsburgh Terminal Coal Company finally signed a union contract (although neither side gained) they negotiated not with NMU but with the nearly defunct AFL's United Mine Workers of America. After categorically refusing to deal with the UMWA for four years, management considered them the lesser evil. Communists could thus claim an impact, though not exactly the one for which they hoped.

National Miners Union post mortems revealed inevitable problems: they prepared inadequately for long strikes and mobilized meager forces; local organizations lacked leadership and suffered paltry membership numbers; they consistently miscalculated when or how to quit or compromise. Heartened, nevertheless, by the mass walkout in the Virginia fields, Communist organizers minimized short-term setbacks and tried again. They trained their sights on loftier goals: to revolutionize workers and recruit for the party.

In 1931, Harlan seemed a likely arena for another NMU effort—with over forty mines producing nearly one third of all Kentucky's coal, and a black hole in union leadership. Acutely deprived of food and morale, miners worked a maximum of three days for a meager four dollars, distributed wholly in scrip. Coal towns trembled with blacklistings, evictions, terrorism, threats on the street, around every corner when the National Miners Union organizers arrived to bring relief and offer some hope to the workers.

Although Harlan and Bell Counties are neighbors, Malcolm Ross noted their differences. Harlan, "new and violent," with brimming coal seams, prided itself when wages soared. Bell, to the south, held more locally owned, older and less desirable mines. Since organizers considered Harlan "too hot" they often based in Pineville, Bell County.[6]

In the summer of 1931, young, energetic northern radicals, some with protective pseudonyms, came to Harlan and Bell Counties in the midst of the bleakest conditions. Dan Slinger (or Brooks), arrived first, followed by Jesse Wakefield of the Communist International Labor Defense League (ILD), Caroline Drew, a relief worker in the textile strikes at Gastonia, North Carolina, and later Doris Parks, Clarina Michaelson, and someone who become very important to Jim Garland, Harry Simms. The organizers encountered a Depression atmosphere thick with distrust, people hungry and frightened. With supplies and food short, scrip useless, miners struggled over paltry tidbits. Jim Garland remembers a store clerk notifying a miner with a large family "everything is gone. All we have in the store is a little pepper and salt." The miner asked the clerk if he had any rope. "A man might as well hang himself as starve to death working if he can't get anything to cook for his family."[7]

In Garland's account of the events leading to the "Bloody Harlan" strike, miners in Wallins and Straight Creeks assembled informal strike committees, hatching plans for an official walkout the first day of 1932. Despite the odds—a weak organizational base, limited miner support (many blacklisted), scant relief commitments, and perpetual harassment from gun thugs—strike activity gained steam. Churches threw open their doors for meetings and housed soup kitchens. By November 1931, walkoffs and work stoppages multiplied; on January 1, 1932, even the last holdout mines stopped. Operators ferociously retaliated by arming more deputies to harass and red-bait miners, burn soup kitchens, and arrest criminals. By the end of March 1932, after months of jailings, starvation, and terrorism, the depleted NMU organizers left Kentucky. The Communist's attempt to drag the masses out of their economic and social morass had failed; John L. Lewis's United Mine Workers of America would, like a phoenix, rise again.

In Draper's analysis, one could predict the strike's failure for a number of reasons, since the NMU's shortcomings held no mystery. The Communist's bane—fragile organization—reared its head. The party and constituent unions, rent by ideological splits, with an impotent rank and file of blacklisted or immigrants workers, couldn't sustain support. The strike continued for too many weeks with undernourished reserves and leadership. Union organizers identified with party recruitment and revolutionary goals rather than with strikers. Unwilling to challenge the more fundamental party line, they tended to fault their own training and methods. Acknowledging the odds against them, Draper remains impressed with their endurance: "In the face of such a phalanx of powerful and implacable enemies, it was more surprising that the Communist organizers were able to fight so hard for as long as they did than that they were unable to win."[8]

A number of subtexts frame the story, and beg a closer look. First, women's involvement in strike activity, second, the miners' embrace and ultimate rejection of the Communists. Third, a complex ideological and power dance entwining five sets of participants—miners, operators, Communist organizers, local newspapers, and radical northern urban writers. Finally, various factions clashed with each other—foreigners and Americans, workers and owners, poor and rich, atheists and believers, urban and rural. Dramatic struggles played out on the Kentucky minefields inevitably burst their seams and exploded onto a large stage.

The National Miners Union structure and policies departed, in a number of ways, from those of the United Mine Workers of America, by democratically electing committees, legitimizing women, and black involvement. Women's auxiliaries insured a parallel leadership (with president, secretary, other officers), formalizing female front-line participation.

Women needed little prodding to walk a picket line or resort to physical violence; they led many of the wildcat strikes in late 1931 and early

1932. Jim told of women who were "fine and serious union folk," not only involved in relief work, distributing clothing and food, delivering messages, but planning meetings to inspire enthusiasm. "Perhaps because of their hand in these rallies, these girls believed that we should strike the whole creek."[9] Tillman Cadle told me of a woman who closed a mine: "Where do you think you're going?" she demanded of a scab. Grabbing his pail and dealing him blows, she threatened him and any others that ventured near the mine.[10] Stories abound about women who wielded and freely manipulated weapons: one of my favorites is about Molly shoving a pistol barrel up a strikebreaker's rear end in Ross, Kentucky.[11]

The community, who supported both the NMU and the strike, in Garland's view, were not simply pawns of the outside radicals: "like any union, we had a certain amount of dissension. But those people who claim that the NMU was nothing more than a tool for the Communist party are simply talking through their hats. The NMU was a bona fide union: its officials were voted in by miners, and the Straight Creek strike, in addition to the later, larger activity, was instigated and voted on by Kentucky miners."[12]

The NMU may have been "bona fide" but it didn't stand a chance. It came to represent "outside" interests, in ironic contrast with coal operators' (despite the high numbers of absentee owners) "inside" interests. Several subplots in the mine war reveal how internal power interests ingeniously constructed the outsiders, and bring us closer to Molly's fateful encounter with the Dreiser Committee and eventual departure from Kentucky.

Outsiders—socially active or radical writers, labor organizers, students, relief workers, clergy—continued to flock to Harlan and Bell during 1931 and 1932. Many met with misfortune, trumped up criminal charges, jailings, a few with death. One incident occurred in February 1932, during the depths of the Communist-led strike. Waldo Frank headed a group of twelve eminent writers, including Malcolm Cowley, Mary Heaton Vorse, Edmund Wilson, and Quincy Howe, to distribute food in the minefields. Within a few hours of their arrival in Kentucky, operators' deputies rounded them up, shoved them into cars, and stranded them on a remote hilltop.

A second episode involved a Jewish New Englander, Harry Simms (born Harry Hirsh). A member of the Young Communist League, Harry rose precipitously in the ranks to District Organizer and came to Harlan in December 1931, where he and Jim Garland instantly befriended one another. A few months later, on February 10, 1932 (the very day of the

Waldo team arrival), an armed deputy, discovering Harry walking with another organizer, shot him in the stomach. Although Harry died in hospital the following day, authorities remained uninterested in locating or punishing his murderer. The Communists transported his body to New York's Bronx Coliseum and placed the casket, surrounded with red carnations, in the middle of the boxing ring. Miners, with caps and lamps, reverently paid tribute to a martyr. A grief-stricken Jim, convinced that the bullet was meant for him, and not Harry, wrote a loving song for his nineteen-year-old friend (which Pete Seeger later recorded, and Molly claimed as her own, although on one of Archie Green's tapes, she acknowledged double authorship).[13] This version appears in Jim's book:

> Comrades, listen to my story,
> Comrades, listen to my song.
> I'll tell you of a hero
> That now—is dead and gone.
> I'll tell you of a young boy
> Whose age was just nineteen.
> He was the strongest union man
> That I have ever seen.
>
> Harry Simms was a pal of mine,
> We labored side by side,
> Expecting to be shot on sight
> Or taken for a ride
> By the dirty coal operator gun thugs
> That roam from town to town
> To shoot and kill our Comrades
> Wherever they may be found.
>
> Harry Simms and I were parted
> At five o'clock that day.
> "Be careful, my dear Comrade,"
> To Harry I did say.
> "I must do my duty,"
> Was his reply to me.
> "If I get killed by gun thugs,
> Please don't grieve over me."
>
> Harry Simms was walking down the track
> One bright sunshiny day.
> He was a youth of courage.

His step was light and gay.
He did not know the gun thugs
Were hiding on the way
To kill our dear young Comrade
This bright sunshiny day.

Harry Simms was killed on Brush Creek
In nineteen thirty-two.
He organized the miners
Into the NMU.
He gave his life in struggle,
That was all that he could do.
He died for the union,
Also for me and you.

(final verse of the original)
Comrades, we must vow today,
This one thing we must do—
We must organize all the miners
In the good old NMU.
We'll get a million volunteers
From those who wish us well,
And sink this rotten system
In the deepest pits of hell.

(final verse which I [Jim] composed later)
Comrades, we must vow today,
There's one thing we must do—
We'll organize all the miners
Into the good old NMU.
We'll get a million volunteers
From those who wish us well,
And travel over the country
And Harry's story tell.[14]

Harry Simms's funeral generated enormous solidarity within the Communist rank and file. It also gave Jim Garland an opportunity to appraise his home-to-be, New York City, as well as validate his enlarged radical worker consciousness:

Before this strike, I had never been out of the mountains, except my trip to Lexington when I took the mine foreman's exam. You can imagine what an experience this trip north was for me. I saw things that before I had only read about in books and newspapers. In New York, I saw people dispossessed because they couldn't pay their rent. I saw the mounted police ride people down with horses. I was struck by the realization that poor people everywhere had the same problems, that the struggles for a place to live and something to eat were universal. . . . I saw boys with college degrees waiting tables for $15 a week. After witnessing all of this, I could no longer think of our fight in Kentucky as purely local.[15]

But months before Waldo Frank's visit, Harry's funeral, and Jim's trip north, a different team of investigators—those most crucial for this story—prepared to journey to Appalachia. The coalfields as a new theater of class warfare had already engaged the radical imagination and the newspapers. The National Committee for the Defense of Political Prisoners (NCDPP) hatched plans in New York City that would lure intense media interest and irrevocably alter the lives of the Garland family.

Theodore Dreiser, head of the NCDPP, novelist, reformer, insisted that only his "own ideas" inspired him, and denied any affiliation with the Communist Party.[16] Perturbed by stories of destitute miners and tyrannical operators, the writer decided to assess conditions firsthand. After several senators declined to join him, Dreiser cobbled together a committee of noted writers including John Dos Passos, Lester Cohen, Samuel Ornitz, Bruce Crawford, Melvin Levy, Charles Rumford Walker and his wife, Adelaide Walker, and Dreiser's woman secretary. The expedition arrived in Pineville, Kentucky, on November 5, 1931, with no formal agenda—just intentions to talk to miners and hold public hearings in local churches to garner media exposure for strikers. They didn't have to cast far for witnesses: miners and wives, hungry, with nothing left to lose and some dignity to salvage, willingly testified. Their wrenching reports became part of the committee's publication, *Harlan Miners Speak:*

Q. How do you manage to live?
A. [Miner's Wife]: We have just managed to exist. . . . We live on beans and bread. . . . [the children] have no shoes on their feet and no underwear on them . . .[17]

One witness, unusually compelling, appeared at the Straight Creek hearing on November 7, 1931. The investigators laid eyes on the middle-aged midwife for the first time and listened to her testimony:

Q1: What is your name?

A: Aunt Molly Jackson.

Q2: What do you do?

A: I am a nurse.

Q3: A graduate nurse?

A: Yes.

Q4: Can you tell us something about the condition of the people in this hollow?

A: The people in this country are destitute of anything that is really nourishing to the body. That is the truth. Even the babies have lost their lives, and we have buried from four to seven a week all along during warm weather. . . .

Q24: Is your husband a member of the N.M.U.?

A: My husband is a member of the National Miners Union, and I am too, and I have never stopped, brother, since I know of this work for the N.M.U. I think it is one of the greatest things that has ever come into this world.[18]

Aunt Molly then punctuated her testimony with a unique contribution, which she would repeat at the next day's hearings—her own song "Hungry Ragged Blues."

1

I'm sad and weary; I've got these hungry ragged blues;
I'm sad and weary; I've got these hungry ragged blues;
Not a penny in my pocket to buy one thing I need to use.

2

I woke up this morning with the worst blues I ever had in my life;
I woke up this morning with the worst blues I ever had in my life;
Not a bite to cook for breakfast, a poor coal miner's wife.

3

When my husband works in the coal mines, he loads a car on every trip;
When my husband works in the coal mines, he loads a car on every trip;
Then he goes to the office that evening and gits denied of scrip.

4

Just because it took all he made that day to pay his mine expense;
Just because it took all he made that day to pay his mine expense;
A man that'll work for coal-light and carbide, he ain't got a speck of
    sense.

5

All the women in the coal camps are a-sitting with bowed-down heads;
All the women in the coal camps are a-sitting with bowed-down heads;
Ragged and barefooted, the children a-crying for bread.

6

No food, no clothes for our children, I'm sure this ain't no lie;
No food, no clothes for our children, I'm sure this ain't no lie;
If we can't git more for our labor, we will starve to death and die.

7

Listen, friends and comrades, please take a friend's advice;
Listen, friends and comrades, please take a friend's advice;
Don't load no more that dirty coal till you git a living price.

8

Don't go under the mountains with the slate a-hanging over your heads;
Don't go under the mountains with the slate a-hanging over your heads;
And work for just coal-light and carbide and your children a-crying for
bread.

9

This mining town I live in is a sad and lonely place;
This mining town I live in is a sad and lonely place;
Where pity and starvation is pictured on every face.

10

Ragged and hungry, no slippers on our feet;
Ragged and hungry, no slippers on our feet;
We're bumming around from place to place to get a little bite to eat.

11

All a-going round from place to place bumming for a little food to eat.
Listen, my friends and comrades, please take a friend's advice,
Don't put out no more of your labor, till you get a living price.

12

Some coal operators might tell you the hungry blues are not bad;
Some coal operators might tell you the hungry blues are not bad;
They are the worst blues this poor woman ever had.[19]

The mountain woman's unvarnished power stilled the foreign observers, who sat transfixed in their seats. Molly's song mesmerized the committee, and inspired, in those moments, some grand possibilities for the miner's wife. Dos Passos would use Molly as exemplar, and lionize her in print as the "high point" of his Kentucky experience as he continued to include her song in writings about Harlan. Less impressed by Molly's performance and somewhat galled by her achievement, Jim Garland (in his book) and Tillman Cadle (in person to me) sarcastically claimed that the Dreiser Committee thought her, "Kentucky herself." Jim had difficulty squelching cynicism when referring to his sister: "During one of their meetings, held at the Arjay Baptist church soup kitchen, my sister Aunt Molly Jackson sang a song she had just recently made up; she called it 'The Hungry Ragged Blues.' The Dreiser people were so impressed by her that they thought she was just about the whole Kentucky strike. In fact she had done very little in the strike aside from going down into Knox County a time or two to solicit vegetables for the community kitchen."[20]

But the writers, skilled at manipulating symbols, didn't question their find: they spotted a gem and slated a purposeful role for her. With her perfect image as a miner's wife, an embodiment of Appalachia, they felt confident that Molly would generate enormous interest—not only in this particular strike, but in the oppression of workers all over the world.

The northerners' attraction to the southern mountains and subsequent embrace of Molly Jackson is a story in itself—an allegory replete with symbols. Bracketed by calamitous depression in the minefields and the National Miners Union's aspirations in Harlan, the writers' portentous visit thrust the Appalachians into a world of intellectual politics. Adjectives depicting miners—gaunt, spent, skeletal, wasted, dissipated, emaciated, withered, starved—peppered the press in the early 1930s and continue to echo in the most metaphorical of class contests.

Although a few Appalachians saw the outsiders as saviors, many others deemed them alien intruders. One incident involving "the toothpick," that occurred during the visit, threw into relief various polarities. A few days after the team arrived in Pineville, local bystanders noticed a woman entering Dreiser's hotel room in the wee hours. The self-styled sleuths balanced a few toothpicks against the door, where they stood undisturbed several hours later. After the writer returned to New York City on November ninth, a Bell County grand jury indicted him on charges of adultery in addition to the more usual "criminal syndicalism (violence with political ends)." Juicy gossip bubbled in the towns, while tantalizing details of the incident in local newspapers eclipsed news of strike conditions. In a rather limp defense, Dreiser claimed to be impotent. Besides the sex scandal, several more weighty criticisms loomed: according to one, the hearings on which Dreiser and the committee based the report *Harlan Miners Speak* actually took place in Bell County, reflecting the observations of the authors more than those of the miners. According to a second, the committee distorted the numbers and heard only "friendly" witnesses rounded up by the union for gullible liberal ears.[21]

Bruce Crawford, editor of the Virginia-based newspaper, the *Crawford Weekly,* and member of the team of investigators (himself shot and injured in Harlan), thought publicity of any sort useful. He wrote in the radical publication, *Labor Defender,* that charges of misconduct "will prove a boomerang. It had served to bring more attention to the Harlan situation than perhaps anything else could have done. . . . Had Dreiser purposely primed the investigation with the high explosive of sex, he could not have detonated greater public curiosity as to the conditions revealed by his committee."[22] But the theme of "foreigner," embedded and embroiled in class and religious antagonisms, whittled away at the miners' trust. Swanberg, Theodore Dreiser's biographer, recounts a clipped exchange between the renowned writer and Herndon Evans, editor of the *Pineville Sun,* hostile to the miners. When Dreiser questioned the large gulf between the editor's income (about $240 a month) and a miner's wages (about $40), Evans in turn inquired how much Dreiser's royalities amounted to. Dreiser answered: "$200,000, approximately. Probably more." Evans: "What do you get a year . . . ?" Dreiser: "Last year, I think I made $35,000." When Evans asked if Dreiser contributed to charity, the writer replied that he didn't, but undertook the present investigation at his own expense.[23]

The committee's endeavors to draw attention to internal class strife faltered as emphasis shifted to the cleavage between "we and they"—mountain people vs. outsiders.[24] The local power elite waged ideological warfare, denouncing the invaders as Communists, throwing suspicion on their motives. The outsiders became everything from rich intruders to devils incarnate, aiming to destroy American freedoms of press, speech, and prayer. All terrorism became justifiable in order to defend these sacred values.

The strike, the union, Communists, and sympathizers formed a single "other" menacing the local power elite. Oakley Johnson articulated the power issues in *The Nation:*

The fact that the National Miners Union is Communist led gives the local officials, controlled as they are by the operators, opportunity to bring in the bogies of "atheism" and "foreigners" and to use the statute on criminal syndicalism in an attempt to imprison for long terms not merely those alleged to have counseled specifically violent resistance to mine deputies, as in the Harlan court cases, but those who are organizing the strike, giving relief to the miners' families, reporting the progress of the strike to the Communist periodicals, or even defending in court the organizers and relief workers who have been arrested— on the ground that one and all are Communist and therefore violators of the statute.[25]

The local media stridently underscored the "foreigner" theme and undermined the strike. Newspapers reported selectively, consistently downplaying the extent of harassment against miners or their sympathizers. No mention appeared regarding the huge attendance (in some accounts, 25,000) at Harry Simms's funeral at the Bronx Coliseum in New York. Items and editorials in *The Middlesboro* [Tenn.] *Daily News,* an organ allied with local powerfuls, diverged from the more sympathetic *Knoxville News Sentinel.* A *Middlesboro News* editorial dismissed the Waldo Frank team's visit as a mere flash in the pan that left the locals unimpressed: "The Crusading Uplifters from New York City have come and gone. . . . Coming into Southeastern Kentucky, heralded by headline blasts, flanked by grinding cameras and self-appointed press agents, prepared to lift fallen humanity out of its misery in the mountains, the Uplifters met a cold, sullen ominous hostility on the part of the Kentucky mountaineers."[26] The paper printed, and doubtlessly agreed with, a local minister's Kiwanis lecture in which he denounced the Communists as God-hating, property-destroying, striking and rioting, revolutionaries.[27]

Jim Garland, in his book, told how the Communist Press turned its own screws. Copies of the *Daily Worker* distributed in Kentucky inflamed even those who were sympathetic:

> Probably what hurt us the most was a cartoon that appeared about . . . the Bell County sheriff. The artist had pictured the man from behind, nothing but a big, wide bottom with two pistols strapped to either side. Actually, Floyd, as we called him, was at that time trying to maintain a neutral stand, so this cartoon made him madder than a wet hen. He demanded that someone retract the statement and apologize for this rendering of him. Trying to calm him down, I told him,

"Floyd, there isn't any way to retract that. Anyway, that shouldn't bother you; it's the office of sheriff that the cartoonist is attacking. And those guys, under our system of government, can draw anything they want to."[28]

The complex relationship between Communists and miners bears some closer scrutiny. In Draper's view, the miners didn't distinguish the Communist union from any other; it just seemed to give them some hope. The "red peril" worked effectively, however, to divert attention from abysmal wages and conditions.[29] But the Communist union meant more than diversion to the miners.

Clearly the miners who embraced the NMU had little to lose and some dignity to gain. As Dos Passos told it, "the situation of the miners is so desperate that they'll join anything that promises them even temporary help. I asked one man if he'd go to work again under the present scale, supposing he could get past the blacklist. He said, 'You starve if you work an' you starve if you don't work. A man 'ud rather starve out in the woods than starve workin' under the gun.'"[30]

The press targeted and labeled the miners. In one miner's words, "If you are hungry, you are a red . . . and if you tell your neighbor that you are hungry that is criminal syndicalism."[31] When antagonizers called miners "reds," some played with the label symbolically; others denied any knowledge or understanding of the meaning of the term, justifying their own innocence. Tillman Cadle told me how one miner reasoned that "they called them Reds was because the miners were so thin an' poor that if you stood one of 'em up against the sun you'd see red through him." Another miner's wife spoke of the naive attraction to the newcomers.

They called 'em [com-mu'-nists] (as in [com-mu'-nal-ists]), which was [com'-mu-nist], but they didn't know the pronunciation of it. They called em [com-mu'-nists], where it should have been [Com'-mu-nists] . . . I don't know what they was . . . just, kind of like the union now, they was trying to get something started, to have an organization, so that people could have something to live on, you know, wouldn't be so badly mistreated. . . . They even gave 'em clothes . . . like the Church of Christ . . . like when they started the Church here. They wasn't but a very few who took up with it. Everybody was scared.[32]

Molly played with the term "reds," finding it easy to weave into song text: "They call us Rooshun Red Necks . . . I wonder why that is? My folks have been in Kentucky for five generations, but one of 'em was a red Cherokee Indian. Maybe that's why I'm a Red."[33] She later wrote about how operators fired her miner husband, Bill, because his "wife's a Rooshian Red." She asserted later to everyone who would listen, that she "never heard of a Communist until I left Kentucky."[34]

Miners and officials, according to Tillman Cadle, used the term "outsider" selectively: "Most people couldn't tell the difference between Communism and rheumatism." He noted ironically, that Communists, rather than absentee owners, were branded as outsiders: "Joe Weber was talking to me about them calling them [the Communists] 'outsiders' and said, 'Why don't we find out about where these coal operators live?' I said, 'The biggest one don't live in the U.S. It is the English land holding company called the American Association.' He said, 'But they don't call THEM outsiders.'"[35]

Of the voices of the time, Jim Garland captured the confusion over terms and labels: "My point was, 'I don't give a damn what you call your union.' People were already calling us names they themselves didn't understand; even some of the working people were calling us the Communist party. If you had at this time said to a group of average mountain men, 'I'm a Communist,' they more than likely would have answered, 'I'm a Baptist' or 'I'm a Mason.'"[36]

Garland writes, of course, with the benefit of hindsight and Julia Ardery's editorial hand. But his soul searching, as he attempts to integrate the alien ideology with his own experience, is almost palpable. We can understand why he and others embraced the party—a melange of innocence, intellectual probing, and pure desperation. Obviously the labels being tossed around were not totally arbitrary, but neither did they necessarily signify real organizational involvements or thought-through ideological commitments. Jim:

> You must remember that I was a religious man at this time, a deacon of the church, and that most of my family was quite religious. But when a person gets involved, truly involved in a labor struggle, it's hard to keep his religious beliefs primary, mainly because he gets so damn mad. And I was mad. I was burned up and hitting out in every direction even though I didn't know actually where to hit. So I hit at the first thing I could see, and that was the coal operators I was working for. It wasn't that I was fighting for higher wages; I was just trying to fight against further cuts in a starving situation.[37]

The party's ideals seemed to give Jim hope and some way of focusing his anger: "When I later was brought before a Senate subcommittee and asked if I were a Communist, I said, 'I don't know whether I am or not, but I sure as hell am going to find out.' Harry Simms said to me, 'Jim, remember everything has a material base.' And that was the one comment that got me thinking about the bases of my religion and the bases of my politics. It led me at that time, 1931, to believe in the Communist party as the organization that might change things for the mountain people."[38]

Ideology aside, Jim explained how desperation and hunger led him to join forces with the Communists: "Part of me was grabbing at straws . . . I was looking for something, some way that conditions might be improved for the miners and their families. Having such a hard time feeding just my wife Hazel and myself, I didn't know what in this wide world a man with a large family could be doing to stay alive."[39]

But the contradictions finally proved intolerable for the miners and their trust in the NMU collapsed. Alessandro Portelli insightfully analyzes various contests over meaning in the Harlan crisis. Miners and operators locked horns in two parallel struggles: one over class issues, the other over the ownership and control of symbolic systems. Each group considered themselves true Americans and even truer believers in God. Religion wove so thoroughly through daily existence that Communism could be another theological variant. The mountaineers thus had enormous difficulty reconciling revelations of Communist atheism with their own fundamentalism.[40]

One such revelation surfaced at the trial (for "criminal syndicalism"—again resorted to by officials when all else failed) of NMU organizer Doris Parks, as reported in the *Pineville Sun*. When the interrogator, County Attorney Walter B. Smith, asked: "Do you believe in any form of religion?" Doris responded, "I believe in the religion of the workers. These workers here have relied on your religion for bread and butter and now they are starving and you ask these workers to believe in religion." Smith: "Do you believe the Bible and that Christ was crucified?" To which Parks replied, "I believe only in the working class and their right to organize and to teach them that they can be led out of this oppression by the Communist Party."[41]

The truth finally out, miners understood the deep chasm between their beliefs and party ideology. The Communist practice of sending local organizers to training courses in northern cities also opened new doors for reflection. Although Jim contends that his studies, the most important learning experience of his life, taught him to "read between the lines," the weight of evidence discloses miners' disenchantment—particularly when confronting Communist atheism. Portelli cites a returning miner who filed an affidavit: "Fellow workers and citizens, the teachings of the Communist party would destroy our religious beliefs, our government and our homes. In their teachings they demand their members to teach their children [that] there is no God; no Jesus; no Hereafter."[42] In one study, the American Friends Service Committee training courses were deemed "'far more effective in smashing the union than the National Guard ever could have been.'"[43] Malcolm Ross agrees "that the strike was broken less by guns and ships than by the rock-ribbed fundamentalism of the miners."[44]

Class and ideological combat aside, the miners' world view thus accorded more closely with mine operators than with urban Communists. Miners proudly defended their rights as Americans, legitimized by God and the Constitution. When operators and their gun thugs mocked these rights, miners felt betrayed. The Communists offered to help the miners resist victimization and to guard these freedoms, and, for a while, the miners listened; but when they realized that Communists believed in a very different system and no God, the tables turned: marked and unresolvable contradictions seeped into miners' consciousness and the Communists, as idealistic and well intentioned as many were, became the betrayers.

While Communists challenged dearly held religious beliefs, they also defied conventional racial and ethnic biases. Although blacks constituted a relatively small percentage of miners, they made up a significant portion of the strikers and blacklisted. White miners, accustomed to living in separate quarters from blacks in coal towns, managed to work alongside them in mines, but balked at prospects of sharing soup kitchens and tables. Since Communist ideology insisted on brotherhood under the skin, deep, long-running antagonisms, only thinly veiled by ideological rhetoric, waited to resurface. Here, another part of the Doris Parks interrogation becomes relevant through a story told by Tillman Cadle. When the attorney asked Parks, "You wouldn't want your daughter to marry a nigger, would you?" she responded, "'I don't tell my daughter who she should marry. I think my daughter can decide that for herself.'" As Portelli points out, Parks's retort would trigger a negative reaction to the idea of miscegenation in opposing groups—officials and miners.[45]

Although weary of party quibbling, Jim vehemently denied that the Communists and National Miners Union simply duped the workers: his belief in the issues remained steadfast. Disenchanted others, however, turned away. Glaring ideological disparities, a disemboweled strike, the NMU's failure to win more power for the workers—all drove the miners to repudiate the union and the Reds. A chorus of voices expressed their bewildered disappointment:

> The unions have made conditions in Harlan County a whole lot worse than they were.
>
> I'm done with the organization—the men won't stick.
>
> . . . after they got us all out and blacklisted, they left us flat.
>
> I'm through with unions. . . . every time I go to get a job they think I'm an agitator and won't take me on.
>
> I am agin' the Reds. They are agin' God and I am agin' them. They caused a lot of trouble through here. They got men out and tore up the mines.
>
> There ain't no use in the world for the poor men to fight the men who have money.[46]

Although history treats the Communists' Appalachian excursion disdainfully, they did manage to offer glimmers of optimism (which manifested themselves physically) in pleasureless times. I'll borrow Tom Tippett's visceral description of the textile workers during the Gastonia strike, which might have applied as well to Harlan: "people were transformed as much and rapidly as a plant brought out into the sun of early spring after a winter in the cellar. The color of their skin changed, they took on weight, sang songs and marched in parades with a tempo that was entirely new. Men and women stood up at meetings and boasted of increased weight since the strikes had begun."[47]

In Draper's opinion, the Communists' ability to attract attention and publicity remained their strongest talent.[48] Whether one agrees with his interpretation, the party's importance in this regard should not be underestimated. They captured impressive press curiosity and played a crucial role in representing Harlan and the coal strikes to the outside world. The exploited coal miner became a metaphor for all impotent workers in the clutches of the capitalist owner. Local papers, such as the *Louisville Courier-Journal* and *Knoxville News Sentinel* dealt with the Dreiser visit fairly sympathetically, unlike the right-wing *Pineville Sun.* Newspaper reporters dogged Waldo Frank and his "independent miner's relief committee" of twelve writers, including the famed Edmund Wilson and Malcolm Cowley. When the gun thugs "took them for a ride," the writers' experience became perfect grist for the publicity mill. Members of the team subsequently published articles in the *New Republic* (Malcolm Cowley, Mar. 2, 1932) and *New Masses* (Edmund Wilson, Apr. 1932). In May 1932 they testified in front of a Senate subcommittee investigating the coal conditions. The radical press—the *Daily Worker, New Masses,* and *Labor Defender*—devoted healthy space to the Kentucky mine wars. New York's major newspapers, the *Times* and *Herald Tribune,* as well as left-leaning journals, *The Nation* and *New Republic,* exposed a substantial educated audience to the miners' plight.

Members of the Dreiser team, however, generated the most precious print on the Harlan scene. Their own powerful documentary, *Harlan Miners Speak,* published in April 1932, intending to expose mine owners' atrocities and miners' victimizations, was to be a classic work. Harlan miners' detailed public testimonies appeared valorous in the pages, paradigms of oppression, paragons of working-class resistance.

Journalist Bruce Crawford crafts the brutalized innocents who were blacklisted, hounded, evicted, starved, betrayed, and terrorized:

> Their eyes stood out like the eyes of hunted animals, and their voices were shrill, but they told their poignant story simply, clearly, unforgettably. . . .
>
> . . . a gnarled, gaunt, miner of perhaps fifty, made an eloquent speech, straight from the bosom. Here was a picture no modern artist could exaggerate—a bent animal prancing furtively to and fro on the platform, his gray face tense with hatred, his eyes emboldened with this opportunity to unbosom his feelings to the world, his voice husky but firm. He looked like a caged animal. . . . There was desperateness in his impoverished limbs, fangs in his mouth, claws in his hands, and revolution in his heart. He had nothing more to lose.[49]

The miners, paradigmatic of an oppressed class, lost in the wilds of an industrializing economy, enlivened writers' imaginations. Sherwood Anderson's prose entwined the miners' conditions with the loss of innocence, a metaphor for industrial tramplings on people's lives. "There is a new world. It is here. It is a machine world. I do not believe there is anything wrong with the machine. Often it is a beautiful, a powerful, a strange and lovely thing in the world. It has got out of our hands. We are not controlling it now. It has really frightened us, unnerved us. We are in a time of transition now, men and women passing out of one world into another."[50] Anderson, too, established his own class identity and empathy, as "the average young American writer [who] comes from a poor family . . . I was a common laborer until I was 24 or 25 years old. I swear I would have been a better artist, a better story-teller now if I had stayed there. I might then have had something to say here as coming out of the mass of people, out of the hearts of common everyday people."[51]

Of all the writers, John Dos Passos represented the Harlan miner most passionately. Images spewed from his pen on the heels of his 1931 visit, graphically engraving locale and people. He wove tapestries of noble poverty, gauntness, and purity of spirit for various popular journals and later for a novel. Dos Passos's painterly impressions of Harlan merely days after the team's visit, allow the reader to join him in experiencing the coal country they would probably never see:

> As we get near Pineville the valleys deepen. Steep hills burnished with autumn cut out the sky on either side. There's the feeling of a train getting near the war zone in the old days. . . .
>
> At the station is a group of miners and their wives come to welcome the writers' committee: they stand around a little shyly, dressed in clean ragged clothes. A little coaldust left in men's eyebrows and lashes adds to the pallor of scrubbed faces, makes you think at once what a miserable job it must be keeping clean if you work in coal.[52]

> Straight Creek is the section of Bell County that has been organized fairly solid under the National Miners' Union. . . . The militia officers who accompanied us were impressed with the utter lack of sanitation and the miserable condition of the houses, tumble-down shacks set up on stilts with the keen mountain wind blowing through the cracks in the floor.[53]

In *Harlan Miners Speak,* Dos Passos, master of dramatic rendering, stages the Wallins Creek hearings—American roots, heroism, juxtaposed with abject poverty, illuminated spirits in a dark, insecure environment:

The hollow was completely black. To get to the Glendon Baptist Church, where the meeting was to be held, we had to cross a high swinging bridge above the creek-bed. . . . The low frame hall was packed with miners and their wives; all the faces were out of early American history. Stepping into the hall was going back a hundred years. . . . These were the gaunt faces, the slow elaborations of talk and courtesy, of the frontiersmen who voted for Jefferson and Jackson. . . . I never felt the actuality of the American revolution so intensely as sitting in that church, listening to these mountaineers with their old time phrases, getting up on their feet and explaining why the time to fight for freedom had come again.[54]

But for Dos Passos, Aunt Molly Jackson, as no other, embodied them all. Excerpts from "Hungry Ragged Blues" became striking frontispieces in his writings—nakedly, boldly anticipating his prose. "I'm sad and weary, I've got the hongry [*sic*] ragged blues, Not a penny in my pocket to buy one thing I need to use."[55]

Aunt Molly's song, reprinted in several major newspapers and journals, caught all of the devastation and anger of the coalfields. After she left Kentucky for New York at the beginning of December 1931, New York's major newspapers, the *Herald Tribune,* the *New York Times,* even *Fortune* magazine, documented Molly's appearances in New York. As one of the only two real "working class" to write for a special issue of the *Labor Defender,* (organ of the Communist International Labor Defense), Molly included one of her songs, "Bound Down in Prison":

It is sad to be bound down in prison
In a cold prison cell all alone
With the cold iron bars all around
And my head on a pillow of stone . . .

She ends her printed page with a call for solidarity: "let us all unite together and fight starvation, wage cuts. Uniting is what it takes to win our liberty and freedom. I remain your true friend and faithful worker. Aunt Mollie [*sic*] Jackson."[56]

Harlan County, paradigm of working-class courage and resistance, overshadowed its actuality. Notwithstanding the failed strike and the dismal conditions that the miners continued to endure, the Communists managed to thrust Appalachia onto a world stage, enshrining for the annals of history a metaphor of class solidarity that cut across culture, region, race, and gender. Aunt Molly Jackson, whom you have already met, figured significantly, if not in the actual strike, in its rewriting, representation, and meaning. In the next two chapters I tell Molly's story, from her Appalachian girlhood through her marriages and midwifery career, as a songwriter and representative of the rural poor in the big city, through her rise and fall as darling of the radical urban left.

PART 2

Aunt Molly's
(and Sarah's) Life

3

"I Was Born and Raised in Old Kentucky": Aunt Molly Jackson's First Fifty Years

Without a twinge of self-doubt, Aunt Molly Jackson reconstructed her past for others and reveled in each elaboration. Leaving Kentucky in 1931, she traveled north to places beyond her wildest dreams. To some, Aunt Molly's memories benefited history, even more than her songs; to others, her flights of fantasy and wild claims rarely bore up under scrutiny.

Since I introduced Molly to you several chapters ago, some points may bear repeating. The stories of Molly's first fifty years in Kentucky arrive from a variety of sources. She told them to all who would listen or help: anthropologist and folklorist John Greenway elaborated them in his chapter on Molly in *American Folksongs of Protest;* Professor of English and Folklore at New York University, Mary Elizabeth Barnicle recorded Molly's voluminous information on mountain culture, intending to write her own book on the Kentucky woman; folklorist-labor historian, Archie Green interviewed Molly with colleagues and students in Sacramento in the late 1950s, while researching *Only a Miner.* I constantly quarry the latter's tapes, notes, recollections for the meat of Molly's story, particularly for her life after Kentucky. Jim Garland's (Molly's younger half brother) autobiography, edited by Julia Ardery, yields a great deal of material on the evolution of coal mining in Bell and Harlan Counties. Garland's personal recall of Molly's early life intrigues me, although their age difference (Molly was twenty-five when Jim was born to Molly's father's second wife in 1905) meant that Jim could only know some of the stories through others' tellings.

Collectors, dozens of interviewers, journalists, broadcasters, musicians, and writers reacted to Molly diversely: some enjoyed her, found her fascinating; others she embarrassed or made uncomfortable. They either ultimately dismissed her, filed her letters in their archives, or intending to write their own books, left us with assorted fragments of her Kentucky years.

Molly contributed to her own portrait through autobiographical notes, written "because I feel it is my patriotic duty in honor of our forefathers and mothers who established our great democratic nation."[1] She wanted her story to appear as a book, which she desperately tried to have published. The handwritten and typed notes, as well as letters, found their way to some archival collections (Earl Robinson, Mary Barnicle-Cadle, Archie Green) but never made it to print. Typists—Mary Barnicle for one—and others anonymous to us, appeared to transcribe Molly's words as she dictated them; a few altered her earthy expressions into more elegant, grammatically correct phrasings, a polish that, when she knew of it, met her strong disapproval. I, too, when necessary for readability, take the liberty to silently edit, but am aware of attempting to retain Molly's spirit and rhythm.

The "facts" as they appear in this entire legacy of stories were often repeated in a variety of contexts. If Molly felt expansive and well received, she would create, elaborate, perform, endlessly weave and texture her tellings. If not, she would tell more compact versions, but just as determined, and repeat them for as many who would listen. Molly didn't merely talk or write, but vividly colored her anecdotes with dialogue, modifying her voice to suit its drama, infusing the narrative with graphic adjectives, grinning and grimacing, spontaneously rhyming.

At times Molly's dates and reporting of incidents confuse, or fail to gel with others' accounts. Some scholars, disillusioned by Molly's inconsistencies, began to suspect her versions. John Greenway, for example, decided after the publication of *American Folksongs of Protest,* which featured Molly Jackson heavily, that she simply lied to him. Archie Green lost patience with her claims to authorship of songs that he felt others wrote or that belonged to "tradition."

We can try to rationalize or explain these discrepancies: Molly's faulty memory; retellings informed by imaginative reconstruction; or even blatant fabrications. Tillman Cadle, convinced of the latter, relished in telling me that Molly "stretched her blanket," the mountain expression for outright lying. Perhaps details of events, simply lost in time, became Molly's elaborations and took on a life of their own. But stories also come from enthusiastic scholars and writers, who created their (our) own mythologies, perpetuating Molly's larger-than-life image. It follows that because we construct history as a social story and negotiate the "truth," we must hold all tellers accountable for their inclusions and omissions. The story I tell here becomes my juggling act of voices: Molly's, family and associates, folklorists, transcribers, ideologies.

Without question, the overarching public portrait of Molly reveals a self-involved and self-important woman. Nevertheless, Molly's personality remains enigmatic. She flaunted her trouble-making, provocative, arrogant, defiant side. She crafted an image as composer-singer of protest songs, as outrageously "foul-mouthed," storyteller, "ferocious" defender of the downtrodden, indomitable organizer and fundraiser for the miners, and the one and only "Pistol-Packin' Mama." But few recognized the other Mollys: the sensitive child who grieved for her mother, remembered her grandmother's ballads, felt neglected by her father and his second wife; or the competent adult, a skilled nurse and midwife, believer in ghosts and spirits and dreams, who mourned the loss of her half-brother, cared for his family, and remained deeply in love with one of her husbands, Jim Stewart.

Molly's awareness of social factors shone through her personal quests—not only the schisms between classes and races, but of gender issues as well. Many of her songs frame the coal struggles in terms of particular consequences for women and children. Despite much in common with other Appalachian women, Molly stood apart and challenged the conservative, mountain culture, constantly testing and stretching the boundaries of appropriate gender behavior.

Beyond the discrepancies and inconsistencies in Molly's tellings, a coherent picture emerges from her first fifty years. Her stories offer insights into the Appalachian coal-mining world with its struggles for food and justice. The following is my attempt, Molly, to hear your voice, to piece together the puzzles, to tell your story using some of your words and some of mine, to understand your desires, and the forces that shaped you.

The long passage below begins Molly's rambling telling of her childhood from one of her autobiographical fragments entited "The Story of My Life by Aunt Molly Jackson, Herself." I'll keep it essentially unedited in order to give you an idea of her prose:

I can remember looking out through a crack in the log cabin where I was born in and seeing high banks of snow. The snow had fallen that night while we were asleep. I remember hearing my grandad Garland saying the snow was six foot deep. I was three years old that past October and this snow fell in December which will prove to you I was three years old when I began to remember. Yes, I can remember sixty-one years ago when I saw my grandad Garland dragging a big pine log through the snow. I remember to this day the color of the scarf my grandad had tied around his ears, and he was making a road from our log cabin to his by pulling that big pine log through the snow with two big yoke of steers, and I remember my mother when she saw this snow so deep she began to cry and weep. Her cheeks were wet with tears because my mother and I was all alone. My father was working away from home. This happened when I was three years and two months old. My daddy was over to my grandads sister's digging coal in a coal mine. . . . That's when my father became interested in coal mining. . . . Then my daddy sold his farm in Clay County before I was four and moved to the first coal mine that was ever opened up in Kentucky.[2]

In September 1880, sixteen-year-old Deborah Robinson and seventeen-year-old Oliver Peoria Garland, of Clay County, Kentucky, bore their first child. Mary Magdalene Garland became Aunt Molly Jackson, a ninth-generation Kentuckian.[3] We know only what Molly tells us about her parents. Deborah's family, the Robinsons, although from Kentucky, originally came from Scotland and Ireland. Oliver's father, Captain William Garland, of English descent, served in the Civil War. Captain Garland's father (also William), Molly's great-grandfather, married a full-blooded Cherokee woman. Molly's sweet story about their romance tells of how great-grandfather, Billy, who worked for an Indian chief in Oklahoma, fell in love with the chief's daughter, who reciprocated: "'Billy, if you leave me here, I'll die from a broken heart.' 'You know I am a white man and if I was to steal you, and they'd catch me . . . they would kill me.' She said, 'You don't have to steal me. I'll hide my clothes out in the fork of the road, in that hollow tree. At four o'clock in the morning I'll meet you there on my filly.'"[4] Billy brought his sweetheart from Oklahoma to Clay County, Kentucky, where they married.

Oliver Garland, who at various times in his life sharecropped, preached (Baptist), coal mined, doctored, and organized unions, farmed in Clay

County at the time of Molly's birth. The new coal mine in Laurel County attracted Oliver, but as a shopkeeper rather than a miner. He and Deborah opened a butcher shop and grocery store in the camp. Extending generous credit to miners, they plummeted into debt within a year. Faced with bankruptcy, a wife, and three children to feed (Molly, John, and a younger sibling—a fourth had died), Oliver reluctantly began to sharecrop, eventually resorting to going down in the mines. Molly revoiced Oliver's concerns (as he reportedly told them to Deborah), in her characteristic poetic form: "Now our youngest son is one year old and oldest daughter is five, and the price the coal operators pay per ton for the coal we are digging today, I don't think it will keep us alive. One thing I know I want our children to live and be healthy and grow, but with prices so high and wages so low, I just don't see how we can thrive."[5]

An energetic, committed Oliver, despite his skepticism, saw hope for the future in unions. He began organizing for the Knights of Labor (according to Jim, "more of a lodge than a union") in 1885. Traveling around to the coal camps that began to mushroom in the Kentucky mountains, he tried to convince miners "to unite into one big union that Jesus Christ Himself called the brotherhood of man." Oliver's longest affiliation, however, with the United Mine Workers of America, began in the late 1890s and continued until his death in the early 1920s. Jim Garland quoted one of Oliver's sermons intertwining religion and commitment to worker's rights: "'Come now, you rich men, weep and howl for your torment that has come upon you. You have heaped up together treasures and the rust of them shall eat your flesh as if it were fire. You have held back by fraud the wages of those that labor in your fields and the cries of them have reached up to heaven against you.'"[6] Molly attributed her own early consciousness about the plight of the exploited to Oliver's sensitivity. "'My dad was a strong union man and a good minister, . . . so he taught me to be a strong union woman."[7] At four years of age, Molly wrote her first song, which pleased Deborah, who rewarded her daughter with a doll house and, according to Molly, often sung it to other mothers.

> My friends and relations, listen if you will;
> The Bible plainly tells us we shall not kill.
>
> If I love you, and you love me,
> Oh, how happy we all would be!

But if I hit you and you will fall,
Then you won't answer me when I call.

Because you will be so mad at me,
You will not want to play under my walnut tree.

So I want to be good to you so you will want to be good to me,
Then we can all be happy—don't you see?

If you love your neighbor, he will love you;
Do unto others what you want them to do to you.[8]

Even at this tender age, Molly reveals her sense of reciprocity.

Although Molly claimed a special talent for spontaneous songmaking, she never hesitated to credit her mountain musical legacy and explain that songs and stories were the ways Kentucky mountain people entertained themselves: "Our ancestors wrote songs about their own lives, their sweethearts, their husbands, their wives, their children and their daily lives. Then they wrote a lot of funny little jigs about their pigs, their donkeys, their cows and their good old hunting dog that treed coons, possums and ground hogs."[9]

Molly's earliest recollections show that her great grandmother (ninety-two when she was four) profoundly influenced her interest in singing: "She took me on her knee and sang the songs to me that my great-great grandmother knew. I want to say I was very proud of my great grandmother that taught me most of the folk songs that I know. Her name was Nancy Mac Mahan which is a good old Irish name. . . . Sometimes it seems I can hear her voice today as she sang 'Lord Thomas,' and 'Lord Bateman' and 'The Gypsy Davey' and hundreds of folk songs to me when I was between three and four years old."[10]

At age six, Molly faced her first losses. Her mother and younger sister died within six weeks of one another. The two deaths, especially that of her twenty-six-year-old mother, thrust Molly all too quickly into adult responsibilities. She never recovered from the wrenching emotional experiences, only the beginning of a series of losses that shaped her understandings. In this graphic autobiographical fragment, Molly discloses her feelings about the tragedies:

My youngest sister died six weeks before my mother died. She was only two years old. She began to cramp in the stomach at three o'clock in the morning. By seven o'clock she was lifeless and cold. My mother wept and cried after her little girl baby. She cried so much she began to have awful pains in her head. She took down with brain fever, and in sixteen days my beautiful mother was dead. The death of my little sister and the death of my mother is the first sorrow I ever knew, since then God only knows all the sadness and sorrow that I have lived to go through.[11]

Although still just a very young child herself, Molly now found herself thrust into a caretaking role:

How well I remember the night my darling mother passed away. It was the sixteenth of November when she called me to her bed side and these were the words she had to say. She told me that she was then dying and that my brother [John] and I would soon be left in the world without a mother. She asked me to promise to be kind and good to my little brother. She said to me 'You're six years old and your little brother is three. Take good care of him and help him to remember me.'. . . The promise I made to my mother that night she died never left my mind.[12]

Stored in her memory, Molly textured the painful details of her mother's burial a half century later:

I remember my poor dad going to a man by the name of Bryce Mobly and give him all the furniture we had for taking his wagon and team and taking us back to Raiders Creek in Clay County. On the eighteenth morning of November this man come and loaded up the lifeless body of my mother and my brother John and I started back to Clay Country to bury my mother. I remember how my mother's coffin was placed in the center of the wagon, and my brother John and I was placed in the wagon on one side of our mother's coffin on a feather bed that my mother's mother had give her when she and my dad was married. Then my dad covered us over with home made blankets that my grandmother had wove for him when my dad was married. It was only fifty five miles back to Clay Country from Laurel Country where my mother died, and the road was so bad it took two days to make the trip. It rained and snowed on us all the way for two days. My mother's coffin was covered with snow and sleet and the blankets that was over my brother and I, and we were plenty cold all the way back to the old home grave yard. She was the oldest child in my grandad Robinson's family. My mother had nine brothers and sisters younger than her. I remember when we got in hearing of the house. I heard my grandmother and grandfather and my mother's three grown sisters screaming and crying because my mother was dead. . . . I remember well the day my mother was buried. She has now been dead fifty years.[13]

Following Deborah's death, Oliver took Molly and John back to his parents' farm, where they remained for eleven months. Molly recalled being happy there until her father married Deborah's seventeen-year-old cousin, Elizabeth, a mere eleven years older than Molly. Oliver's second marriage to a close relative upset his mother. Molly explained "Back in thar days it was a terrible sin for a boy and a girl to get married if they were kin. . . . They claim they had the same blood run through their children veins through the fourth and fifth generation. My grandmother told my dad that he would be cursed all the days of his life for marrying his own uncle's daughter."[14] Oliver (whom Jim Garland described as five foot six, but not afraid of anything)[15] apparently closed his ears to objections.

Since Oliver traveled and preached extensively while his teenaged wife Elizabeth stayed much of the time at her own mother's house (the couple lived on her mother's farm), neither parent spent much time with the children. Tensions between Molly and her stepmother surfaced quickly. In Jim Garland's account, Molly was headstrong, distorted the truth, and caused her parents, particularly her young stepmother, no end of grief: "Once when Molly went to a neighbor's house to spend the night, she told these folks that my mother wouldn't let any of the children eat meat. Molly said Mother would take a meat skin and rub it all around our mouths to make my father think that all of us had eaten. Molly also claimed Mother would tie a meat skin to a piece of string, force us to swallow the meat, and then pull it back out of our throats."[16]

Molly's own narrative shows a different side. Vulnerable after her mother's death, she felt rejected, even abused, by her new stepmother.

A first cousin to my own mother, but she was a stranger to me and my brother, so we was awful unhappy. We used to sit around and talk about our own mother and cry. Our step-mother was only a child herself, only sixteen. I often thought she was the prettiest woman I ever seen, but my brother and I thought she treated us awful mean because she went away and left us every day. . . . I used to roast 'taters and parch corn and cry and wish I had never been born. I set traps for snow birds all day long while my step-mother and daddy was gone. I was seven years old then and my brother John was four. I was always so badly frightened when we was alone. I was afraid we would never be able to see our dad any more. I was afraid some wild beast like a wild cat or panther would come up to the door. Yes, I would watch through the cracks of the log cabin and look and listen for wild animals to come out of the woods and tear me and my little brother to pieces some day while my dad and step-mother was away. We lived up that dark hollow for two years after.[17]

On the first anniversary of her mother's death, Molly composed this song:

> I was young but I remember well
> The night my mother died
> It was a cold night in December
> When she called me to her side
>
> She told me then that she was dyin'
> And that I would soon be left alone
> She asked me to take good care
> Of my little brother after she is dead and gone
>
> I remember it well as if it was yesterday
> And that lonesome old willow tree
> Was blowing and I yelled out,
> Sadly blows that weepin' willow
> Just like me she stands alone
> I've had no one to love me
> Since my mother's dead and gone[18]

Molly painted her loneliness vividly, shared with her brother, John, whom she felt responsible for:

> We used to say we felt like two old fishermen that had been struck by a big ship and wrecked with no one to guide them to safety. We was awful depressed from neglect, because our dad left home every morning before it was even daylight, and he did not get home from his work on the farm til ten o'clock in the night. . . . We used a woolen blanket on our bed that our grandmother gave our dad for a sheet. These wool blankets were white, and every night the blood would run out of our frost bitten feet, then our stepmother would scold us and mistreat us because she found spots of blood on our sheet. One day my little brother said, "Why can't we die now that our mother is dead?"[19]

Molly told of how poverty compounded her feelings of isolation and rejection. During the first dreary winter of Oliver's remarriage, she and John, shoeless, "had to use a hot board to set our feet on when we had to go out behind a stable or a rock pile which was the only kind of a toilet we had to use them days . . . we used a corn cob for toilet paper." Survival struggles, a constant theme in Molly's life, began early, with money for the barest essentials difficult to come by.

> I had one little cotton dress that cost five cents a yard and wore that dress till I had to tie the ragged strings together in the front for weeks before I could get ten cents worth of eggs saved up before I could buy another cotton dress. . . . Eggs was fifteen cents a dozen. . . . I know it will be hard for some people to believe that times had ever been so hard that you just could not get a hold of any money at all, not even ten cents to buy a cotton cloth enough to make a dress. . . . You had to save up eggs to buy your coffee, soda and sugar, and if you didn't have any hens to lay eggs you would have to sell corn.[20]

Oliver, who cast around for a variety of ways to support his family, couldn't subsist on the dearth of remuneration for back-breaking labor. Molly would later call on her father's example as a rationale for organizing workers: "My poor old dad worked that winter twelve hours a day for a bushel of corn and then he would carry that three miles on his back to the mill to get it ground into cornmeal to make into bread. Then the miller would take a peck of corn out of every bushel. . . . Nobody knows child as I was how sad I would feel when I began to realize my dad had to work twelve hours a day for only three pecks of cornmeal or five pounds of meat, that was when my daddy said that a union could never be beat."[21]

Molly (eight) and John (five) spent carefree moments during this period, hunting rabbits and squirrels in the mountains with their stepmother's youngest (twelve-year-old) brother, Dickie Lucas. Dickie would call Molly "Joe," lend her his old britches, coat and coonskin hat "so if any other boy met us in the woods when we was out a huntin' they would think I was just another boy. Dickie Lucas had a wonderful voice. He had one song he would always sing when he wanted my brother and I to meet him half way between his house and our house . . .":

> "Come in little stranger," I said,
> as she tapped at my half open door

She had a blanket pinned over her head
and I never had saw her before.
She had a basket hung over her arm
She looked like she was ready to cry
As she said, "I have matches to sell,
and I hope you're willing to buy.
I need money to buy milk and bread
for my invalid mother and I."
My mother is an invalid she said
My father was lost in the sea
And I have these matches to sell
To buy food for my mother and me
I pity this poor orphan child
This story she told was so sad
I looked at her kindly and smiled
Then I bought all the matches she had
Now, go home, little stranger, go home
Go home to your mother I said
Then the little girl bid me good bye
With a blanket pinned over her head.[22]

Molly recalled other happy times, like when she and her friends Molly Rogers and Sally Ann would stay up all night and sing to each other.

Two years after his second marriage, Oliver left the farm and moved to the coalfields, where he remained for a while. His young wife Elizabeth (who Molly always refers to as her "stepmother" in her writings) gave birth every year, adding eleven more children, with Molly acting as a surrogate mother. Jim Garland (born in 1905) and Sarah Garland (born in 1910), were the tenth and twelfth. Of the fifteen children that Oliver sired, only six survived to adulthood and four remained alive when Molly wrote her life story in the 1940s. "Every twelve and thirteen months my dads last wife would have another baby, and I had to take care of them all. . . . They seem much more like my own children rather than my brothers and sisters."[23] Although very young girls were expected to care for siblings, Molly was clearly resentful about responsibilities, particularly because she felt her mother was shirking her own, and was determined to get an education. "My own dear mother's brother told me that I would grow up to be a fool if my stepmother kept me home to work all the time and would not let me go to school. But I went to school for three months after my mother died and I learned to read and write."[24]

With domestic chores weighing her down, the rebellious Molly need-ed outlets for fun. Despite Oliver's warning that dancing is a devil's activ-ity, she found ways to defy him, and stole away to her first dance party on Christmas Eve just after her ninth birthday.

> My dad was peeping in at the window when he heard John call out "Swing your partner and skiptumalue." Then my dad jumped in and grabbed me by the hair of my head and drug me out and took me home. He beat me in the head with his fist and slapped me in the face til I felt dizzy all the next day. But that did not stop me from slipping out and going to parties and places to dance. I always loved music and dancing. My mother's [Deborah's] father was the best fiddler in Clay County, Kentucky. I used to never be able to keep my feet still when my grandad was playing the fiddle. When I was three years old I was afraid to let my dad see me move my feet when my grandad was playing the fiddle. . . . We would go into the taverns and restaurants and dance for money. Somedays we would have a whole pint cup full of silver peo-ple would give us. I was between eight and nine years old when I would slip out and dance for money. I used to win prizes for hoe down dancing. . . . My dad was never able to find out about me slipping out and dancing, because we never did offer to dance in the town where we lived. My dad used to think I was going to Mistress Brown's house to help her in the garden and sweep and wash dishes . . . so after I growed up I realize that I had been forced to lead my life as a lie.[25]

Molly constantly worried, however, about the consequences of Oliv-er's wrath and didn't freely go to parties until she married Jim Stewart and moved ninety miles from home and well away from her father's scrutiny.[26]

One of Molly's formative and most told experiences, which she tends to elaborate slightly differently depending on her audience, led to the composition of Molly's earliest multi-versed song. At age ten, while living at her grandparents' (Robinson) farm on Big Sexton Creek, Molly played a Christmas prank. Smearing her face with charcoal, she fashioned horns, and donned her grandfather's trousers and rifle. Her grunts and howls terrified children at a farmhouse down the road, and one actually faint-ed. His father summoned the sheriff, and, invoking the law against the use of "disguise," he arrested Molly, sentencing the unruly child to ten days in jail. In her autobiography, Molly explains how she coped with this ex-perience:

The County judge married a first cousin to my father, and he felt awful sorry for me, and he asked me what on earth caused me to do such a thing as to disguise myself in men's clothes. He asked me if I didn't know that was strictly against the law. I told him I did not know anything about the law and that I didn't mean any harm. I only thought that I would have a little fun out of the children on Christmas eve. Then the judge told me the best he could do was to give me the lowest penalty which was ten days in jail and a twenty-five dollar fine, and I asked him, "How do you think that I could go to jail, and me a little girl as I was?" I told him, "you know there has never been a stain on my whole generation's christian morals, much less to go to jail." Then the jailer told me I would not have to stay in jail, that I would just go to his house and stay with his wife, who was a first cousin to my mother. I decided if I pretended that I had no mind [was crazy] that she would get sorry for me and have her husband send me home. So when I went in the house I began to act foolish like.[27]

Molly then changed her mind and decided on another strategy—she appealed to the sheriff in a song that she wrote and sang to the jailer and his wife at supper that night, which we could see as her first protest composition.

> The day before Christmas I had some fun
> I blacked my face and took my gun
> I went up to Bill Louis's and made them run
> Mr. Cundif turn me loose.
>
> The next Monday morning old Bill Louis got out a writ
> When I found this out, the wind I split
> Mr. Cundif turn me loose.
>
> It was just three weeks til I come back to play
> Old Cotton arrested me the very next day
> Mr. Cundif turn me loose.
>
> Then I thought my case would be light
> Cotton took me before Judge Wright
> Judge Wright told me I'd done wrong
> For blackin' my face and puttin' britches on
> Mr. Cundif turn me loose.
>
> He listened to me 'til I told my tale
> Then he give me ten days in Cundif's jail

When I went to jail they thought I was a fool
They didn't offer me as much as a stool
But the jailer's wife, she treated me kind
Because she thought I had no mind
Now, what she thought I did not care
I knew I was just as smart as her
Mr. Cundif turn me loose.

Well it ain't no use to cry and snub
While I'm eatin' old Cundif's grub
Tho' very much better I would do
If old Cundif would furnish me "tobaker" to chew
Altho' I am healthy, young, and stout
If I can't get "tobaker," I can do without
Mr. Cundif turn me loose.

Hello, Mr. Cundif! If you'll open the door
I won't put my britches on anymore
Mr. Cundif turn me loose.

The old hymn book lays on the shelf
If you want anymore song
Compose it yourself
Mr. Cundif turn me loose.[28]

There were, apparently a few verses that didn't make it beyond that first singing:

A jailer in London is a very fine man
Mr. Condor[sic], won't you tarn me loose?
A jailer in London is a very fine man
and he feeds his prisoners the best he can
But old thee, doggone his soul
We will scratch his eyes and throw sand in his hold
Pete Condor, won't you tarn me loose?

The nits and lice they are hangin' to the jiste [joists]
I heard one turn over and say "Jesus Christ!"
Mr. Condor, Won't you tarn me loose?[29]

In Molly's explanation of the impact of her song to Barnicle, she revealed, "It was very much against the law to hev lice in the jail and when I sang those verses he got busy and got judges and ever'body to hear me sing the other verses to keep me from singin' this stuff." When Barnicle asked if there were lice in there, Molly responded, "Naw, there warn't none."[30]

Molly's song apparently so impressed the jailer that he called the county judge and attorney, as well as other officials, to hear it. Although they offered her no reprieve, people requested repeat performances, bestowing her (to her delight and surprise) with money and gifts. She proudly recalled, "At the end of ten days I had thirty seven dollars and twenty seven plugs of 'tobaker' and the jailer's wife made me a satin dress with 'yeler' butterflies, and she bought me a high top pair of fine button shoes and a handbag. . . . Then I was ten years and six months old."[31] Describing the dress slightly differently to *Daily Worker* reporter Valentine Ackland in New York, Molly remembered it as "the beautifullest dress that ever I did have."

Although Molly claimed to have written earlier songs, Hazel Garland told me that she believes "Mr. Cundiff" stood as her only pre-Harlan strike composition, and that Molly considerably polished and altered it before performing it for New York audiences in the 1930s. Despite the various elaborations of the story's details, the incident must have influenced Molly's perception of the power of performance, and of how persuasive, personally rewarding, and politically useful, songwriting can be.

After her jail episode, Molly began working for "Miz" Lizzie Jarvis, the wife of another jailer in Barbersville, Knox County, Kentucky, washing dishes and sweeping floors for fifty cents a week. There Molly luxuriated in an affluent lifestyle and some rare nurturing.

> Miz Jarvis took me up-stairs and give me a bath in the first bath tub I ever saw in my life. Then she shampood my hair and plaited my hair in braids and tied red bows of ribbon in my hair. Then she dressed me up in her little girl's clothes and put a nice little pair of slippers on my feet. These slippers had silver buckles and I thot they was the prettiest things I ever had saw, in fact, they was the first pair of slippers I ever had saw in my life. I had come to town bare footed because no children had any shoes to wear being the summer and fall and only the well to do families bot shoes for the children at any time them days. Miz Jarvis give me a nickname. . . . She called me "Patsy."[32]

Miz Jarvis, unfortunately became disenchanted with Molly, and fired her for interfering in her relationship with another employee, by an act that Molly saw as simple kindness. She gave an "old colored lady, Miz Jarvis' wash woman, two dollars to buy something to eat for her children," which Molly insists was indirectly, but ultimately, responsible for some good fortune and for leading her into her future profession as a nurse. Shortly after starting her new job at the county clerk's house, helping to tend fifteen children and twelve bedrooms, Molly contracted whooping cough. Miz Jarvis's grateful washerwoman visited Molly, bringing a compound of honey, garlic, garden horehound, and whiskey. Molly avowed that this mash cured her and inspired her to take up nursing. She told the story to illustrate how good deeds paid off:

> I have cured many cases of whooping cough with the same remedy since I have been a nurse. So you see the two dollars I gave this wonderful kind old colored lady caused her to come to see me and bring this wonderful remedy that saved my life, and teach me how to save many cases of whooping cough, and this gave me such a desire to become a nurse and by the time I was eighteen, I was able to make a first class diploma for a mid-wife and nurse. And from that time to this day, I have always done by others just what this dear old colored lady done for me. That is, I mean I treat every human being just as I would have them treat me.[33]

Molly's stories invariably illustrated how she managed to convert negative into positive experiences. They provided moral or ethical lesson material, supporting the effectiveness of her resistance against injustice. The theme of others' racial bias and Molly's *lack* of it threaded through them: "If a boss mistreats one working person, that should give all the rest of the working people to understand that that boss should not be trusted I have learned this is true by experience, because I learned this lesson when I was a small child. And this is something else important that I learned when I was a child; that if a colored person is your friend, they will do more for you than your own white race."[34]

Jim Garland tells us that Molly married John Mills in her early teens, whom "she found so foolish and stingy that he lived only on corn bread and jallop, a gravy made from cornmeal."[35] Molly preferred to forget this first marriage, and fails to mention Mills in her autobiographical notes. She told John Greenway that Calloway Clance stole her heart as "the first boy I ever loved in my life." In her own pain-filled words, "His aunt separated us cause they wanted him to marry a rich widow woman that had a husband who had died and left her a big farm and a lot of money. We were planning all that summer to be married and when his parents split us I thought of committing suicide . . . you should see the sad love songs I wrote from that."[36] Seeing Calloway again a few years later, "her knees commenced just trembling."[37] In April 1894, Molly married coal miner Jim Stewart, the date recorded in an announcement in the Pineville newspaper. She was thirteen and a half.

Finally able to claim independence from her father and stepmother, a still innocent Molly just started to menstruate and claimed to know nothing about sex. When husband Jim "raised her nightgown," she'd tie it down or jump into her mother-in-law's bed for protection.[38] At fifteen and a half she bore her first child and at seventeen (fifteen months later) her second son came. Since I found no further information about Molly's babies, they probably died in infancy. Molly, however, talks about raising two of Jim Stewart's children (son, Jesse Willis and daughter, Lillian Lee, both from other women), and four of Bill Jackson's.[39]

The Stewarts followed work to various coal camps (Tucky Hole in Bell County, Ely Branch, Black Raven), where Jim mined and Molly nursed and practiced midwifery. They both attended moonlight school in Clay County (established by northern women), where Molly learned the alphabet in a day and read the primer in a week. No longer subjected to Oliver's disapproving eye, Molly adored dance parties. She and Jim developed some fancy footwork, entered contests, and, according to Molly, regularly won the prize money.[40]

Molly's midwifery career began at age twelve helping Doctor Pennington deliver babies. Tillman Cadle told me an amusing story that he heard about her youthful fearlessness. When the doctor was late, the unflustered Molly stepped in. Responding to the father's question about how many babies she delivered, Molly claimed, "I caught fifty!" The baby successfully out, he gasped, "Well, I guess you caught one hundred, not fifty!" When the doctor finally showed, he was delighted to see the intact newborn but encouraged Molly to reveal her birthing inexperience to the family. "Well," Molly retorted, "I was talking about rabbits!"

Although mountain people usually call midwives "Granny," "Aunt" seemed more applicable for the young Molly.[41] By age eighteen she had a diploma (it's not known who certified this, probably an apprenticeship), then nursed and delivered babies at a Clay County hospital for ten years, after which she set up an independent practice in Harlan County. At age twenty-three, after fourteen months of training with an Indian herb specialist, Molly patented an Indian herb medicine. Assuring others of her considerable healing skills, she wrote, "I set up my own office and became a doctor myself, delivered eight hundred and seventy eight babies without losing one baby or one mother. I rode all over them Kentucky mountains delivering babies."[42] She earned twenty-five cents for each birth certificate she sent to the Louisville state board, received in the form of a check once a year—a total of thirty-five or forty dollars.[43]

Jim Garland, generally skeptical of Molly's reportings, acknowledged his half-sister's success and reputation as a midwife, as she "delivered far more babies during those years [1910–32] than did all the doctors on both Horse Creek in Clay County and Straight Creek in Bell County." And, "According to Molly's own estimate, she attended over 5,000 births."

> Midwives, usually middle-aged or older women, were mostly tough old girls. . . . Even if mountain women took care of the birth themselves, they generally wanted a midwife to check them over, to be on the safe side. Lots of times, granny women would stay over after the women had delivered their babies, doing the housework until the mothers could do for themselves. Aunt Molly was highly thought of as a midwife; in fact, many women preferred her help to that of a doctor. Serving at the births of two of my children, she did quite nicely.[44]

Barnicle, particularly curious about Molly's midwifery experiences, recorded detailed accounts that reveal her extensive knowledge of and competence around childbirth. Molly's story of Shelby Baker's wife displays a willingness to take risks, as well as skill, sensitivity, and calm.

> I risked my life acrossin' over the dam jist across Horse Creek because she had this baby misplaced and pitched four different times between the seventh and ninth month. The last time she pitched in a way that the hips would come first so when the child come she might die. That is why I bridged the water to git this case. And sure enough, it was a feet-foremost case. I got the right foot at 1:30 but then the little leg was in such a way that I had to wait until the rump expanded and it was wide in order to take out the foot and leg without lacerating the mother. It was then 6:30 the next morning before I could safely git the other leg. I took the left foot then I jist took it by the little hips and I worked him down until I could git my fingers under the arms and the next labor pains expelled everything but the head. Then I took the little

thing and give it a shake and out come the little head. The afterbirth was tangled round his neck and I was afraid he'd choke. I said to the grandmother, "Hold the covers up until I unwrap the baby from the neck." She got worried, "How was it born?," she asked. I just answered, "Oh, it was born alright," because I didn't want to excite the mother. After I dressed the child and took care of her and put her off to sleep and the mother was OK, I took the grandmother aside: "I couldn't afford to answer you and excite Sally. Mebbe she'd hev hed a hemorrhage and died."[45]

As always, stories contain a point and a lesson for Molly, as they often, too, unveil her service and self-sacrifice:

Git this point down [to Barnicle] thet the most important thing in the world is havin' an intelligent set of plans and good judgement. . . .
    I hev larned more from practice and experience than I hev ever larned from a doctor's book. I say thet will power and intelligence and guts is the important thing. The greatest pleasure in this world from a little child for me was tryin' to relieve sufferin' humanity. Anybody thet was sick. When other children would hev a great deep sincere desire to be out playin' ball I would like to be sittin' by the bedside of my neighbors thet was sick, helpin' around the place to help sufferin' humanity; and I was bred from thet kind of a man with thet kind of a principle. And I couldn't be nothin' else.[46]

As midwives in other times and places, Molly intimately understood the relationship between mind and body, knew of birth control and abortion methods, and pragmatically used them. Cynicism would surface, though, when she talked about the consequences of blind religious belief: "You know these cleanings that people take up here after they've had sexual intercourse with a man, they figure down that its murder and they think the'd never git forgiven for wilful murder. It's religion they makes them hev all the children. They hev nothing to take but there is weeds that grows that you can make tea out of at the first start of labor."[47]
    Although, as I mentioned above, Molly's own two children most likely died in infancy, she defined herself as a mother, loving and protecting those of her husbands (six children in all), taking credit for her ability to provide for them. Shortly after she married Jim, Molly dreamed that his dead mother asked her to care for Jim's seven year-old sister, Fannie. Molly took this "warning dream" very seriously and felt responsible for Fan-

nie's welfare. Fannie stayed with some relatives in Knox County, away from her home district, and couldn't attend the local school. When the local schoolmaster's wife informed her that Fannie wasn't eligible for admission, Molly raged, "'Oh, yes she'll go to school.'" "I went up and got the books and paid for them and put them under my arm and picked up Ed Hendrick's rusty old .45 and I blacked the earth up and I shot hell out of the ground." Threatening to "bust the fat belly" of the offending woman, Molly showed her "she can't chase me no place." Fannie went to school.[48]

Molly also adopted Jim Stewart's infant son, Jesse (the result of his union with a known neighborhood prostitute), who was sent to Molly to cure his spinal injury. Although Molly knew Jim fathered Jesse, and blamed him for his irresponsibility, she couldn't let the baby suffer for the sins of his parents. "I got me three night bottles and three day bottles and malted milk for food. Five weeks after I took him I went and got the beef brine which was recommended the best in the world to rub the spinal cord to help the paralyzed nerves." Molly became very attached to the infant, who began to regain movement in his limbs: "Oh, I never was so proud and relieved in my life and by the first of April what a big sparkling fat baby . . ." She then adopted Jim's younger child, Lillian Lee, cured her of head lice, and took great pleasure in watching her grow: "I kin jist see her now how she used to sing and hum and she was jist a little thing eight years old and she was so particular in washing little hankies and feel them was they dry and then arn [iron] them and put them away. So along with the bad I hed some good."[49]

Molly relates in her autobiography that Jim Stewart's poor health prompted the couple to move to Florida in 1907, when Molly was twenty-seven. After Jim found work for a lumber company, they reconciled themselves to living away from the mountains. Molly's Florida experiences threw into relief her reactions against injustice. For example, she witnessed a shop owner's violence against a young black employee, understood it as racism, and responded accordingly. When she threatened to "'blow [the white boss'] stinking brains all over the floor,'" he called the police and demanded they "'arrest [the] white woman for taking sides with the niggers.'"[50]

Dismayed to find that Floridians didn't think much of Kentuckians, Molly submitted a poem to the *Pineville Sun,* attempting to communicate her perception of their misunderstandings.

My dear old mountain friends
You are far behind the news
I write to you a line or two
About these Florida peoples views.

The people here in Florida
Seem to think the mountain folks are fools.
They claim we are poorly equiped for churches
And poorly equiped for schools.

They seem to think we make a living
By running moonshine stills,
But thank God we have a more excellent way to live,
In our dear old mountains and hills.

You don't know how my heart ached
And how it distressed my mind,
When a lady in a Baptist church
Read a story about a mountain girl.

Her name was Becky Lyon,
Becky was pictured in her Mother's old faded bonnet
And a faded calico dress
When if she had been a moonshiners daughter,
She would have been dressed in the very best.

Just like these whiskey sellers here in Florida
And these men with big race tracks,
They have always got plenty of money
And good clothes on their backs.

You need not go to our dear old mountain home
To find your household gods
To look on whiskey sellers
You need not go a rod,
Right here in Florida
Where gosple is shining all around.

If you will look for whiskey sellers
and whiskey stills
I'm sure they can be found.[51]

Unexpected rewards again followed. She showed the poem to a Baptist pastor, who, worried about negative implications for the church, begged her not to send it to the newspaper (a request that she disregarded). However, recognizing and hoping to co-opt the mountain woman's verbal gifts, he offered her (and she accepted) a preaching job for the royal sum of seventy-five dollars a month. Although the money enticed her, Molly already claimed a new calling to follow in her Baptist lay preacher father's footsteps. Molly told Barnicle of the time she and Oliver came across some Holiness people preaching in a grove (she doesn't indicate when this happened). When Oliver contradicted their teachings, they called him a "wicked man." Defending her father, Molly mocked the congregants, especially their strange habit of speaking in tongues. Her husband's sister, Julie, warned Molly that God would punish her unkindness.[52] In 1907, after arriving in Florida, Molly dreamed she ran a backyard prayer service to which she welcomed "colored folk" (again, the theme of Molly's color-blindness weaves through her stories). She understood her destiny (not uncharacteristic of women in mountain religious culture)—to join the Baptist Church and lead services.

During her Florida sojourn (1907–8, for about a year), Molly continued working as a nurse, tending the sick child of a local wealthy couple, the Gaddies. Although they tried to compensate her with money, Molly refused, saying that she might need their help in the future. The opportunity came when Jim contracted malaria. When the family learned of it, they immediately sent over groceries and money, took Molly shopping for clothes, and invited her to parties where they introduced her as "their Kentucky pal." Fortune once again emerged out of adversity—and Molly's good deeds. She proudly wrote in her autobiography about the presents and letters she received "from people all over Florida for my songs and for my funny jokes. . . . You could not pick up a paper in the state of Florida them days but what you could read something about me."[53] Despite these flattering allures, she pined for the Kentucky mountains. After warnings from the doctor that if Jim was to make it back to Kentucky alive they shouldn't waste any time, they packed up to go home.

> Old Kentucky, Old Kentucky, my dear old mountain home,
> You are the grandest spot of earth to me, no difference where I roam.
>
> Florida has a lot to be proud of, her warm clime and her fine fruit trees
>   and her flowers,
> But to me the grandest spot of earth, is that grand old state of ours.

I long to be at home, I do, I'm lonely every hour,
I can not enjoy a sunny day, I can not enjoy a flower,
I can not enjoy my new made friends, I had rather be alone,
Thinking of my friends and loved ones I left behind me, And my old
    Kentucky home.[54]

When Molly sent her poem to the Gaddie family, who held a soft spot
for Molly ("They like to hear me tell rough jokes"),[55] they supplied the couple's train fare back to Kentucky in June 1908 and promised them a house.
Jim, too ill to work for three months after arriving home, stayed home,
tended their few pigs, cows, and chickens, and planted corn. In September he returned to the Bell-Knox coal mines, while Molly diversified. She
continued to nurse and attend births, but also "sold jewelry and silk hose
and done quite a bit of fancy picture framing, and painted pictures and
also doctoring with my Indian Herb tonics."[56]

Molly told of curing convict railroad workers who contracted small-
pox and of how they rewarded her, still again stressing her lack of racial
prejudice.

> I cooked and took care of them all, white and colored the same; I de-
> livered their babies, washed their clothes, cooked for them and done
> their mending for both white and colored just as though they had been
> my own family. . . . When that railroad job was finished and the rail-
> road workers both men and women started to leave Ely Branch they
> come to tell me good buy [sic] and every one of them brought me a nice
> present of some kind. One colored women brought me the nicest pair
> of gold ear rings that I ever had, and another colored lady, one of the
> mothers of twins, gave me a wrist watch with a solid gold case.[57]

Later, in the throes of a sweeping flu epidemic at Eagle (Ely) Branch,
Molly treated the victims, traveling "day and night as a nurse and doctor,
doctoring and nursing the people." But, by then, Molly's religion became
a motivation for doing good deeds:

> I would rise at four o'clock in the morning . . . when I got to the last
> house comin' down, it would be as late as four o'clock in the evening.
> I would find little children a-crying for something to eat and their fa-
> thers and mothers so sick they could not get out of bed to feed their
> little ones. I cooked and fed as high as seventy five little children lots

of days. All the rest of the people in that country that had not already took the Flu was afraid to come in a house where anyone had the Flu, even. Despite the fact that they claimed they was God fearin' people and was willing to do unto others as they would have them do unto them, so I asked them after the epidemic was over if they would like to have the Flu and lay without anyone come in and even give them a glass of water, and I told them that the old time religion was good enough for me and that I followed the teaching that Jesus Christ teached the people when he was here on earth. . . . Believe it or not, I always fit in every vacant place when I was asked. Any time I felt I was doing some unfortunate person a favor.[58]

In 1910, a strike lasting for over six weeks took place at the Hughes mine in Ely Branch, where Jim worked. Molly responded to the events by composing her first mining "protest song."

> Oh Fair ye well old Ely Branch,
> Oh, Fair ye well I say,
> I'm tired of livin on dried beef and tomaters and I am going away.
>
> When we had a strike in Ely this spring,
> These words old Hughes did say:
> "Oh, come along boys, go back to work,
> We'll give you the two weeks pay."
>
> When they put on their mining clothes
> Hard work again they tried
> And when old pay day rolled around
> They found old Hughes had lied.
>
> When Hughes thinks his mines is going to stop,
> A sight to see him frown,
> There's gas enough in old Hughes today
> To blow these mountains down.
>
> Oh, take your children out of Ely Branch,
> Before they cry for bread
> For when old Hughes' debts is paid,
> He won't be worth a thread.[59]

After making several copies of the song, Molly decided to casually drop them by the spring where miners' wives come for water. But, of course, she found the opportunity irresistible and couldn't keep the song's authorship a secret. Jim Stewart was soon fired.

Molly's story of the "grocery shop" incident epitomizes her savior self-image. Molly noticed a starving family standing in front of a company store in a Bell County mining town, lacking money for food. She went inside and insisted that the grocer supply them with provisions. Jim was again fired.[60]

John Greenway repeated this story with embellishment, either his own, Molly's, or both, and it's worth retelling despite its length, since it illustrates how Molly's end justifies her means:

> When Aunt Molly was walking with her little son, Henry, toward the coal camp, she stopped at the cabin of Daisy Allen, a miner's wife. She saw Daisy's smallest girl sobbing for food, and asked Daisy what she was going to do for the child. "I can't do nothing for her," wailed Daisy, "I don't have any more to eat in the house."
>
> "Is it possible that I will do more than you will for that child?" asked Aunt Molly, . . . When she came to the commissary she strode confidently in and greeted the proprietor with an expansive smile that meant money. "Well Mr. Martin, it seems that no matter how hard times get, I can always find enough to tide me over. Give me twenty-four pound of flour." She gave the bag of flour to Henry and told him to meet her at the tipple. Then she had Martin fill a sugar sack with groceries. With one arm loaded, she began to edge her way out of the store.
>
> "Now, Mr. Martin," she said, "I'll see you just as quick as I can raise $5.90. I have to feed some children, and they can't wait on a collection."
>
> "Don't you offer to get out of here without paying," warned Martin, and he started around the counter. Aunt Molly reached under her coat and pulled out the .38 Special that she carried for protection on her rounds through the coal country as a midwife.
>
> "Don't you try to stop me, Mr. Martin, or I'll shoot you six times in a minute," declared Aunt Molly, and she backed out of the store.[61]

Other stories flesh out the fashioning of Molly's identity—especially that as balladeer of working people. For example, Molly professed that her famous "Poor Miner's Farewell" emerged out of personal grief. On one visit with Archie Green, she recalled the death of her half-brother, Richard Garland: "[He] was mashed up in the coal mines; it took fifteen men to raise a piece of slate off of him, till they could get his body out, . . . every bone in him was just mashed."[62] She told Green that she penned "Poor Miner's Farewell" only three weeks after the tragedy, when, "I just found myself a walkin' along there singing: 'Poor hard workin' miners their troubles are great, so often in mining they meet their sad fate, killed by some accident that no one can tell, Miners, oh poor miners farewell.' Then I said 'He's only a miner killed under the ground, Only a miner and one more is gone. Only a miner, one more is gone, leaving his wife and little children alone.' I think you know that my whole life is just a poet by nature. I was just born like that."[63] When Green asked Molly if that was an old mining song, she insisted, "No, no!" that she was the original author and everyone else "messed it up."[64]

While Molly freely supplied dates and details of her compositions and life in response to others' questions about them, confusion arises in pinning down chronological sequences. Green deals extensively with the contested issue of authorship in *Only a Miner,* but the discussion below provides a small example of how Molly's flexible memory, and/or recording errors, make historical reconstruction difficult.

Molly told Archie Green that Jim Stewart died of a broken back while working at Black Raven mines in Bell County at age twenty-three,[65] while John Greenway reported that Molly and Jim were married for twenty-three years, which would place the year of his death in 1927,[66] leaving only a few years for Bill Jackson (the husband that she left in 1931). She also told Archie Green that the actual date that she married Gus (Tom) Stamos was 1924, rather than 1946, as everyone thought.[67]

Molly wrote a song after Jim Stewart's death, which Barnicle included in her notes, in Aunt Molly's words, "composed by me and dedicated to Jim Stewart, the father of my children," disclosing a tender side, which some call "mawkish," far from the tough image she publicly displayed.

How sad and quiet it seems
wish that I'd fall asleep
and see you in my dreams
but my heart is so full of sorrow tonite
I cannot lay on my bed
I have no one to love or care for me
now that you are dead

I often think of by gone days
when you were still in life
when you was my loving husband
and I was your adored wife
you would always stay at home with me
you never would leave me alone
I have no one to keep me company
now that you are dead and gone
It's no use for me to try to be happy
since I am left alone
with strangers I can never be happy
I had rather be alone
Thinking of my loved ones
In days past by and gone
Its the last nite of love
O how sad and quiet it seems
O how I wish that I could fall asleep
and see you in my dreams.[68]

We don't know the date of Molly's second marriage (according to Jim, her third) to coal miner Bill Jackson (descended, according to Molly, from Andrew Jackson),[69] but it probably took place in the middle 1920s. Tillman Cadle, the Garlands' close friend, thought of Jackson as the only one of Molly's husbands who could dominate her. Jim Garland agreed, depicting Molly's second husband as "quite a character, a large cross-eyed man with a big red nose, and the only man Molly married whom she couldn't control. When my sister got to raising Cain with him, he would get out his old .45 pistol and shoot under her feet. No wonder people called him 'Forty-Five Bill Jackson.'"[70]

Molly and Bill separated in 1931 or 1932, reportedly because of her union activities, and this coincided with Molly's departure from Kentucky. John Greenway claimed Bill divorced Molly,[71] but it's unlikely he ever formalized it. Little exists in Molly's own notes regarding Bill's importance to her, or of her feelings for him. We know that she raised four of Jackson's children[72] and continued to know of his whereabouts. Besides keeping his name, though, Molly seemed to derive little benefit from their union. One story relating to their relationship, though, became elaborated to tell of how she inspired the 1943 Tin Pan Alley song, "Pistol Packin' Mama." With characteristic bravado, Molly asserted that her husband's cousin, Jesse Baker, composed the song in 1915 based on her pistol packin' behavior.

> One Saturday evenin' Bill Jackson, he slips off from me and went to that [his cousin's moonshine] still and I went to the foot of the hill and told him to come down. I had a permit to carry a pistol; I carried this Smith and Weston .38 for protection over them hills for delivering babies . . . he was scared of me when I had that pistol in my hand and I was scared of him when he'd get to drinking. . . . "now Mol, put that pistol down. I'm not coming down, not until you lay that pistol down." So I laid the pistol down and Jess Baker . . . made up that song. "Lay that pistol down, you pistol packin' momma, lay that pistol down." When I come to New York, I sang that song and before six months after that they had it in the cabarets.[73]

Contradicting Molly's version, Tin Pan Alley composer Al Dexter took credit for writing the commercial "Pistol Packin' Mama" in 1943 after watching a brawl in a barroom (totally unrelated to Molly).[74] But Molly's claim to the song and its meaning for her prompted me to use it to title my book.

In chapter 2 I discussed the intensification of the coal struggles and events that led to Aunt Molly's departure from Kentucky. Here I will briefly review conditions that led to the Harlan strike. Despite their relative advantage as coal counties, Harlan and Bell mines began, in the late 1920s, to decrease production and slash wages. John L. Lewis's United Mine Workers Union, rife with internal politics, let its members down. Mine operators hired scabs to replace the men unwilling to work, and subjected them to harassment and violence. Many blacklisted miners, starving and desperate, found hope in the Communists' National Miners Union—a number of local and wildcat strikes broke out before the major "Bloody Harlan" on New Year's Day 1932.

The NMU legitimized wives' support through auxiliaries. Women played vital roles, organizing strike meeings, doing relief work, and leading wildcat strikes.[75] Molly, as usual, placed herself at front and center of the action. She told *Daily Worker* reporter Valentine Ackland in New York how she organized the women and children and "one day they marched, one and all, to the pits and went underground," and how the men heard them coming singing her own "Hungry Ragged Blues."[76]

Crawling out of their holes, hardly able to stand upright in the narrow passage, the men crowded together, amazed and afraid. "What in god's name," [they asked of the women], "do they want down there?" [Women weren't allowed in the mines then—it was considered bad luck.] And Aunt Molly answered. "We've come to fetch you up. You're doing no good here." They told her to go back and she said "We've nothing to do at home, no food to cook no clothes to wash. We stay right here till you come up with us." They said that meant losing the job, and she answered them, "You've nothing to lose. You'll live longer in fresh air and sunshine without food than you will down here. Throw down your picks, empty your water-cans and come right up and say you won't strike another pick till you get a living wage!" and they followed her.[77]

Motivated purely by hatred of injustice, Molly swore no connection with any outside manipulation or formal ideology. "'I joined the Auxiliary and organized the women, but when I marched into the pit that time I hadn't so much as heard of a Communist Party or a radical. I just knew we could do nothin' at all until we'd organized those men.'"[78]

In her autobiography Molly provides another illustration of her pivotal leadership ability:

the coal miners used to go in the coal mines and work all day and then when they come out of the coal mines at night all cold and wet when they would try to draw one dollar in scrip the bookkeeper would tell them they was in debt, and in debt for what? Not for milk or for bread we had got, it was for the carbide [needed for lighting lamps and to blast the surface of the rock—they could buy this but not food on credit] that he had got from the company store to make them a light, and for the powder they had shot, the coal operators call that carbide and powder the miners expense, and that was my reason for telling the coal miners if they worked and slaved for the coal operators and their wives and children dying from starvation by the thousands that they didn't have a speck of sense, and because I pulled the coal miners out of the mines and put them all on the picket line carrying a slogan . . . "Our children must have milk and bread."[79]

Molly declared that she fought with the others at the Battle of Evarts, May 5, 1931, "right between them," and offered her usual detailed memories to Archie Green:

I'm left handed and I was pulling the Colt .45 in this hand, .38 Special in this hand, and I had a belt full of cartidges around me and an apron around me and it full of cartridges. It was so smoky between them coal miners and them scabs and thugs that nobody knowed who shot who nor nobody knowed who killed who. . . . . The officials offered the leaders of the strike to choose between prison for twenty one years and a day or banishment from Kentucky. It was seven years before I was allowed to go back to Kentucky after.[80]

Molly was always willing to suffer the consequences of her political activism. The following is a prime example of her way with words, while bringing it all back to the essentials: food and children.

The coal operators in Kentucky began to call me a "red," and when I asked them what the word "red" meant, they told me a "red" was a person that went around thru the coal operators camp here, thar, and yonder, a-pulling the coal miners out on strike with their Russian Redneck Propagander. Then I told them propergander, or propergoose, that for working the coalminers without paying them for the labor that they had a poor excuse, then I told them, "Mr. Coal operator call me anything you please, blue, green, or red, I aim to see to it that these Kentucky coalminers will not dig your coal while their little children are crying and dying for milk and bread."[81]

Molly's centrality as leader of the miners' resistance emerges from her own narrative and perspective, while others, especially family members, cast doubt on her involvement. One of Jim Garland's stories, though, confirms his half sister's fearlessness. Jim recounted the miners' growing disaffection with John L. Lewis in the 1920s, fury at the scabs, and one incident involving his sister:

Company sucks [strikebreakers] were stripped naked and whipped with switches in the presence of women. One particularly effective tactic was used later at Ross, Kentucky, when a group of scabs and gun thugs approached a picket line that had been set up by the local women. These women grabbed the gun thugs and stripped them naked while some of the local men took off through a cornfield after the strikebreakers. After four women had managed to hold down one of the gun thugs, my sister Molly took his pistol and shoved the barrel right up his rectum. Never did this particular thug show his face there again; even when I met up with him years later, he told me this had taught him a lesson he could never forget.[82]

Although women, and Molly particularly, were not loath to use violence, less dramatic actions characterized the daily work of the union auxiliary. When Dreiser's "National Committee for the Defense of Political Prisoners" came to Kentucky to investigate the coalfield conditions in November 1931 (see chapter 2), Molly most likely participated in mundane but indispensable women's auxiliary strike activities, running the soup kitchens set up in Harlan and Bell churches, and distributing relief packages. It soon dawned on Molly that other women could run kitchens and deliver messages—her mission became more important than daily drudgery. The opportunity presented itself that would, as we know, lead to enormous changes in her life.

The northern investigators, anxious to hear the miners speak for themselves, began their hearings in churches and meeting halls. After listening to and recording miners' disturbing stories of hazardous work conditions, accidents, operator abuse, relentless hunger, and grueling pay cuts, there was no doubt left: Harlan's and Bell's struggles epitomized, and cast into vivid relief, class warfare. Even though they knew this in theory before coming to Harlan, they heard it now from the mouths of the oppressed.

The committee's hearings, and their journalistic legacy, allow us a fascinating window to the past, to visualize and recreate the power of those times and moments, when miners and their wives portrayed to outsiders the extent of degradation and terrorism suffered at the hands of mine operators and gun thugs. The group's visit offered, too, a propitious opportunity for the writers to place local events in Kentucky in the context of an international class struggle.

John Dos Passos, who would mine this other-world experience for years, captures the setting at the Glendon Baptist Church, the stage for Molly's dramatic appearance:

> Straight Creek is a narrow zigzag valley that runs up into the mountains from Pineville. The mines are small and often change hands. The houses are low shacks set up on stilts, scattered in disorderly rows up and down the valley floor. They are built of thin sheathing and mostly roofed with tar paper. A good many have been papered with newspaper on the in-

side by their occupants in an effort to keep the wind out. The floors are full of cracks. . . . The visitors form a motley straggle through the little dooryards. . . . The A.P. [Associated Press] man and the gentleman from the *Courier-Journal* have a harrowed look on their faces; they keep looking around behind things as if they felt the houses had been put up to hoax them. They refuse to believe that people can be so badly off as that. They crowd into the door of one shack to hear what Aunt Molly Jackson, the local midwife, has to say, but you can see them getting ready not to believe what she says, what their own eyes see.[83]

As part of her fateful testimony on November 7, 1931, Molly decided to sing one of her own compositions, which she thought of as a folksong, and which she sensed captured the miners' urgent plight more effectively than simple words. In her most creative meanderings, though, she couldn't anticipate the enormous consequences of this performance for herself, for the writers, and for their political cohorts. (See chapter 2 for the entire text.)

> I'm sad and weary; I've got these hungry ragged blues;
> I'm sad and weary; I've got these hungry ragged blues;
> Not a penny in my pocket to buy one thing I need to use.
>
> I woke up this morning with the worst blues I ever had in my life;
> I woke up this morning with the worst blues I ever had in my life;
> Not a bite to cook for breakfast, a poor coal miner's wife.[84]

Molly's song, delivered in rough, cracked, Appalachian style, instantly piqued the committee's interest and tugged at their hearts: they knew they had struck gold. They invited the mountain woman to become the miners' emissary, to travel to the north and raise funds for the cause. As Tillman Cadle put it, Theodore Dreiser and John Dos Passos "thought Molly was Kentucky herself." The writers recognized the enormous symbolic power and potential of this bone-weary, aging miner's wife, as spokesperson not only for this specific cause but for larger ideological interests. Dreiser would place "Aunt Molly Jackson's Kentucky Miners' Wives Ragged Hungry Blues" at the very beginning of the committee's published report and subsequent book, *Harlan Miners Speak,* and Dos Passos and others used it to color and texture their writings about the coal struggles. Molly's song changed, or at least had a significant impact on, the New York left-wing world in the 1930s.

Aunt Molly in New York City, ca. mid-1930s

Aunt Molly with Theodore Dreiser, Kentucky, 1931

The label from Aunt Molly's only commercial recording, December 1931

Aunt Molly, holding a copy of the *Daily Worker,* with Tom (Gus) Stamos, at home in New York City, 1937

Matrix Number	Catalog Number	Original Recording Date	Title	Artist
W152031	2578-D	December 8, 1931	TOO LATE	GUY LOMBARDO AND HIS ROYAL CANADIANS WITH KATE SMITH
W152032	2578-D	December 8, 1931	RIVER, STAY 'WAY FROM MY DOOR	GUY LOMBARDO AND HIS ROYAL CANADIANS WITH KATE SMITH
W152033-2			HOME	DORSEY BROS. AND ORCH.
W152034	2581-D	December 9, 1931	BY THE SYCAMORE TREE	DORSEY BROS. AND ORCH.
W152035	2589-D	December 9, 1931	(You Knew You'd Hurt Somebody) WHY DID IT HAVE TO BE ME?	DORSEY BROS. AND ORCH.
W152036	2581-D	December 9, 1931	OOH THAT KISS	DORSEY BROS. AND ORCH.
W152037-2	2580-D	December 9, 1931	TOO LATE	RUTH ETTING
W152038-3	2580-D	December 9, 1931	CUBAN LOVE SONG	RUTH ETTING
152039		December 10, 1931	THE UNMARKED GRAVE	BOB FERGUSON
W152040	15731-D	December 10, 1931	KENTUCKY MINER'S WIFE (Ragged Hungry Blues) (Part 1)	AUNT MOLLY JACKSON
W152041	15731-D	December 10, 1931	KENTUCKY MINER'S WIFE (Ragged Hungry Blues) (Part 2)	AUNT MOLLY JACKSON
W152042			THE PRISONERS LOVE LETTERS	JACK MAHONEY
W152043			OUR BLUE HAIRED BOY	JACK MAHONEY
W152044	2587-D	December 14, 1931	I FOUND YOU	"RED" McKENZIE
W152045	2587-D	December 14, 1931	I'M SORRY DEAR	"RED" McKENZIE
W152046			POOR MINERS FAREWELL	AUNT MOLLY JACKSON
W152047			I LOVE COAL MINERS	AUNT MOLLY JACKSON
W152048	2585-D	December 18, 1931	ALL OF ME	BEN SELVIN & HIS ORCH.
W152049	2585-D	December 18, 1931	I FOUND YOU	BEN SELVIN & HIS ORCH.

An excerpt from the Columbia studio listing, December 8–18, 1931

Sheet music cover for "Pistol Packin' Mama"

sep the 2 1989

n y c

o mr alin lomax
in ancer to yow letter
i am not interested in you
usl in eney of my storys
or songs as i am rite ing
a book of my own i
wont to usl oll of my
songs an storys in my
own book so do not usl
eney of my songs or story
whatever you do if you
do i am shurl you will
be sorry

from malley Jackson
$16 east 9th st apt 7
n y c

Aunt Molly's September 2, 1939, letter to Alan Lomax

aunt molly JACKSON   June 10 1943

I'm Working with Uncle Sam!

Earl Robinson
Dear friend i have wrote
a new war song that
i have ben sing ing a mong
grapes that sells stomps
on bonds on they all say
it makes a big hit in
selling bonds on stomps
so they told me to send
this song to the tretoril
De fort ment in washington
to be used on a national
scoil m inter torments
over the radio
so if you will be abble
to writ the music to this
song for me you will be doing
me a grait for war so if you can
Do me this favor Please let me kenal
what time i can come to your
house to get the music to this
song writer. so i will be
abull to send it to the tresore
De fort ment your trul friend
or ever ount
√ Jackson Molly

Aunt Molly's June 10, 1943, letter to Earl Robinson

Aunt Molly with her niece, Mamie Quackenbush, New York City, 1939–40

Aunt Molly with Gus, New York City, 1943

Aunt Molly with Gus at Camp Unity, ca. early 1940s (Courtesy of Tillman Cadle)

Aunt Molly and Gus in front of their Sacramento home, ca. 1955

Jim Garland and Sarah Gunning, 1974

Aunt Molly with Archie Green, Sacramento, 1957 or 1958

Sarah Gunning with Pete Seeger, Newport, R.I., 1964 (Courtesy of Ellen J. Stekert)

4

"Christmas Eve on the East Side": Aunt Molly Moves to New York City

Aunt Molly Jackson's bus pulled into New York on December 1, 1931. John Dos Passos and Charles and Adelaide Walker, the couple who planned to host her, met her at the station. Welcoming messages flooded in to the Walker's Park Avenue apartment from a gamut of celebrities—Sherwood Anderson, Theodore Dreiser, Waldo Frank, Lewis Mumford, Lester Cohen, and Melvin P. Levy.

The next day, Ben Robertson Jr., a young journalist for the *New York Herald Tribune,* heralded her arrival in print:

> MINE "AUNT" HERE TO HELP DREISER BY "BLUES" SONG:
> Mrs. Molly Jackson Brings "Powerful" Thanks of Kentuckians for
> "Foreign Aid"
> Put Harlan Plaint in Verse
> Mountain Woman to Take Part in Meeting Sunday

> Mrs. Molly Jackson, wife of a soft coal miner, a woman known in southeastern Kentucky in the fold between Pine Mountain and the Cumberlands as "Aunt Molly" Jackson, midwife and general nurse, arrived in New York yesterday "to be on hand in case" Theodore Dreiser, John Dos Passos and the several others should need her help in the effort they are making to have conditions improved in the Harlan and Bell section from which she comes.

> Aunt Molly left the mountains on Sunday evening. She came all the way by bus and had not slept since Saturday, but she made no com-

plaint. "I had a right nice trip, I reckon," she said to Mr. Dos Passos. "No bad luck nor nothing like that on the way."

She said the men and women in the mountains "'were powerful thankful' to Mr. Dreiser and his party for the foreign help they had given them. . . . If they hadn't come from New York when they did, the Lord only knows what would have happened to us. They came to us and found us in the midst of the worst destitution on earth."[1]

Robertson, quite taken with Molly, portrayed the tall, thin coal miner's wife, wearing a cotton print dress and gold earrings as "pleasant and friendly, and [one who] still knows how to laugh." He noted her colorful expressions, "enriched with allegory with frequent idiom and colloquialisms. . . . She drew many similes from the woods and from the Bible. She spoke bitterly of the lot of the miners." Molly told Robertson how she composed "Kentucky Miners' Hungry Blues" (which he reprinted in full), when "feeling blue" one morning: "'All [I] did was just to open my mouth and sing.'"

Molly told Robertson that her first husband, a miner (Jim Stewart), died several years ago, and after him, she lost her two children. "Then I married a widow man and I raised his four children from the time they were wee mites. [Note: If Jim Stewart was only dead a few years, Molly wouldn't have had much time to raise Bill Jackson's children.] Now they are grown. . . . I'm almost ashamed to tell you how old I am—I look so old. I was forty six years old the 30th day of last month [born in 1880, Molly was actually fifty-one]. I know I look tough, but I am not tough. Wait until I get a little sleep."[2] Robertson's article, according to Archie Green, served to "reintroduce [Molly] to a contemporary audience" and "honors both the subject and the author."[3]

Molly's first opportunity to tell her truths came Wednesday, December 2, on a grand scale. The Communist-led Unemployed Councils sponsored a farewell rally for the three hundred who took part in a National Hunger March on Washington. The *New York Times* (Dec 3, 1931) reported that "'Aunt Molly Jackson of Harlan, Ky., chanted a miners song,'" before an audience of eight thousand at the Bronx Coliseum. On Sunday afternoon, December 6, the "National Committee for the Defense of Political Prisoners" held a meeting at the Star Casino, 107th Street and Park Avenue. In the illustrious company of Sherwood Anderson, John Dos Passos, Lewis Mumford, and Waldo Frank (for some reason, Dreiser failed to show up [*Herald-Tribune,* Dec 7, 1931]), Molly sang her by-now-famous

"Ragged Hungry Blues," receiving, according to the *Daily Worker* (Dec 8, 1931), a big ovation. The crowd of some three thousand heard another composition, which was to become Molly's "introduction" song:

> I was born and raised in old Kentucky;
> Molly Jackson is my name.
> I came up here to New York City,
> And I'm truly glad I came.
>
> Some friends of mine came to Kentucky;
> I sang for them a song I made.
> They invited me to New York City,
> And I came out soliciting aid.
>
> I am soliciting for the poor Kentucky miners,
> For their children and their wives,
> Because the miners are all blacklisted,
> I am compelled to save their lives.
>
> The miners in Bell and Harlan counties organized a union;
> This is all the poor coal miners done,
> Because the coal operators cut down their wages
> To 33 cents and less a ton.
>
> All this summer we have had to listen
> To our hungry children's cries;
> Through the hot part of the summer
> Our little babies died like flies.
>
> While the coal operators and their wives
> All went dressed in jewels and silk,
> The poor coal miners' babies,
> Starved to death for bread and milk.
>
> Now I appeal to you in tender mercy
> To give us all you have to give,
> Because I love my people dearly
> And I want them all to live.[4]

During her first few days in New York City, Molly met Margaret Larkin, musician, writer, and member of the Worker's Music League. Originally from the Southwest, Larkin gravitated toward New York and left-wing circles. She played a key role in bringing Ella May Wiggins, union activist and songwriter, murdered during the 1929 textile strike in Gastonia, North

Carolina, to the attention of the New York Left. On December 10, 1931, eight days after Molly arrived, Larkin accompanied Molly and Margaret Young (a writer with the Dreiser group, who possibly arranged Molly's maiden recording session) to the Columbia studios on West 12th street. With Larkin on guitar, Molly made her first and only commercial record "Kentucky Miner's Wife" ("Ragged Hungry Blues"), released as a two-sided record on 10" 78 RPM.[5] A week later, she recorded a second, with "Poor Miners Farewell" on side A and "I Love Coal Miners" on B, which Columbia apparently never released. The newly arrived mountain woman traveled in good company—Guy Lombardo and his Royal Canadians with Kate Smith, the Dorsey Brothers and Orchestra, and Ruth Etting used the same recording studio during the same month.

During the following months, in the early part of 1932, Molly busied herself with a constant whirl of political and social activities. She and her brother, Jim Garland, who came north for Harry Simms's funeral at the Bronx Coliseum (in February) became ubiquitous presences at progressive rallies and meetings, dramatizing through song the Kentucky miners' circumstances. Molly's early experience as a union supporter and spokesperson could not have been unlike Jim's, who told it this way: "At some of the larger meetings, various committees spoke and solicited money, but usually I would speak to three or four smaller groups or clubs each day by myself. I would talk for about five minutes about the miners' families and then ask the group to send us any amount they wanted to donate."[6]

For the next year, Molly traveled widely to fundraise for the miners, until a bus accident in Ohio incapacitated her, forcing her to return to New York City to her East Side apartment and bed. (There is some question about when this accident actually happened, since she dated the bus wreck for Archie Green as January 6, 1932, which would have been within six weeks after arriving in New York City. She may have meant 1933.)[7] Although mobile again after a few months, Molly claimed she never fully recovered and proceeded to (unsuccessfully) claim damages from the bus company.

Despite the brief periods Molly spent in Kentucky during those early years, her home became the Lower East Side of Manhattan, with living conditions only marginally better than those in the mountains. The area consisted of two square miles of tenements, sweatshops, and squalor, described in the Federal Writers' Project *Guide to 1930s New York* as "typical" of the city, magnifying "all the problems and conflicts of big-city life."[8]

Although Jim Garland prepared himself for the worst before he left Kentucky (for visits in the early thirties and then relocating with his family several years later), the reality both unsettled him and allowed him some perspective. He saw poverty, worker problems, and anger with injustice and "could no longer think of our fight in Kentucky as purely local."[9]

Molly's desperation for money drove her, at times, to creative solutions. A typewritten note came to me via Archie Green from Dick Reuss, who passed along some "information" from Lawrence Gellert, telling of a young Elizabeth Baldwin who came to New York with Molly. As the story goes, the party no longer needed the women's help when the Harlan strike settled in early 1932, so they asked them to go back to Kentucky. But, Baldwin, happy and "buxom" after a few months, hesitated to leave. Setting up shop in an apartment on East Third Street, she became a prostitute, with Aunt Molly as madam, and Jim Garland playing the harmonica in the front room to muffle the bedspring creakings. According to Reuss (ultimately Gellart), the Communist Party frantically paid the women a monthly stipend to leave New York and continue their union work in the South. Although they did leave, Molly and Jim soon returned. Woody Guthrie apparently told Gordon Friesen of (another?) whorehouse run by Molly in 1940 or 1941.[10]

These stories, whether true or not, testify to Molly's reputation as a defiant, untamable mountain woman, an image that Molly herself encouraged. Far from confined to Molly's immediate circle, the "wild woman" persona infused the consciousness of academic folklorists and song collectors, becoming fixed in historical memory long after Molly was gone.

Molly constantly flaunted convention through irreverence for authority. When Jim and Hazel decided to move to New York (at Molly's invitation) in December 1935, they arrived at the dark apartment of an infuriated Molly, who had locked horns at that time with the city's electric company, which would not turn on her power at Christmas time. In characteristic way, Molly fumed to folklorist John Greenway in the 1950s: "Just because Jesus Christ was born nineteen hundred and thirty-six years ago I can't get no electricity today."[11]

Molly's reports of expanding resistance activities and sense of herself as an activist fed each other. Family and close friends like Jim and Hazel Garland and Tillman Cadle, who rarely sang her praises, validated Molly's defiance of authorities. They seemed to enjoy her contests, probably didn't disagree with her causes, and her interventions allowed them, if they desired, to remain on the sidelines. As Cadle put it in an interview with me, Molly's reputation in New York outshone the one in Kentucky, and Jim wrote: "She had spoke all over the state for relief for striking miners and had become active on the East Side in the Workers Alliance, a relief organization. She had also led a demonstration to City Hall, and demanded that a fence be erected along the East River, after a child had fallen in and drowned."[12]

Hazel Garland described Molly to me as she went to the Home Relief office to protest a family's lack of clothing and food, standing outside and taunting the bureaucrats by waving her underpants around on a stick.

Songwriting became the irascible mountain woman's special and powerful trademark. Even though he accused Molly of claiming his songs as her own, Jim believed Molly's composition talent was one of her greatest virtues. He loved her ability to take stances again injustice, to burrow in and stick it to the powerful: "[She] wrote many union songs and many other types of songs as well. She was at the height of her glory when she was giving someone she thought was no good a hard time. If she believed someone was taking advantage of his or her position in life, whether that was a coal operator, a husband who beat his wife, a man who would not work to support his family, or a bookkeeper who denied some needy family scrip to buy food with, she made her feelings known. These troublemaking instincts led her to write many a fine song."[13]

Molly switched the focus of her songs to suit the political times. She wrote "I Am a Union Woman," either before leaving Kentucky, or just after she arrived in New York in the early thirties, as a rallying song for the National Miners Union. Molly's shift in union affiliation also signaled a shift in the Communist Party line to Popular Front positions around 1936–37.

> I am a union woman
> As brave as I can be;
> I do not like the bosses,
> And the bosses don't like me.
>
> [*Chorus:* Join the NMU, come join the NMU (later, Join the CIO)]
>
> I was raised in old Kentucky, in Kentucky born and bred,
> And when I joined the union, they called me Rooshian Red.
>
> [*Chorus:* Join the NMU; come join the NMU.]

When my husband asked the boss for a job these is the words he said:
"Bill Jackson, I can't work you, sir, [your] wife's a Rooshion Red."

[*Chorus:* Join the NMU, Join the NMU.]

This is the worst time on earth that I have ever saw,
To get shot down by gun thugs and framed up by the law.

[*Chorus:* Join the NMU, Join the NMU.]

But we are many thousand strong and I am glad to say,
We are getting stronger and stronger every day.

[*Chorus:* Join the NMU, Join the NMU.]

If you want to join a union
As strong as one can be,
Join the dear old NMU and come along with me,

[*Chorus:* Join the NMU, Join the NMU.]

The bosses ride fine horses while we walk in the mud;
Their banner is the dollar sign while ours is striped with blood.

[*Chorus:* Join the NMU, Join the NMU, Join the NMU, Join the NMU.][14]

New York of the 1930s must have made an enormous impact on Molly Garland Jackson from Kentucky. Wealthy radicals invited the Appalachian guest to their elegant houses, lavished food and drink, and earnestly listened to her performances. Despite hardships, the depression years inspired a cultural flowering. Roosevelt's New Deal encouraged creative expression through the Writers Project, Federal Arts and Music Projects, while a bewildering assortment of left-wing movements sponsored events attracting the city's intellectual and artistic elite. According to Michael Denning, the Popular Front was a social movement and radical historical bloc "uniting industrial unionists, Communists, independent socialists, community activists and 'emigre' anti-fascists around laborist social democracy."[15] An expansive awakening defined the 1930s in America, supporting and elevating the "common man." Writer Joe Klein described the decade as one of the "happiest, most accessible, demonstrative, and inspirational periods in American cultural history."[16]

Nowhere was this energy more intense than in the political Left, with all its permutations and schisms. Irving Howe captures the Left's impact on New York City's social and cultural life: "New York was always 'the party center,' no matter which party it was; here you could listen to the leaders and intellectuals, and here it was possible, usually, to fill a fair-sized hall so as to soften our awareness of how small and futile we were."[17]

Broadcaster Henrietta Yurchenco fleshed out for me the attractions of Communism, the feeling of belonging, and the sense of hope that the radical community provided for intellectual New Yorkers in the late 1930s and 1940s.

> It was the only viable answer of the time. . . . There was hardly a paint-er, writer, musician, architect that didn't espouse more than liberal thoughts . . . this was in the air everywhere you went, it was something that everybody talked about. When there was a picket line, a demonstra-tion . . . any party that you went to, all the professionals were lined up . . . that was the feeling of the time. . . . You really felt that a change had to take place. At that time we were not prepared to listen to the neg-ative aspect. That was our dream as it appeared to us at the time. It was a time of great optimism, despite the hardships of the Depression. The optimism came from the belief that we ourselves had some control over our destinies. If we got together and fought or changed and aroused all sectors of the population we would do it. The WPA transformed the cultural life of the city. Concerts were cheap, theater, newspaper, topi-cal reviews, ballet. There was optimism in the air, despite the poverty. No one had any money, we were helping each other with rent parties.[18]

New York became the center, too, of Molly's new universe, and despite lingering weakness from her accident and sheer struggles for survival, her political will and determination never flagged. She mesmerized a number of journalists who paid court and diligently recorded her tales of triumph. *Daily Worker* interviewer Valentine Ackland was clearly taken with the "tall and handsome woman; her hair is grey and her eyes are grey and look at you directly and wisely; she smiles an amused and affectionate smile and puts her hand on your arm and leans forward to talk. She talks hon-estly, without boasting."[19]

In the same interview, Molly told of her triumphs over New York bu-reaucracy. One day Molly heard a neighboring woman scold her children. "Go to school I can't give you dinner. Put toothpicks in your mouths as if you'd had some, and run on." Molly knocked on her neighbor's door, and finding her crying, advised her to get an emergency relief card. Afraid and too proud to go alone to the welfare office, the woman asked Molly to accompany her to the welfare offices. "What do you want here?" the officer asked. "These ain't your children . . . I know you, you want to overthrow the government of the United States!" "Yes, Sir!" blazed Molly, "So I do. If I'd my way I'd turn it bottom upwards. I think it'd look better that way." The officer took Molly's threats seriously and the woman's children ate a hot meal that night. Molly's story completely convinced the reporter: "Wherever she goes the same things happen; the police shift uneasily and take tight hold of their sticks and their guns, and the workers gather in hundreds, in thousands, they sing her songs, listen to her words, take her advice because it is shrewd, courageous and they can trust her absolutely."[20]

With futile attempts to find paid work, Molly subsisted on New York's welfare, or Home Relief. In search of a job, she went to WPA headquarters. She tells the story of her encounter with an ignorant, rigid clerk, and how the system failed her (note that Molly often rhymes her prose).

> "Lady, I would like to get a job as a composer so I could earn my daily bread." Then this lady looked me over and this is what she had to say. "You have to have a birth certificate today, to prove you was born in the good old U.S.A. before you can get a job on our W.P.A." "Lady," [Molly responded] "I was born and raised in the hills of old Kentucky, believe it or not, but a birth certificate, I have not got because they didn't make any birth certificates in Kentucky til many years after I was born, the parents kept their childrens age in the family bible til after I was born." Oh yes, I was a married woman and a trained nurse and midwife before I ever saw a birth certificate in all the days of my life, but I am a quarter American Indian born here in the U.S.A. and when it comes to refusing to at least let me work for a living I must say that I am tired of being treated this way, because I am an American by birth, if there ever has been one on the face of the earth. But because I had no record of my birth this lady turned me away, and I was not allowed to work on W.P.A. so I had to mostly depend on home relief from 1933–43 and no one on earth will ever know how cruel the fascist minded rulers in my home of the brave, and the land of the free has actually treated me.[21]

John Greenway retold the story slightly differently:

> While applying for home relief for herself in 1941, she was asked for her birth certificate. In the argument that followed Aunt Molly's expressed indignation that she had to have a birth certificate before being eligi-

ble to eat, the clerk said to her, "You talk like a radical. I believe you are a red."

[And quoting Molly:] "This is what a young American learned girl said to me in this land of the free. Oh, how foolish some people can be! You see, we did not have any births registered till 1912—a man just came around taking names; then we knew we was borned, but we didn't know when."[22]

The incident, of course, deserved a new song: "Disgusted Blues."

Since I left my home
In the mountains in 1931
I believe I've had more trouble
Than any woman under the sun.

And today my whole life is wrecked;
My health has been destroyed,
And I come from one of the oldest families
That's in the U.S. today;
But after all they refused
To give me a job
On a government project today.

When I applied for a job on W.P.A.
The words I heard them say
You must have a birth certificate
Before you can have a job on W.P.A.

I have never had a birth certificate
To her I proudly said,
And the Kentucky mountaineers that was living when I was born,
Most of them are dead;
But if you please I would like to work
To earn my daily bread.

Now my heart is filled with sorrow
Trouble, pain and grief
Because today and tomorrow
I must exist on home relief;
But comrades I refuse to lick the boots
Of those lousy Wall Street Bums,
While they are living at their ease
I shall refuse their crumbs.

Next Sunday is Christmas day in 1938
I cannot express my feelings,
My trouble is so great,
I have nothing to be thankful for,
Nor one penny of earth to give,
Nobody knows in this wide world
What a miserable life I have to live.

Yes I have suffered all my life,
And I'll tell you the reason why,
I have had to see the worker's children
That lived around me starve to death and die.
Because their parents were afraid
To unite and fight for freedom and bread,
Afraid some boss would accuse them
Of spreading foreign propaganda
Or call them some kind of Red.

So come all you laboring people wherever you may be;
Unite yourselves together and fight for liberty.[23]

Another version, or a different song that Molly wrote in 1941, calling it "My Disgusted Blues," appeared in John Greenway's book:

I get up every morning
Feeling so disgusted and blue,
Because I have no money
And I don't get no work to do.

Refrain:
Trouble, trouble, is all I ever see
Because I met so many people that tries to make a slave out of me.
Trouble, trouble, I worry all day long
Because everything I do something goes on wrong.

When you have a lot of money
You have a lot of friends come around;
But when you are broke and disgusted
Not one friend can be found.

Yes, trouble and disappointments
Is all I ever find;
I believe that trouble and disappointments
Will destroy my worried mind.[24]

We can understand Molly Jackson's significance in the matrix of music, class, and political resistance. Her "discovery," involvement in the Left, contributions to changing musical aesthetics, become important symbolic stepping stones. She both sang and composed traditional and "political" songs. The latter spoke to conditions of economic deprivation and class inequality, intriguing her political friends. No anecdote furnishes a more apt metaphor for the stark contrast and awkward alliance between sophisticated urban musicians and the reality of the "folk" than that of Molly's encounters with the Composers Collective.

The Composers Collective, formed in 1932 as a branch of the Pierre Degeyter Club (named for the French composer of L'Internationale), was a sizable group of radical musicians. Affiliated with the Communist Workers Music League, the collective became an umbrella organization for radical choral and orchestral units.[25] With a shifting membership during its four or five year history, of Elie Siegmeister, Charles Seeger, Henry Cowell, Aaron Copland, Mark Blitzstein, Earl Robinson, Ruth Crawford Seeger, Henry Leland Clarke, and Norman Casden, the group engaged in "'round-table criticisms of each other's current productions in proletarian music,'" with a formal "beaux arts aesthetic orientation."[26] Attracted to classical style, they found models for creating people's music in European worker choruses. One of its inner circle, Charles Seeger, writing under the alias, Carl Sands, expressed the sentiment of the group in his view of folk tunes as "'complacent, melancholy, and defeatist—originally intended to make slaves endure their lot—pretty, but not the stuff for a militant proletariat to feed upon.'"[27] Seeger later changed his mind and realized that the collective was simply out of touch with the people: "Everything we composed was forward-looking, progressive as hell, but completely unconnected with life."[28] Mike Gold, writer and *Daily Worker* columnist, less kindly quoted a worker's reaction to the collective's music as "'full of geometric bitterness and the angles and glass splinters of pure technic,'" composed for the classically trained musicians as if they were "an assortment of mechanical canaries."[29]

In the winter of 1933, a little over a year after Molly first came to New York City, the collective invited her to one of their meetings. Her songs, new texts set to traditional tunes, baffled the musicians, while her style and voice violated their classical aesthetic tastes. Molly herself thought them stuffy and rejected their work.[30] I will deal further with the dynamics of Molly and the collective in the next chapter, placing them in perspective of the Left and music. For now, though, the orientation of the collective began to change dramatically by the middle 1930s when the party moved toward broadening its base (Popular Front), and by 1935 began to appreciate the usefulness of folk or people's music as a mechanism to reach the masses. Aunt Molly's style intrigued Charles Seeger, who wrote to Richard Reuss in 1971 that he recognized that "she was on the right track and the Composers Collective and the Communist Party the wrong as far as music as a 'weapon in the class struggle' was concerned."[31] The mountain woman's keen sense of performance also impressed him, as he noted how quickly she was able to alter her repertoire and style to suit the context and audience.[32] When Charles Seeger introduced his fifteen-year-old son, Pete, to Molly Jackson, she sang for him the traditional Appalachian song "Wedding Dress." Young Pete, struck by Molly's rendition and moved by her presence, later credited her as one of his major influences.[33] David Dunaway, in his biography of Pete Seeger, claims that the young urban singer met Molly through folklorist Alan Lomax, who brought him to her East Side apartment, where "her rough clear voice bowled Pete over, the first live 'protesty' songs (based on folk tunes) he heard. Her songs had fire and direct, everyday lyrics, and Pete immediately sat down and transcribed them."[34] Years later, when I spoke with Pete, he portrayed her as a "woman with strength and energy" with a "voice the combination of soprano saxophone, oboe, and bassoon." "We're going to make a new world for you to grow up and fight in," she told him during that first meeting. But Molly couldn't resist an attentive audience. Pete also remembered Molly's particular delight when his scarlet face revealed his reaction to her sexual explicitness. Molly and her family, for Pete, were great storytellers, folklorists' dreams.[35]

Molly's encounter and relationship with mentor Mary Elizabeth Barnicle, professor of English and Folklore at New York University, remains one of the most pivotal during her New York years. When Barnicle, as her friends called her, heard about Molly's traditional mountain songs and stories, she felt compelled to interview her and invite her to her folklore class. Enchanted with the mountain woman as a motherlode of Appalachian lore, Barnicle spent hours with Molly, recording her stories, songs, and midwifery experiences. She noted how Molly reflected Appalachian culture and womanhood, and yet observed and appreciated her uniqueness. The similiarities between Molly and Barnicle strike me—both tall, direct, open women of Scots-Irish ancestry. But even more obvious are their contrasts: the cultivated, educated New Englander and the earthy Appalachian. Barnicle brought Molly to life for me through her intuitive, insightful (although often illegible) handwritten notes she gleaned from her own interviews with Molly and prepared for an American Folklore course in the middle thirties. I'll extract and compact them as if they were a quote, but Barnicle uses outline form for lecture purposes.

> . . . naturally intelligent, not self-conscious, raconteur, a repository of family lore, believes in ghosts and spirits, luck-tokens and charms, herbs, does ballads and songs of all ages from remote antiquity to modern blues, songs of her own, hymns, has memory, is musician, creative source, midwife, herb doctor, showy vivid language, uses concrete words, smiles, not accustomed to reading lickety split like we do, immersion in her own culture—the mountain woman, looks, accent, manner of thought, culture, humor, manner of telling stories and singing, many happenings, tales and stories to corroborate every belief, a richness and fullness of belief. . . . (Appalachian) Culture has produced fiery independent men and women, farmers, miners, hunters, religionists. . . . Possible to see how easy it is to develop. Might have been with good education great speaker, actor, musician, writer. Aunt Molly not an exception, some women and many men like her in the mountains. Compares to peasantry, tradition of independence, poor yeomen to any lord master like the peasantry of the English countryside in Dorset.[36]

Molly's sexual joking, outrageousness, and irreverence particularly delighted Barnicle—so different from conservative New England culture! She began to accompany Molly back to Kentucky (first in 1934) to meet her family and collect songs and stories of other mountain folk. After one such trip in 1937, she recorded enthusiastic impressions of the Appalachian natives, seeing even more clearly how Molly could emerge from this environment.

Over the years Barnicle became one of Molly's foremost patrons, and was totally fascinated by the Kentucky woman whose independence of mind and spirit paralleled her own. Some biographical "facts" about Barnicle intrigue me. A shoe-manufacturer's daughter from Natick, Massachusetts, with an Irish father and Scots-Irish mother, Barnicle acquired a master's degree in English at Bryn Mawr, specializing in medieval literature. She subsequently held a variety of faculty positions, the longest at New York University, where she taught for thirty years. As comfortable in a mountain cabin as a college classroom, Barnicle met and married coal miner Tillman Cadle in New York and retired to a cabin in Rich Gap high in the Smokies in 1949. She taught for a year at the University of Tennessee and remained in the mountains until her death thirty years later.[37]

Willie Smyth, in a biographical portrait of Mary Barnicle accompanying an album of her collected songs (produced in 1986 by the Tennessee Folklore Society), speaks of the folklorist's political motivations and involvements to the (implied) detriment of her scholarly activities.[38] This interpretation infuriated Tillman Cadle, her ex-coal miner husband and co-collector (ninety plus years old and still living in Rich Gap, Tennessee, when I interviewed him in 1990; he died in 1995). He insisted that Barnicle's orientation wasn't "political" but "humanitarian."

Mary Barnicle became a channel through which Molly met other scholars and musicians. The mountain woman, though, didn't reciprocate by introducing the professor to her family, perhaps, as Jim Garland later concluded, because his half sister was "a little bit jealous."[39] Barnicle finally met Jim, who in 1937 introduced her to his Kentucky friend and fellow union organizer, Tillman, who became collaborator and husband. Molly did bring Barnicle to Sarah's cabin on one trip home to Kentucky (in 1934 or 1935), but shared little about her younger sibling (and even less about her singing talent) prior to this time. When Barnicle suggested that Sarah and family move to New York (which I'll speak about in the next chapter) Molly probably wasn't thrilled at the prospect. She did enjoy the invitations, along with Sarah and Jim, to Barnicle's folklore class in the middle to late 1930s, and enjoyed regaling students with stories and songs of home. Molly later made much of these classroom experiences, and when journalists and collectors interviewed her in Sacramento during the 1940s and 1950s she spoke of her "teaching" stints at New York University.

In 1935 Barnicle brought nineteen-year-old college student and budding folklore collector, Alan Lomax, to Aunt Molly's apartment. Together they recorded a comprehensive singing biography that included seventy-five of the Appalachian woman's songs, ranging from traditional and indigenous ballads, women's, children's songs, and her own protest material, using Molly's accompanying annotations and reminiscences. These would later prove to be a sore point for Molly and Sarah, too, who wasn't informed that the recordings would be donated to the Library of Congress without compensation for either of them.

Lomax [handwritten in left margin]

Lomax would become a pivotal figure in the folk-politics of the 1930s and 1940s, and head of the Archives of Folk Culture at the Library of Congress. With his father, folklorist John Lomax, he introduced traditional musicians and singers like Leadbelly to New York audiences, championing rural people's music and promoting it for urban tastes. Molly so entranced Alan that he called her the finest traditional singer he met in the United States (along with Texas Gladden), and characterized her singing as "wild, strident, highly emotional." Lomax's admiration for Molly went beyond her music. In the Molly Jackson memorial issue of the *Kentucky Folklore Record* he described the Appalachian singer as a "social satirist and a person of broad sympathies and understanding; completely aware of the role she could play for the good in her own time, and not sparing herself ever, in it."[40] Never losing interest in his Appalachian jewel, he painted with words (in a phone interview with me) that capture the wildly diverse facets of her personality: "incredible narrative fictionalizer, hellcat, hard drinker, wonderful, meaner than a nest of rattlesnakes, ten feet tall."[41]

Barnicle intended to use her notes for her own biography of Molly, but never completed the project for reasons one can now only speculate. Perhaps she became suspicious after Molly sang to her (completely from memory) a lengthy "Robin Hood Ballad," which she first claimed to have learned at the age of four from her ninety-two-year-old grandmother. Molly's version turned out to be remarkably close to one in a book by Kittredge and Sargent that Barnicle lent her.[42] Molly never denied, though, that the book inspired her song, the melody of which "comes to me with the words."[43] Or perhaps Jim, Sarah, and Hazel, who found Molly's accounts about various events and exploits difficult to swallow, persuaded Barnicle of their sister's crass opportunism.

When Barnicle translated Molly's colorful colloquialisms to grammatically "proper" talk, the mountain woman bristled. She began to see the folklorist as just another collector who "messed up" or "mommicked" her words. For whatever reason, Barnicle interviewed her Appalachian source extensively, took down the most meticulous details about her life experiences and cultural lore, and never published her material. Fortunately for me, and those that follow, she left her notes to archival posterity.

Perhaps Alan Lomax's intrusion into the Molly-Barnicle relationship contributed to or made it difficult for Barnicle to write her own version of Molly's story. The ubiquitous young collector, according to Tillman, magically appeared in Barnicle's apartment when she was interviewing Molly, which reportedly hampered her progress. Barnicle and Lomax, in a way, struggled over "ownership" of Molly. Another interesting possibility: Alan and Tillman seemed to compete for Barnicle's attention. Did Lomax think Tillman Cadle an inappropriate mate for his friend, seeing her attachment to the Appalachian former coal miner a way of "going native?" Lomax, who intended (perhaps still intends) to write his own "Molly" book, chastised me, when I contacted him for help, for writing her story or doing secondary research, when I could be using my time more fruitfully, collecting "new" folklore material (field recordings).

By 1935 Aunt Molly had entrenched herself in New York left elite circles, embraced by academics, writers, and artists with a social conscience. Wealthy supporters like Clifford Odets and his wife Louise Rainer courted Molly and the Garlands, inviting them to gatherings, often held in their honor. Molly could be counted on to entertain, even flabbergast her hosts with vulgar jokes. At one party, according to Tillman's telling to me, Molly explained the difference between Democrats and Republicans:

> Back when they didn't know what indoor plumbing was they kept a pot in the house. An old lady in the house was cooking a big kettle of pumpkin and set it on the hearth. The children upset it and it hit the outhouse pot and the pumpkin was mixed up with the contents of the pot. The old man said "Lord, I hate to see that nice looking pumpkin wasted . . . do you think you could save any of it?" The woman took a spoon and tasted what looked like pumpkin. "Is this pumpkin? No, it's shit." The old man said, "Well I guess we'd better throw it all out. It got so mixed up you can't tell the pumpkin from the shit." That's the Democrats and the Republicans!

Molly loved the attention but resented patronizers who treated her as a token representative of the oppressed. Reputed "to like her drink," party givers prepared for Molly's visits by stocking up on cheap wine. On one occasion, Tillman reluctantly accompanied Molly and Barnicle to a woman's club party. Molly, sitting next to him whispered angrily, and probably loud enough for her hosts' ears: "Tim, them goddam bourgeous [*sic*] shits think they know more than me, don't they? . . . Well, I'll show em!"

Two marvelous stories that clearly epitomize the mountain woman's attitude toward her bourgeois hosts come from writer Alice McLerran, who visited and recorded Molly in Sacramento in the late 1950s. Although almost eighty years old and considerably enfeebled, the ever theatrical

Molly charmed and textured her voice for her enchanted listener. She told Alice of a party given for her in 1940 in Washington, D.C., by Library of Congress lawyer John Vance, a "blue grass Kentuckian," which Alan Lomax also attended:

> I had a nice suit, a blue wool gabardine. When we got to the door . . . Margaret Vance, [who] met me at the door, said, "Aunt Molly, now we're just both about the same size. If you want an evening gown for the evening, why you just go up in my bedroom and pick out any evening gown you want to put on." Now, being a poor Kentucky coal miner's child and twice a coal miner's wife, and her talking to me about an evening dress. I looked at her. I didn't say "Mrs. Vance." I said, "Margaret Vance! My great-grandmother's never seen an evening dress, my grandmother's never seen one, and my mother, we all have never seen evening dresses." I said, "They was just as fine women as pissed through hair." That poor Allan Lomax . . . "Aunt Molly!" he said. I said "Don't 'Aunt Molly' me." "Now, if what I've got on is not nice enough for this thing, I can turn right around and go back!"[44]

The same evening yielded a second quintessential vignette illustrating Molly's scorn for upper-class snobbery. Her hosts asked her to stand at the head of the table and speak about 1931 Harlan coal conditions:

> This Lord Morley's wife [he was a Lord from England, Molly subtitled], she had bracelets of diamonds and pearls around it. When I began to demonstrate that sometimes I would have to take a little string and put it in the bacon fat in a lead pan to make a light, to hold a little dying child in my hands and see him die, she jumped up rattling them diamonds. "Oh," she said, talking that proud English, "that couldn't happen." I said, "Madam, it *did* happen, but if I would have had some of those pearls and diamonds that you have hangin' on your stinking person, it wouldn't have happened." I said, "I would have throwed them pearls and diamonds in a pawn shop and pawned them and got milk and bread for them babies and saved the lives of them." I said, "Now you sit down before I knock you down!" [exclamation point and emphasis mine, following voice inflections].[45]

Molly's impatience with Barnicles's students' naive questions about her Communist affiliations revealed itself in the following snipe:

"What do you mean Communist?" I asked. "You know what I mean," he says, "a Red." I said, "No, I don't know what you mean, but I'll tell you what I mean. If a Communist or a Red, whichever one you want to call it, if they believe in treating everybody just like you want the other fellow to treat you and believe in standing together for a right to live in this world and not just a little handful hold everything and the poor men that works for a living and sheds their blood and sweat to feed their children, if them people is Reds," I said, "Boy, I'm one of the Reddest Reds that you've ever looked at in the days of your life, now figure it out for yourself," I said.[46]

Molly's New York community included family and friends in close proximity. Jim Garland and his wife Hazel joined Molly in the middle 1930s. Sarah and her family moved to the city at Barnicle's urging in 1936, becoming Molly's neighbors on the Lower East Side. Huddie Ledbetter (Leadbelly) arrived with the Lomaxes from Louisiana on New Year's Eve 1934. Although he would be in and out of town for several years, Leadbelly found a kindred spirit in Molly. He identified with the Kentucky clan and recognized the similarities between their proletarian music and his topical songs.[47] Archie Green recorded Molly's rendition of a ditty Leadbelly wrote for her:

Aunt Molly Jackson,
It gives me great satisfaction
To work with Aunt Molly Jackson.
She walks, she talks, she fights;
She unites the working class.

Bless her old soul,
She's worth millions of gold,
Bless her old soul,
She's worth millions of gold.

She's brave and bold,
And if you fool her,
She'll knock you cold.[48]

Woody Guthrie, who came to New York City in 1937, applauded Molly's singing talents and noted her and Leadbelly's special affinity for one another. Referring to Aunt Molly Jackson and her clan:

"[They] all come to Leadbelly's house almost every day. . . . Molly is the woman Leadbelly. She is in her cotton apron what Leadbelly is in his bathrobe. She talks to him exactly as to her reflection in her mirror. He speaks back to her like the swamplands to the uplands, the same as his river would talk to her highest cliffrim. She loves him in the same half-jealous way that he loves her, because he sees and feels in Aunt Molly the woman who has found in her own voice the same power on earth that he has found."[49]

Woody, too, was fascinated with Molly and her clan—"from the fascist country of Harlan County, Kentucky,"[50] a term that he and others used to describe the Garlands, underscoring Molly's role as dominant family "representative," an image that she fostered. For him, as for Leadbelly, Molly seemed a comrade in arms. Woody lauded Molly as "the best ballad singer in the country." He headed his notes to eight of her songs, *Hard Hitting Songs for Hard-Hit People,* "Hell Busts Loose in Kentucky." Woody wrote: "I know Molly well. She's strong and she's good, and she ain't afraid of the police. She says what she thinks when she thinks it. The big guys call her a red. Well, Molly, it looks like if you always say just exactly what you think is right, they'll jump up and say you're a red . . . you ain't a'scared of nobody, Molly."[51]

The Kentuckians and their friends lived in starkly contrasting New York worlds. One consisted of parties in fancy homes of upper- and middle-class patrons, another, the meeting hall rally and union circuit, and the third in their poor, densely populated neighborhoods. Woody described living conditions by noting that "filth and starvation and disease is just as bad, only thicker, than anywhere in Kentucky."[52] Jim Garland's wife Hazel, in softer but equally despairing terms, reported, "We had expected things to be better in New York than they were in Kentucky, and to a certain extent, things were better. Not as many people were starving, but the struggle for food, clothing, and shelter was having to be fought there also."[53]

Molly's apartment on East Ninth Street on the Lower East Side, through the eyes of an interviewer in November 1938, contained a "conglomerate of knicknacks from second hand shops . . . and with five other people from Harlan County . . . it was clean but poor." Molly herself, the interviewer told us, went to "primary school but otherwise was self-educated, a midwife, organizer, minstrel singer and composer of ballads. . . . At one time she was a religious woman but I doubt whether she is now.

Her religion is of a peculiar type: the bile and the fighting for miners rights are interwoven into one whole. She is a strong mountain type with weather beaten face."[54]

Molly's marriage to a Greek man, Tom (also known as Gus) Stamos (her third and last husband if she didn't marry John Mills) still holds some mystery. She told Archie Green during one interview in Sacramento that she actually married Tom in 1924 when he came to Appalachia, but kept it a secret because the mountaineers didn't take kindly to foreigners. According to all other sources, she remained married to Bill Jackson until she left Kentucky in 1931 and most likely met Tom at Camp Unity, an upstate New York Communist Party country retreat, where he worked as a chef.

People remarked on their stormy relationship, with Tom usually on the receiving end of Molly's belligerence. Despite his Greek background (a culture that normalizes male dominance), Molly intimidated her husband, who felt privileged that a real American—and famous singer and songwriter—deigned to marry him. Taking pleasure in drinking, cavorting, and tale telling in front of visitors, Molly would become extremely irritated with Tom's (apparently frequent) interruptions. She once shouted at him, ignoring the company. "Don't I have no goddam democracy in my own home? Well, keep your damn mouth shut then!" On another occasion, she treated him, according to Tillman Cadle, like a dog: "Don't you bark until I pull your chain!"[55] But clearly, Woody and others adopted Tom as one of their own, as "he loved Martha and Leadbelly, danced with everybody, laughed and cried, and came to this house [Leadbelly's] because it was the only place that he could find all of his whole tribe at once."[56]

In 1940 Molly and Tom opened a restaurant on Fulton Street in Brooklyn. Tom cooked, with Molly's help, an odd combination of Greek-Kentucky food, and Molly sang for the customers (which, Hazel Garland wryly told me, drove them away). Pete Seeger described the place to me, which he visited once, as about twenty by twenty-five feet, with a juke box playing Kentucky music. Tillman described the sizable sign displaying "Aunt Molly Jackson of Radio Fame." The *Daily Worker* (May 4, 1940) quoted Woody Guthrie saying that "her eats are swell . . . and I know [Walter] Winchell [a New York columnist] won't mention her, so I say, for an exasperation inhalation of groceries, or a superb sip of something, go to Aunt Molly's—Proletarian Potatoes, the best in town." Despite Woody's enthusiastic advertisement, the venture floundered, and to make ends meet

Molly and Tom offered the place for union meetings. Molly wrote to some of her influential friends, Alan Lomax and composer Earl Robinson, seeking loans to sustain them, but whether or not they received responses, the restaurant went bankrupt after a fairly brief period, and they returned to New York City, and Home Relief.

The Kentuckians, despite their integration in the left-wing political and artistic scene, generated formidable tensions among themselves, particularly between Molly and Jim, Hazel, and Sarah, which involved personality differences, jealousies, and mistrust. Barnicle arranged for Jim to run a radio program on WNYC for four months in 1938, providing an arena for the Kentuckians in which Molly apparently didn't appear.[57] When Jim formed a group to represent Kentucky at the 1939 World's Fair, where "the women donned bonnets and long skirts and men dressed as farmers one day and coal miners the next, complete with hats, lamps and dinner pails," he didn't include Molly.[58]

The way Molly saw it, the other Garlands owed her a great deal. She took them in, introduced them to her fancy New York friends, was available when they needed her. Sarah, after all, met her savior Barnicle through Molly's efforts, and should be beholden to her older half sister for this good fortune. Molly not only cared for Sarah's family when her child was in hospital, but delivered Hazel's and Jim's child, Jim Jr., at home. She offered to nurse Hazel and Jim in 1938 when the doctors diagnosed both of them with tuberculosis.

A string of bad experiences, however, aroused Hazel's suspicions of Molly and provoked her disillusionment: "We got an apartment just next door to Molly. I think it was on Broome Street. Well, I thought that was the most wonderful thing that had ever happened . . . her offer to take care of three kids and also me. She had charge of everything, all the money that we had . . . I never seen any of it. When she found out Jim was coming home she took the money and we couldn't even buy the baby's milk. She turned around and destroyed all the good things she'd done."[59]

Molly continually embarrassed the Garlands and they deeply distrusted her motives. While she could be interesting, even amusing, according to Hazel, she could also be, the "meanest, awfullest person on earth." Jim disclosed his cynicism to Tillman, who told it to me this way: "I was staying in New York. Jim and I was together quite a lot and one morning we went to the pushcart market to do some shopping. We were on the street where Aunt Molly lived and Jim suggested that we go up to see her. Aunt

Molly was out of sorts and was ranting and raving. 'Nobody is any good, sons of bitches.' . . . When we left, I asked Jim what the problem was. 'Don't you know what was wrong with her?' Jim asked. 'They forgot to put her picture in the paper today!'"[60]

Another of Tillman's stories about Molly's self-serving behavior illuminates the severe strain between her and the Garlands. During one December in New York some wealthy benefactors sent Molly and Tom three turkeys and trimmings for Christmas dinner, meant for all the Garlands. The couple, however, never distributed them. When they found out about it from a cousin who noticed the cache of cranberry sauce under the bed, Jim and Sarah were infuriated. Sarah composed a funny, venomous song about her rotten half sister, accusing her of lying, home wrecking, bigamy and theft, lacking redeeming qualities. Willie Smyth included Sarah's song in his recording of selections from the Barnicle-Cadle collection for the Tennessee Folklore Society. Tillman vociferously objected to Smyth's choice, insisting that Sarah wrote the song for Molly's ears alone and not public consumption. But, more about this in chapter 5, Sarah's story.

The others who noted Molly's opportunism were less affected by it than her family; they generally dismissed or found it amusing. Henrietta Yurchenco, then broadcaster for WNYC, who met Molly and her clan in 1940, compared Molly with her family and friends: "Molly was the weirdo, you never knew what she was going to do, she might be nice, unctious, say a bunch of nasty things. Sarah and Jim were always reasonable. Woody was the poet, Leadbelly the musician." Henrietta told me of the time she, the Garlands, Woody Guthrie, Alan Lomax, and others, enjoyed a day in the country. "Molly sidled up to me and said 'Miss Jenco, I've been hearing some bad stories about you. They said you're a snob, real uppity.' 'Molly, next time I have a broadcast you'll come up.' Molly couldn't be more delighted. Leadbelly, standing near us, leaned over and said, 'She's the one spreading the rumors.'"

Yurchenco thought Molly an ornery, self-important, disagreeable woman "who would do anything to stay in the limelight," but also appreciated her unique talents.

But [here's the other side]. . . . There is no question as an observer, she was terrific. When she talked about her life, it was some of the greatest stuff about miners and miners' lives. She rhymed so easily . . . at parties people would make up verses, Aunt Molly's was always spectacular, it was poetry. She was central, she made herself so. She was a very visible woman. I still remember the ease with which she spoke, the graphic language that she used, that kind of inner poetry.[61]

The three year period from 1939 to 1942, Serge Denisoff's "proletarian renaissance," "represented a subculture and a style of life which fitted into the working-class ethos of the Communist party."[62] In this musical revival, real folk and urban appreciators consolidated under the common banner of folk consciousness expressed through music, the theater, and art. Actor Will Geer organized one of the revival's pivotal events, the "Grapes of Wrath" concert, a benefit for agricultural workers on March 3, 1940. I'll discuss the concert and its implications in chapter 6 but note here for the first time, traditional singers (like Molly Jackson), previously marginalized and little known or appreciated outside of their own circles, performed together with urban revivalists (like Pete Seeger) in front of a mainstream audience.

After this benefit, enlivened spirit infused the folk music community. Promotors arranged more concerts, creating a new demand for singers. Alan Lomax's CBS radio program "School of the Air," became an avenue for revival folk artists to educate the public about their roots. Earl Robinson's "Ballad for Americans," composed in 1938, played a number of times during the late 1930s, and Will Geer performed in socially relevant theatrical productions. In the early 1940s the Almanac Singers formed, with Pete Seeger (then Pete Bowers), Millard Lampell, and Lee Hays (later joined by Pete Hawes and Bess Lomax, Woody Guthrie, Sis Cunningham, and others). In its various permutations, the group traveled the country, singing at union meetings, writing, recording, and performing—representing a community committed to instilling political consciousness in the masses. They hosted hootenannies in a rented loft near Union Square, charged a small admission, and sold beer. As many as a hundred people in all might show up, including Leadbelly, the Lomaxes, Josh White, Sonny Terry, Burl Ives, Aunt Molly, and her clan.

But, despite the vigor injected into people's music for large audiences, with Molly angling for a central place in the revitalization, her personal circumstances sorely deteriorated; she sank deeper into poverty and desperation. Regarded as more of a symbol than a singer, her audiences shrank, most preferring to hear the more polished sound of Josh White and Burl Ives. In the view of Woody's biographer, Joe Klein, "The *idea* that

Aunt Molly Jackson was singing the people's music was a lot more palatable than the harsh, nasal reality of her voice."[63] And in Richard Reuss's view, although Aunt Molly "was revered as a militant example of the Kentucky proletariat, admired for her ability to blend class sentiments with old mountain tunes, yet few radicals other than some of the Lomax singers really enjoyed the harsh, tense sound of her voice, or the modal or minor-key tunes of many of her songs."[64] Invitations for Molly to perform became rare.

Molly's associates and patrons, trying to respond to her continual appeals, arranged benefits for her. Earl Robinson organized at least one in 1941, and in January 1942 her friends held a large concert "in her honor," where Earl, Leadbelly, Burl Ives, Josh White, Woody Guthrie, the Almanacs, Sis Cunningham, Will Geer, and English balladeer Richard Dyer-Bennet performed. Gordon Friesen, whose tribute to Molly appeared the day before the concert in the *Daily Worker* (Jan. 10, 1942), reported that the mountain woman still has her "fighting spirit" and quoted her saying "You know, we're a hard-punching people, and we aint' never been licked. We pack a mighty wallop, and when we hit them something happens."

An endless series of disillusionments beset Molly in her northern home, beginning with the Columbia recording experience during her first New York days. Convinced that the company distributed the record but never paid the promised 15 percent, Molly never forgave them. She wove a story for Archie Green, with her usual mix of wry humor and anger, about how she inadvertently discovered Columbia's secret and the fate of her recording during her first trip home to Kentucky:

> After the strike was over I went up to the Columbia Broadcasting Company and they said there hadn't been a record sold. Professor Barnicle and me, we went to Kentucky in '34. That's the first time I was back, and I had a great aunt that lived in Clay County [who] was ninety-four years old. I was going along and I heard this record playing in the mining camp. . . . It was on Christmas Eve and I went up and listened. . . . They had got the news that I was dead and they was all gathered up around that record now like it was a funeral or something. They believed, them old people you know, in ghosts and hags. Martha Currie, she was crying "I'd give anything in the world if I could see the poor old thing. That's all I want for Christmas is just her blessed face." I kicked the door open, I said "OH, YES!" I scared the socks off them and they was paying a dollar and a half for second-hand records of that, and

them lowdown cheaters, they had shipped into Harlan Country six hundred of my records. They'd shipped to Bell County five hundred and they'd shipped to Manchester and Clay County seven hundred of them records. All I could do about that record was just to stop it and I didn't get a penny.[65]

Although her public statements swaggered with self-serving bravado, the series of letters she wrote to Alan Lomax and Earl Robinson in the late 1930s and early 1940s tell another story: her rising sense of victimization and depression. Her own scratchy handwriting, or occasional dictated typewritten pages (rendered grammatically intelligible by people she managed to draft as temporary helpers), revealed how she entreated those she perceived in a position to help her. As heartrending narratives of disappointment and exploitation, they bear reprinting. I offer a sample here, with the first two essentially as written and the others slightly edited for spelling and readability, since Molly's text ran on without puntuation or capitals. All letters and poems to Lomax cited here are in the Archives of Folk Culture, Washington D.C.; those to Earl Robinson in his papers at the University of Washington, Seattle.

> To Alan Lomax in July 1939:
> Dear Friend, I have not received anything for the recording I have done for you yet please see that I get my pay at once as am very sick, and haft to get out of this . . . city if I live. I've not been able to make a penny since you left New York and the death of sister Sarah's little boy has made a nervous reck of me. The doctors say my life depends on getting out of the city so please help me get a few dollars together so I can go to the country for a while til I can live over this shock of my sister's little boy's death. . . . Kiss your sweet little wife for me . . . closed with love as ever from Aunt Molly Jackson.

She admonished Lomax for not publishing a labor song book that was to include a chapter on her as well as Jim and Sarah, and pleaded with him to compensate her for songs, to help her write (type, edit), and publish her autobiography. In another letter, written on July 31, 1939, a less supplicant, more assertive Molly asked for her due:

> Mr. Lomax Sir: I am to old to be fooled the second time by a young [?] . . . like you. You rote to me last week that my check was on the

way. . . . You rote and ask Miss Barnicle if you should pay me . . . so if you can not make up your mind how to pay me and how much to pay me I will haft to rite to the new superviser of the Library of Congress, a member of the American riters legal and at least I can learn from him how to get pay for my recording so if you don't send my check in return mail I will haft to try to collect. from Aunt Molly Jackson

Molly's communications became more irate as she realized Lomax wouldn't publish her book; she threatened him not to use her material. She attempted to invoke his guilt for deserting a union sister, and stood together with Jim and Sarah, protecting their interests against an exploitative outsider. On August 7, 1939 (handwritten by someone else, but still in Molly's stream of consciousness style), she wrote:

Sir, in answer to your letter dated August 4, how do you expect me to remain your friend when you have proved by your actions that you are not my friend, or even a friend to any poor person as far as that goes. As for me wanting to work with you again or even corresponding with you ever any more is out of the question, for I could never trust you ever again. Since you have proved so false to me and also my brother and sister. You agreed to put out a labor song book for me and Jim Garland and Sarah Ogan and each of us was to have a chapter and get royalty for our songs. Now you want to use only 2 of my songs and some of my stories. So I warn you not to use one word of my material or any of Jim Garland's or Sarah Ogan's either. Until you first get a written agreement from them. The songs and stories you recorded from me was for the Library of Congress and I expect them to pay me for all of my songs. Mr. Lomax you thought you were doing me a favor as I am a poor home relief victim by having the Library of Congress to send me only $30 for all the songs I recorded for them. I am sorry that I ever got acquainted with you or any of your kind for that matter. I assure you that I would be better off financially and in better health. Speaking as my part in the spirit of good unionism and democracy or class loyalty I assure you there has never been anyone any more loyal to my class than I. I have been a sincere union woman all my life and I will remind you I am too old to be a scab for anyone. I still feel that you have not been square with me and I am more than glad to drop the whole matter as I do not want any of my songs or stories coming out in any other books or pamphlets because I do not want the sale of my own book damaged. From a real comrade, signed Aunt Molly Jackson, 816 E. 9th Street N.Y.C.

With Molly's and Tom's Brooklyn restaurant plummeting into financial crisis, she again sought Lomax's aid. An August 1940 letter compliantly related distress, lack of work, jealousies of Sarah and Jim, and how other mentors disappointed her:

> You are the only ones that I can depend on for help. Everything was going fine til Tom got robbed by a pickpocket. We are building up a good trade now and the Brooklyn truckmen are coming out on strike the 24 of this month and my restaurant will be headquarters, that is if I can keep my place open till the 24. I can if I can pay my rent for August in the next ten days so please help me out of this pinch. Also I am so disappointed and heart broken I don't know what to do. I have not been able to make one cent from singing or entertaining this whole summer. Earl Robinson promised to get me some bookings. He disappointed me. Leadbelly Woodie and Jim Garland and sister Sarah has had lots of bookings through Barnicle but I was one of the hillbillies group that was asked for often by the people and Miss Barnicle tells them I went back to Kentucky. Please send me a few dollars so can keep my place. Give my regards to your beautiful wife and your sweet little sister [Bess Lomax Hawes] for me so I will close hoping to see you or to hear from you soon from your true friend and comrade, Aunt Molly Jackson.

On the flip side of the letter, Molly scrawled a saccharine love poem with the title "In Rememberance of Alan Lomax":

> I am thinking of you
> Are you thinking of me
> Your two big brown eyes
> I am longing to see
>
> Your brown eyes that
> Sparkle love
> Shine down on me like
> Stars from above
>
> I love to meet you
> With your sparkling brown eyes
> How I hate to leave you
> Yet I hate those goodbyes
>
> Some times those goodbyes
> Last for too long

Excuse me old pal
If you think I am rango [wrong?]

I am your true friend
And I always will be
Please keep a little cozy corner
In your heart for me.

I found one letter from Lomax to Molly in Earl Robinson's papers, written in 1942, in which he held out hope that he would work on Molly's book and asked her to send some material. But we can assume nothing came of it. Molly eventually transferred her affections to composer Earl Robinson (in whose personal papers drafts of Molly's autobiographical typescript turned up). With hope that this other famous patron might help her sell songs or publish her story, she corresponded with Earl extensively from New York and Sacramento, after he moved to Los Angeles. The series of letters disclose the ways Molly tried to wheedle money and favors from "important" friends, ranging from self-abasement to sympathy and guilt. On the other hand, they project the desperation of a once useful, now discarded "other." Struggles with poverty, the desire to help Jim and his family, and a declining relationship with Sarah become clear from this 1941 letter to Earl:

> Dear Friend,
> My sister Sarah is mad at me because I am sick my self and cannot come to the hospital to see her and she is going to report to the home relief that I got money from a benefit that you ran for me and I do not need relief. Please Earl, if you are asked by the home relief about the benefit, say I was only the guest of honor at this benefit for I have spent every cent for my brothers sick wife and her little children. If they stop my home relief I will have to starve and if you can find someplace where I can entertain for a few cents. Please let me know for I need a few dollars now worse than ever in all my life. My brother Jim Garland has little and his family is on home relief . . . one quart of milk a day for three children. So you see I must have more milk for them some how. Regards to your wife and wonderful son. Hoping to hear from you soon. Aunt Molly Jackson.

Molly enclosed one of her new songs, which like others during this period, were mainly autobiographical accounts, reasserting her accomplishments and reminding Earl, and others whom he might influence, about the key role she played in organizing the workers.

> This is a true sad story
> About a woman from the hills
> She labored hard for her living
> Around the coal mines and mills
>
> She was a trained nurse and a midwife
> In the same state where she was born and raised
> In the hills of old Kentucky
> Where she was always loved and praised
>
> From eighteen to fifty
> She traveled day and night
> Nursing and delivering babies
> That was her greatest heart's delight
>
> In 1931 she was forced to leave her home
> Hard times and misfortune
> Forced her to roam
>
> She was fifty years old
> The day she went away
> Now she is sixty-one
> Her hair is turning gray
>
> She lives today on the East Side in New York City
> And there she aims to stay
> Till death comes along
> And calls her away
>
> She serves the laboring class with great satisfaction
> And the name of this woman is Aunt Molly Jackson

Another composition, in the same autobiographical vein, emphasizes her undying support for the union:

> I'm a coal-miner's daughter
> And a coal-miner's wife
> I was borned and raised in old Kentucky
> And lived there all my life
>
> Until hard times and low wages
> Caused me to roam

Then I left my relations
My country and my home

I was born in Clay County, Kentucky,
Sixty-one years ago
I'm a member of the coal-miner's union
Affiliated with the CIO

I am a union woman,
One that really fights
I teach all my fellow workers
To stand up for their rights

I have marched on lots of picket lines,
I've called miners out on strike
Low wages and long hours
Are two things I do not like

We called the strike in Harlan County, Kentucky, in 1931
Because the wages was so low that's all that could be done
They had cut the coal-miner's wages down to 30 cents a ton

When we struck for living wages
The coal-operators chased the organizers away
But I am still an organizer,
That's why I am here today

Some of our organizers was sent to prison
And some of the coal miners lost their lives
They was fighting for bread and butter
For their children and wives

But that did not break our spirit,
Our union is strong today
And I for one do not regret
The price I had to pay

I covered twenty-eight states
Of the Union in 1931 and '32
As an organizer and writer,
I did all that I could do

In a December 18, 1941, letter, a profoundly depressed Molly lets Earl know how far she's fallen, abjectly begging him for money, but stressing that she wants to sell her songs in the interests of patriotism.

Dear Friend,
This is to let you and your wife know I am very sick and am suffering with my heart and stomach. The doctor put me on a diet but I do not have any money to buy the food which means I will get worse instead of better, so if you can get everyone interested in the kind of songs I compose or can help me to get a album of records out in order to enable me to feed my self as I should so I will be able to do my part in this war. I sure will thank you a lot. All I get from the Home relief is 35 cents a day for food and I cannot live much longer on that.

In 1942 Molly tries another poetic tack, employing guilt, humor, and, as usual, patriotism:

Earl: I will sing you all a song if you want to hear it. I sure haven't lost my spirit. I can sing and compose to you I declare. I am a good broadcaster if you put me on the air, I am a tough old yankie a quarter Cherokee and all the Nazis in the world can't tantalize me. (sung to tune of Davie Crocket).

By 1943 Molly's political affections transferred to the Democrats and Franklin Roosevelt, whose praises she wrote in songs for the war effort and forwarded to Earl:

Dear Friend, I have wrote a new war song that I been singing. It will make a big hit in selling bonds and stamps. So they told me to send this song to the Treasury Department in Washington to be used over the radio. So if you will be able to write the music to this song for me you will be doing me a great favor. So if you can do me this favor, please let me know what time I can come to your house to get the music to this song written, so I will be able to send it to the Treasury Department. Your true friend, as ever Aunt Molly Jackson

Oh, Mr. Roosevelt
It's the nation's cry
We still want you for president
Please don't deny
Mr. Roosevelt you must run again
Yes Mr. Roosevelt you must run
You must carry on the fight our forefathers begun
Mr. Roosevelt you must run again.

The enemy of democracy
Screams day and night
Crying the things you do are not right
But Mr. Roosevelt you must run again.

In 1943 Molly and Tom Stamos left New York for the West Coast, relocating like Jim and Hazel, first to Vancouver, Washington, where Tom found work in the shipyards, then finally to Sacramento. Far from regretting the move, the embittered Molly craved to abandon the eastern city that abandoned her: "They framed me up from 1931 to 1943, they beat me up on the streets of New York City, they spit in my face, they had me put in jail . . . they called me Jew lover, a nigger lover, and a trouble maker for nothing more than teaching the brotherhood of man. . . . I believe I have been treated worse by the rulers of our country than any other poor woman that has ever lived under the sun."[66]

We know little of Molly's life in Sacramento, California, especially during her first five years, except through her correspondence. Poor health kept her fairly close to her little house on Fourth Street. She stayed in touch with Earl Robinson and kept hoping he would come to visit, help write her book, find her a publisher, and arrange for appearances at festivals. Molly never failed to assure Earl of her devotion to working people's causes.

Molly amused and fascinated Earl, who responded to her letters even though he might not have done her bidding. Increasingly more desperate, but not without optimism, the sixty-five-year-old Molly wrote (with someone's help) the following letter to the composer in Los Angelos, dated September 1, 1945. Well-cultivated wiles—flattery, coaxing, flirting— would convince Earl, she thought, to save her from obscurity.

I received your letter and glad as always to hear from you, and also glad that you thought probably that it would be possible for me to appear in one of the folk festivals as in New York. Now that the gas rationing is over it certainly would be nice if you could run up here and take me down to Hollywood. Any time that it would be convenient, I certainly would be honored if I could make my appearance in one of your folk festivals in Hollywood. I have always wanted to go to Hollywood as you know. I have been delayed with my manuscript on account that I could not get any typist to type permanently. As soon as I can get the manuscript finished, if you do not have a chance to drive your car up here, and take me back with you then I just will get on the train, and come any time you think you would like me to appear in one of your festivals and I will bring the manuscript of the book with me, so that you can correct any thing that you think should be corrected. In the mean time while I am there, if your sister can write the music to the songs that I have composed that is not copywritten yet, I certainly will be grateful to you both. You said in the last of your letters, let's be sure to keep in touch with each other, and you bet I will. I have been following you up ever since I heard you on the program "What's Doing Ladies" as a guest of Art Linkletter's program last year. You would have a hard time getting away from me "Boy!" I am sure we will both remain in Calif. Remember I will always be glad to appear in anyone of your programs any time you will arrange a part for me. Kiss Perry [Earl's son] and your wife for me. Tom sends you his regards and says he hopes it will be possible for you to come to Sacramento to visit us sometimes in the near future. Hoping to hear from you soon, as always, love from your one and only Aunt Molly Jackson.

An excited Molly, soon after sending this, dashed off another (typewritten) letter congratulating Earl on the radio performance of the now classic "The House I Live In" (probably in October 1945): "I cant help writing you and telling you how proud I am of you." And then in her characteristic verse style, merging passion and politics, lavished her approval and love on this icon, as she did on Lomax before him.

I hardly know how to start.
First, I want to say you are a man after my own heart,

What I mean, you are just my kind,
You are not afraid to speak up and tell the world your mind,

And believe me you sure can put your feelings in a song,
Which I think is the best way on earth to teach what is right and what is
    wrong.

That song you wrote "What America is to Me:"
Is as powerful as any song can be

Please keep on composing songs, don't stop at all
For that is the best way on earth to bring around all for one and one for all

That one big solid union that is so easy to understand
That Jesus Christ himself called "the brotherhood of man"

Yes, Jesus told the people to love each other
like a father loves a son, and like a daughter loves her mother,

He said "Do unto others as you wanted them to do unto you"
He did not say for the Gentile to love the Gentile, and the Jew to love
the Jew,

He did not say a thing
about the black or the white
He just said for us to treat each other right

And that is just what I aim to do
I am fed up on division among races and colors, what about you?

The letters in Earl's papers cease in 1948. Molly probably sent him parts of her autobiography that she retrieved from Mary Barnicle (since some of the same pages appear in both archives) but Earl, as Barnicle and Lomax, disappointed Molly and never wrote, or helped her publish her story. In the early 1950s Molly corresponded from Sacramento with Rae Korson, then head of the Archives of Folksong (Now the Archives of Folk Culture), in Washington, D.C., obviously answering a request for a signature on a release form. Tom had died a number of years before (probably in 1948) and Molly seemed muddled, but she took the opportunity to tell Korson something about her place and her mission, ever hopeful that she would be asked to sing again and thus convey her message to future generations.

Dear Friend: I am sorry I did not understand that I was supposed to sign this form you sent back for me to sign, so I signed my name. If anything else is to be done I give you permission to fill in for me anything that I did not understand. My nerves is all shot and my memory is bad and I don't have anything left in my old age pension. All my husband left me was my house on a lot in the city and a lot of doctor bills to pay and my fire insurance. I sure am glad to get any money I can at this time and I'm still glad to help in every way I can to help the young generation to learn the songs that our ancestors sang before we even heard of a nation. In the hills of Kentucky my ancestors just composed their own songs about their life, their husbands, sweethearts and their pleasures and sorrow. I have hundreds of songs in ballads that I have composed my self that I want to give to our good friend Archie Green to teach from after I am resting. I want my union songs to build a union spirit in every youngster's breast after I've been laid to rest. I would like to come to Washington and record some more records when I get my voice back. I have such shortness of breath now, it is too hard on me to sing like I used to. Thanking you for your past favors and for anything you can do for me in the future, your true friend as always, Aunt Molly Jackson.

One of the last to interview her, Archie Green, located Molly in her Sacramento home in the late 1950s. He returned many times between 1958 and 1960, the year of Molly's death, accompanied on different occasions by Zonweise Stein, Page Stegner, Billy Faier, and others whom he tried to interest in Aunt Molly. Researching *Only a Miner,* Green thought the old woman an amazingly fertile, if not reliable, informant. Grilling his Appalachian source, the folklorist gleaned detailed information about her versions of traditional songs, methods of composition, relationships in Kentucky and New York. Archie Green concluded that Aunt Molly remained less concerned that her songs didn't "enter tradition" than with their potential political impact. She passionately wanted her composed music to offer future generations power to resist oppression. But tradition for Molly was simply her *being*—she embodied the "real thing." In Green's words, "Molly Jackson's preface [to 'Poor Miner's Farewell'] is as good as her song—perhaps better. . . . She reviled others who 'messed up' her songs and professed a most conservative loyalty to old forms."[67] John Greenway, too, commented on Molly's rigidity about the authenticity of her versions, even though she would vary them: "she has a genius for alienating collectors. More even than coal operators she hates collectors who 'fix up' her texts, and it is impossible to avoid offending her in this matter. One takes down a song as accurately as possible, submits the text to her for checking, and immediately receives the fury of her monumental rage for 'messing' up the song. She cannot be convinced that she never sings a song the same way twice. Not only words but tunes also change without provocation."[68] Molly denounced Greenway's treatment of her in *American Folksongs of Protest,* as she had Barnicle and Lomax before him. But Greenway, despite concluding that Molly was an unreliable informant, still thought her a "great" one.[69]

Molly, in a letter to *Sing Out!* magazine shortly before her death in 1960, bitterly ranted about her lack of recognition and remuneration for her traditional songs. Despite it all, she affirmed her continuing loyalty to the cause of justice and equality:

I am 3,000 miles away from my old Kentucky home, barely existing on the old age pension. Nobody seems to pay me any attention. Only the folksong collectors that want me to teach them the songs I learned from my Kentucky ancestors 75 years ago. But if I ask them where I can get a few pennies for the songs I teach them, they just don't know. . . . I have had the songs I composed translated in five different languages and records made of my songs, but I have never received one cent from anyone out of all the protest songs I have composed. . . . Some of the people that is putting out records and using my songs think I am dead and I am forgotten. But I am not. All said and done, I am still standing by my union, one for all and all for one, even if I am almost eighty-one.[70]

The letter exhibits Molly's overriding hope to be remembered, not as an Appalachian traditional singer, but as a champion of the downtrodden whose personal experiences and songs captured the tragedies of class oppression. Near the end of her life, vulnerable Aunt Molly invoked the painful sorrows of so many burdens and tragedies, but made sure that she emphasized her contribution:

So from 1919, I have never been happy. Many be the time since my brother was killed, I've laid awake all night and cried. But this is sure, one thing I always knew that it was my duty to struggle and do my very best to see that the workers' little children had milk and bread and a decent shelter over their heads, even if I lost my life by some gun thug putting a bullet through my chest . . . I have realized if working people lived in peace at all, they must first be organized. For the last fifty years I have surely done my best. I first began to build unions in the South; then next I built unions in the East and North, and today, I am here in the West, and if I cannot do it well as some other organizers may do, I will always be able to truthfully say, I have done my very best.[71]

Aunt Molly Jackson died on the last day of August 1960, shortly before her eightieth birthday. Scraps of paper with notes and songs disappeared, most likely discarded with her shabby furniture, Barnicle's dog-eared copy of Kittridge and Sargent with the contested "Robin Hood" poem, and photographs of Roosevelt and Pete Seeger proudly placed on her wall. Obituaries in the *Sacramento Bee* (September 2) and the *New York Times* (September 4), the *San Jose News,* and *St. Louis Post-Dispatch* (September 4) all honored the original and famous "Pistol Packin' Mama." John

Greenway, in his *Sing Out!* obituary, said, "If Aunt Molly has made it to Heaven I am sure her fight goes on . . . the songs she is singing are like nothing the heavenly choir ever heard before."[72]

Molly's funeral, held in the Sacramento Memorial Garden Chapel, arranged by her niece, Lula Holcolm, drew a surprisingly respectable crowd of about fifty assorted people. Writer Alice McLerran lovingly remembers the mountain woman as she lay in an open lavender and blue casket, with withered, hawklike features, still haunting despite softening efforts of the embalmers. Molly's final theater would have brought her joy—the wafting soulful organ music, rocks and streams decorating the front of the chapel. She would have disdained the minister who grabbed the opportunity to warn mourners that they too might fall from grace. As he orated, "In my father's house there are many mansions . . . ," Alice could almost see Molly rise and proclaim, "Mansion?! My mother never saw a mansion. My grandmother never saw one either. And my great-grandmother? They none of them saw a mansion . . . and they was just as fine a women that ever pissed through hair!"[73] And Mary Magdalene Garland (Mills?) Stewart Jackson Stamos would have certainly written a song to mark the ironic conclusion to her extraordinary life.

Molly's closing, in a way, meant Sarah's opening. A shadow thus far in my telling, Sarah receives attention in the next chapter, mostly as frame for Molly, but also as unique life story. We will, reader, be revisiting some happenings and people in Appalachia and New York, but this time from Sarah's standpoint.

5

"Girl of Constant Sorrow": Molly's Sister, Sarah Ogan Gunning

"I am a girl of constant sorrow, I've got trouble all my days." Sarah Ogan Gunning's plaintive words floated over the audience at the 1964 Newport Folk Festival. Newport proved a turning point for Sarah, a festival Cantwell calls "the supreme moment in the national seance of the folk revival."[1] Overshadowed by dominant Molly during her younger years, middle-aged Sarah finally emerged after her big sister's death. As Molly's setting in the 1930s accented relationships among Communism, music, region, class, and gender, Sarah's involvement in the commercial folk music revival of the late 1950s and early 1960s allows us to further explore cultural, political, and musical webs. Those who knew both sisters highlighted their differences—rambunctious Molly, self-possessed Sarah. But they also lived in historically different times. Theodore Dreiser and his cohorts visited Appalachia in 1931 (when Sarah was merely twenty) and drafted a middle-aged Molly as their miner's angel in the North. As we know, the fit between the prototypical mountain woman and the progressive writers' needs couldn't have been more ideal. With the dust of "Bloody Harlan" settling, Molly remained on New York's Lower East Side for the entire third decade. Though the Kentucky miners' struggles faded, she continued to perceive herself as a front-line warrior until her death. During her last fifteen years of her life in Sacramento, California, far from the coal mines of Appalachia, Molly's vision of a better world and role as savior persisted. Wrestling with physical infirmity, poverty, and obscurity, she never deserted her commitment to radical goals. In the final few years before death in 1960, an enfeebled Molly brightened at the rare arrival of visitors, ever hopeful that someone would publish her story, record her songs. When Archie Green, pursuing song origins, perched in Molly's Sacramento living room with colleagues and students, another opportunity arose for her to shine. The old woman, voice crackling and fragile, twinkled her eyes, embellished, cajoled, insisted, admonished, reassured the folklorist that she, and only she, told the truth. Green, like others, remained skeptical.

Although much of Sarah's life in New York during the middle and late 1930s paralleled those of Molly's and Jim's, she left Kentucky for different, more personal reasons than her siblings, and shied away from the limelight. By the time Sarah arrived, Molly had already established herself in the big city as a family head, an elder, with Sarah and Jim Garland as younger siblings. Acquaintances in New York would consider the Garlands a unit and often invite them all to the same gatherings. When Molly, and husband Tom, and older brother Jim and his family moved west to find war work in the early forties, Sarah soon followed, staying for a while before settling in the Midwest. Archie Green learned of the younger Garland's whereabouts from Molly in the late 1950s, and tracked her, by that time Mrs. Joe Gunning, to a Detroit basement apartment in 1963. Archie would return with folklorist Ellen Stekert soon after to persuade Sarah to record and perform. The private Sarah would introduce new audiences to "traditional" Appalachian song at festivals and see young urban folkies appreciate and try to emulate her.

Despite their obvious similarities as Appalachian coal miners' wives, the sisters' lives, personalities, and politics diverged significantly. Molly, drawn to New York in 1931 by radical and Communist sympathizers, fashioned herself as their proletarian firebrand. By 1936, when Sarah moved north, the National Miners Union had vanished, and the Communist Popular Front's broader based policies replaced Third Period sectarian rigidity. With radicalism muted, Sarah vehemently disassociated herself from the uncomfortably close links between folk music and the Left. One of her songs, originally entitled "I Hate the Capitalist System," became, with music producer Moe Asch's urging, "I Hate the Company Bosses." Motivated by concern for husband Andrew's health and her children's welfare, Sarah denied interest in or connections to Communism. While Molly claimed she wrote songs as a child, Sarah proudly admitted to writing her first one only after moving to New York City.

Although the sisters encountered many of the same outsiders in New York, their understandings and relationships couldn't have been more dissimilar. Molly died before the beginnings of the sixties commercial folk revival, an arena that provided Sarah with novel opportunities. The younger Garland met and mingled with budding folk singers like Joan Baez, Bob Dylan, and festival promoters who had never encountered her controlling older sibling. I'll tell Sarah's story here—her childhood, motivations for leaving Kentucky, her feelings about Molly, and perspectives on the folk revival.

Born in 1910 to Oliver Perry Garland and Elizabeth Lucas, Sarah was one of eleven children from this second marriage. Although the family moved frequently during Sarah's early years from her birthplace in Ely Branch to various coal camps, Straight Creek in Bell County, Kentucky, became more of a "home" than the others. Continually battling health afflictions, Oliver succumbed in 1923, after which Elizabeth coped by taking in washing. In a 1976 *Sing Out!* article, Sarah told how little ones helped the family by "baby trapping," opening mine shaft doors for mules and carts: "My two oldest brothers started working the coal mines when they was so small a man's suit coat would make them an overcoat."[2] At fifteen years of age, Sarah married twenty-year-old coal miner and unionist, Andrew Ogan, and gave birth to four children. As mining conditions worsened during the late 1920s, constant scarcity and fear for her family overwhelmed Sarah, who, as other miners' wives, could only pray for survival.

Religion and song nurtured Sarah during childhood and young adulthood. Although she respected Oliver's impassioned Baptist preachings, the spirited Holiness church piqued her interest. "The ladies used to shout and the old ladies they used to have bonnets and aprons and they used to get happy. In church they used to throw their bonnets and they'd just clap their hands and praise the Lord. Holiness people, they jerk with a power, they say, and they speak in other tongues, in an 'unknown tongue,' they call it. Everything is more faster."[3]

While church music garnered collective enthusiasm, Sarah's mother (Molly's hated stepmother) provided an exemplary role model. Elizabeth Lucas, in her daughter's eyes, resembled the good fairy—golden blond, blue-eyed, and fair-skinned, who sang "while she worked, walked, or sat." Elizabeth's song bag embraced old ballads, funny ditties, and children's verses, while Oliver's (with jet black curly hair, according to Sarah) favored hymns or religious songs. Although Sarah placed both parents on a pedestal, her mother shone as the sun: "a real hard working Christian woman, a wonderful mother and true friend and neighbor to all who knew her. She taught us most of all the old ballads and spirituals and other songs we know. She also told all kinds of folk stories and riddles and called them 'tales.' We really was very happy when we was children, living in a coal-mining camp. We was very poor and didn't have money or fancy food and clothes, but we were a real close family with lots of love."[4] Sarah tended to minimize the depressed side of Elizabeth but recalled Jim saying she sounded like her mother "just like a sad, tired person."[5]

Nourished by family and heritage, Sarah claimed no special musical expertise. "Everybody nearly in Kentucky sang," Sarah assured Green and others, "and some made up songs."[6] "Mostly we sang at church. Other times we sang mostly just for our own amusement. Whatever mood we was in we sang. You sang when you washed dishes, you sang when you worked. Even the men folks, they sang. They used to say that if you had a very difficult something to do and it was really hard to do, if you would start a good old spiritual song you could get it done a lot easier."[7] "My mother said the Garlands has all got a big mouth and they're always open with singin' or something."[8]

Sarah's song learning came easily, "practically the first time I heard it,"[9] and this facility became a safety net. "Sometimes I think being able to express my feelings in song has kept me from going nuts."[10]

Molly's younger half-sister's migration to New York City is linked, of course, to her older sibling's story. I'll set the stage for Sarah's move. Recall that in 1932, a year after Molly left Kentucky (1931) to tour for striking miners, a bus accident hobbled and confined her to a Lower East Side Manhattan coldwater flat and in-town activities. Although physical disabilities hampered her movements, Molly's archetypal image as feisty miner's wife (husband Bill never left Kentucky) propelled her to near celebrity status. Reveling in attention from wealthy benefactors, collectors, and intellectuals, Molly made the rounds with Jim Garland, appealing for coins for the cause. By the middle of the decade, with the United Mine Workers of America again in the saddle, and Communist and radical groups shifting to a popularist position, Molly's fund-raising activities dwindled. Two of her closest New York acquaintances, Professor Mary Barnicle and young folklorist Alan Lomax, remained enthralled with the Appalachian woman for another reason: as treasure chest of traditional song. Molly happily sang her extensive repertoire into Barnicle's recording machine, spending hours with the collectors, who reveled in her traditional and composed songs, mountain anecdotes, midwifery exploits, and witch stories (for the book that Barnicle would never write).

In 1935, with hopes of discovering further untapped southern mountain material, Barnicle arranged to accompany Molly on a trip home to Kentucky. Sarah, then twenty-six years old, burdened with a fourth pregnancy, an ailing husband, and housemaid's job an hour's walk each way, apprehensively awaited the visit from sister Molly and her illustrious friend.

Despite numerous conversations with Barnicle, Molly had shared little with the folklorist about Sarah or her singing talents. In mere moments, though, after meeting the younger woman, Barnicle's empathetic antennae assessed Sarah's circumstances: coal-mining accidents claimed two brothers, hunger and illness beset her husband and children, and she was mourning the death of her fourteen-month-old daughter. When Barnicle heard of the Louisville doctor's pessimistic diagnosis of Andrew's tubercular condition, she urged Sarah to bring him to New York City for good hospital care. Despite an intense attachment to the mountains and her beloved mother Elizabeth, Sarah felt little choice. Relentless poverty would destroy her family: "When she was four months old my daughter got sick. She was a fat little baby and then she got sick. She had scarlet fever I guess. As far as I know that was the beginning of it and I just couldn't get a hold of the money to buy the milk and the things that a sick child needs to bring them out of something after they have had it."[11] Molly, Jim Garland, Hazel, and their children already relocated to New York City's East Side, where economic conditions, although depressed, seemed an immense improvement over those of Kentucky.

Within a year after Barnicle's portentous visit to Sarah's mountain cabin, she returned in a station wagon (chauffeured by Leadbelly) to collect Sarah and three remaining children (Bill, six, Dorothy, four, Jimmy, less than a year). Andrew stayed behind to dispose of furniture and install Sarah's ailing mother at another daughter's house, then followed by train. He never saw much of his adopted city, since he spent most of his two final years in a New York hospital. In 1938, Sarah took Andrew's body back for burial near his mother's home in Brush Creek, Kentucky, as he requested. Herself ailing with tuberculosis, Sarah chose to remain in New York, where outpatient care enabled access to her children:

> I didn't want to go into hospital for the shadow on my lung because of the kids, so they let me go to the hospital boat on the East River near

Bellevue hospital every day. They had a nursery school and a school for the children, not just mine but other people's too, on this boat. Then the mothers, they could lay out on this deck and rest and they served you your lunch and they give you hot cocoa and they serve the kids their lunch and everything and then I took the kids and went home in the afternoon to my apartment.[12]

Just ten months after Andrew's death, Sarah suffered another loss—Jimmy, a mere infant, sickened and died. The paltry sum squirreled away behind a picture frame on the wall of her apartment would be emptied for his funeral.[13] Barnicle's station wagon again traveled the road to Kentucky, this time with Jimmy's two-year-old body beside his grief-stricken mother. Sarah's brother Bill dug a tiny grave for Jimmy near her parents, Oliver and Elizabeth. Alone now with two (four- and six-year-old) children, Sarah appreciated the considerate hospital workers and offers of clothing from affluent New York acquaintances. The heartache and deep sadness, though, never again lifted.

Songwriting became Sarah's solace in which she fused her personal grief to the general conditions of life in Kentucky. Adapting "Boy of Constant Sorrow," which she thought she heard on a Jimmie Rogers or Stanley Brothers record (the latter recorded it), she wrote her version with the same tune: "Girl of Constant Sorrow":

I am a girl of constant sorrow
I've seen trouble all my days
I bid farewell to old Kentucky
The state where I was born and raised

My mother, how I hated to leave her
Mother dear, who now is dead
But I had to go and leave her
So my children could have bread

Perhaps dear friends, you are wondering
what the miners eat and wear
This question I will try to answer
For I'm sure it is fair

For breakfast we had bulldog gravy
For supper we had beans and bread
The miners don't have any dinner
And a tick of straw they call a bed

Well, we call this hell on earth, friends
I must tell you all goodbye
Oh, I know you all are hungry
Oh, my darling friends don't cry.[14]

In another composition, "An Old Southern Town," Sarah connected personal loss and homesickness with economic and political conditions in Appalachia.

I'm thinking tonight of an old Southern town
And my loved ones that I left behind
I know their ragged and hungry, too
And it sure does worry my mind

Poor little children so hungry and cold
The big mighty bosses, so big and so bold
They stole all our land and they stole all our coal
We get starvation and they get the gold

I know how it feels to be lonesome
And I know how it feels to be blue
I know what it is to be hungry
And I've sure been ragged, too

I'm thinking of brother and sister
From the loved ones who I had to part
I'm thinking of their little children,
who is so near to my heart.

I'm thinking of heartaches and starvation,
That the bosses has caused me and mine.
I'm thinking of friends and neighbors,
And the loved ones that I left behind

Now if I had these rotten bosses
Where the bosses has got me,
What I wouldn't do to them rascals
Would be a shame to see.[15]

The popular Tin Pan Alley song, "That Old Feeling" inspired Sarah again to remember Kentucky and hard, hungry times—"I saw you last night and got that old feeling, when you came in sight I got that old feeling." In Sarah's version:

I saw you last night and got that old feeling,
My supper was so light
I had that old feeling
[she explains the "feeling" as hunger][16]

Social and musical activities in New York eased some of Sarah's pain and focused her energies. She joined Jim's "Kentucky Mountain Singers," with Hazel Garland, niece Mamie Quackenbush, and Dorothy Buron, appearing with them on Henrietta Yurchenco's program on WNYC and at the 1939 World's Fair. Sarah recalled the outfits: "The men had overalls and checkered shirts and straw hats and red handkerchiefs, the women checkered gingham, long dresses, and bonnets."[17] The community that encircled Sarah—Kentuckians, urban friends and acquaintances—provided some comfort, relief from loneliness. Jim and Hazel, Molly and Tom, Mary Barnicle and her Kentucky husband Tillman Cadle, Alan Lomax, Will Geer, Pete Seeger, Woody Guthrie, Burl Ives, Leadbelly, Josh White, and Lee Hays, gathered in each others' flats for visiting and hootenannies.

Sarah, like Molly, felt particularly attached to Leadbelly and Woody. "I lived up there on 10th street. Leadbelly and Marthy they lived on 8th street. Woody he came to Leadbelly's, and my two children used to go to Leadbelly's house and he used to put them on the piano and have 'em talking and people was playing the piano."[18]

Woody, who frequented Leadbelly's apartment when he sojourned in New York City, clearly adored and admired Sarah, but saw her in a very different way than he did Molly. In his quote at the beginning of "My Name Is Sarah Ogan Gunning," in *Sing Out!* magazine, Woody explained the younger sister's almost spiritual magic:

I heard Sarah Ogan sing her songs about getting together and shaking hands, organizing around this whole world once, and twice. . . . In the whole crowded room of all tones and colors of faces and eyes, it was a high feeling when Sarah would set forward on a couch and sing in her natural voice and key with no music box to back her up. I heard her voice, dry as my own, thin high, and in her nose, with the old outdoors and down the mountain sound to it. Singing out to her skies had made her voice a thin one, but with that unknown gift of carrying up and out to the several directions. Singing to us as she had sung into the rifle fire of Sheriff Blair's [of Harlan] deputies, Sarah Ogan got the house of people to keep so still that the cat licking his hair sounded like a broomstick rubbed against a washtub. . . . I heard Sarah, and I watched every move she made.[19]

Woody's introduction to Sarah's songs in *Hard Hitting Songs for Hard-Hit People* couldn't praise her virtues more highly. He idealized her as wife and mother, yet her resistance to the oppressors remained strong.

> She's a housewife and more than a housewife. A mother and more than a mother. She's worked and slaved and fought to save the children of her own home and to keep her own house, and she was so full of the Union Spirit that she found time to get out in the wind and rain and the hail of bullets from the deputies guns, and make up her own songs and sing them to give nerve and backbone to the starving men that slaved in the coal mines. . . . Sara, there aint a man a living that can give you as good a write up as you need . . . nor tell the love and the hate that is a beating in your heart. I done my best. I'm just a praying and a hoping that your songs will "mow them rich guys down"—and I know they will.[20]

In 1941, three years after Andrew's death, Sarah met and married an Irish New Yorker, Joe Gunning, who—as she tells it, "wanted to raise my children." Yet Sarah would move several times before experiencing a "home" again. During the war, she and Joe went west, to California and Washington, following Jim, Hazel, Molly, and Tom, in search of jobs. But the damp western climate would play havoc with Sarah's health and force the family back to the Kentucky mountains, where she underwent lung surgery. Physical infirmities aside, Sarah apparently never stopped doing what she loved. In his "Biography" of Sarah in the brochure accompanying her *Silver Dagger* album, Jim (whose adoration for his sister knew no bounds) remarks: "it's hard to believe that she has only one lung when she sings."

Leaving Sarah to recuperate from her operation, Joe tried his luck in Detroit, the path of other Appalachians seeking work. By 1948–49, Sarah, again well enough to travel, joined him. Daughter Dorothy married and moved nearby, while her son Bill joined the navy. After a series of odd jobs, Joe secured an assistant building manager job, which came with the basement apartment where Archie Green located Sarah in 1963.

Green, familiar with Sarah's field recordings and struck by the younger sister's artistry, found her through Molly. On his first visit to Detroit the folklorist discovered that Sarah hadn't sung for twenty years except in church and while "doing housework." With his colleague Ellen Stekert, Green began to unearth Sarah's extensive traditional repertoire. Stekert invited Sarah to speak and perform in her English class at Wayne State University, while Green approached Sandy Paton's fledgling record company, Folk-Legacy, and asked if they would issue an album of Sarah's songs (*Girl of Constant Sorrow,* recorded in January 1964). The folklorists also arranged public radio appearances and various concert and festival venues for their Appalachian discovery: Carnegie Hall, the University of Chicago, the Smithsonian Festival of American Folklife, a Detroit banquet for Walter Reuther, and the Newport Folk Festival.

Sarah obviously beguiled Archie Green, who thought she never strayed from her mountain traditional cultural style. Finding Sarah "incapable of dissimulation, exaggeration, or self-pity" with a "towering personal honesty,"[21] he would depict Molly to me in exactly the opposite, negative terms.

Although Sarah resigned herself to northern life in Detroit for fifteen years before Green's first visit and another twelve afterwards, the lure of home pulled her back to the mountains. She made summer pilgrimages to Kentucky until 1961, and then only for family crises: "I've been away a long time and lived in New York and a lot of places but when it starts to get springtime I get so homesick, I can't hardly stand it, even now."[22]

In *Sing Out!* magazine's twenty-fifth-year publication issue, sixty-five-year-old Sarah (finally a "cover girl") poignantly reflected on her life. Residing in Hart, Michigan, with one remaining lung, she tells of her church, vegetable garden, and how she spends her time: "help all people as much as I can" and "go to all the folk festivals." She credits Molly, although with a slightly reluctant tone, for Barnicle's rescuing her family from the mountains in the middle 1930s: "I guess you could say she kept us from starving to death." Between the time of writing and publication of the article, Joe Gunning, who had been hospitalized for a stroke, died. As she spoke of her life in the Detroit suburb, Sarah's sense of self and irony never faltered. "The people are very friendly, but they 'know about as much about folk songs as a hog knows about a side-saddle,' as Ernie Ford says."[23] As for the U.S. government and unemployment, "I am getting scared, afraid that some of the things that happened in Hoover's time will happen again. Only I don't think the people will just sit down and take it this time!" Sarah's song "Come All You Coal Miners," which she recorded on Rounder records (album title the same), accompanied the article:

Come all you coal miners wherever you may be
And listen to a story that I'll relate to thee
My name is nothing extra, but the truth to you I'll tell
I am a coal miner's wife, I'm sure I wish you well
I was born in old Kentucky, in a coal camp born and bred
I know all about the pinto beans, bulldog gravy and cornbread
And I know how the coal miners work and slave in the coal mines every
   day
For a dollar in the company store
for that is all they pay

Coal mining is the most dangerous work in our land today
With plenty of dirty slaving work,
And very little pay
Coal miner won't you wake up, and
open your eyes and see
What the dirty capitalist system is doing to you and me

They take your very life blood
They take our children's lives
They take fathers away from children, and husbands away from wives
Oh, miner, won't you organize wherever you may be?
And make this a land of freedom for workers like you and me

Dear miner, they will slave you till you can't work no more
And what'll you get for your living but a dollar in a company store?
A tumble-down shack to live in,
snow and rain pours in the top
You have to pay the company rent,
your paying never stops

I am a coal miner's wife, I'm sure I wish you well
Let's sink this capitalist system in
the darkest pits of hell[24]

Sarah's story, so briefly capsuled, holds great significance. First, her similarities to Molly: they shared a father, both grew up in coal-mining communities, married as adolescents to coal miners, bore and raised children. Although Molly's own two babies died in infancy, she raised two of husband Jim Stewart's sons, and several of Bill Jackson's. The sisters scrubbed grime and coal dust off cabin floors and tattered clothing, squirreled away scarce morsels of food, toiled for miserly wages, nursed injured and sick family, grieved tragic early deaths of close kin and friends, and actively resisted coal bosses' tyranny. Supported and encouraged by outsiders, the mountain women made their ways in strange cities, using song as a vehicle to tell their stories. Both sisters' texts emerged from personal experience but moved beyond it to larger social and political statements.

Sarah, like Molly, dismissed the categorizations of her repertoire or definitional discussions surrounding "folksongs," a term Sarah never heard in the mountains. "They just call them songs. They call them love songs if they was about love, and they call them religious songs if they was about religion, and they call them funny songs or somethin' like that if they was funny. They didn't call them 'folk songs.'"[25] Sarah, like Molly, whose extensive repertoire of traditional songs astounded collectors, bridled at others' citified alterations or interpretations of her music.

But then there are the differences. While Molly professed a songwriting history rooted in her early childhood, Sarah's inspirations came as an adult, following her move to New York. Sarah explained later to interviewers that burdens of work and family back home left her no time to create. When she came north, she felt inspired by (and jealous of?) her siblings' successful efforts and yearned to tell her own version of the coal-mining "reality." "When I first went to New York, my brother Jim, he had composed this song about the death of Harry Simms and Molly, she had composed some songs. I decided I would compose some songs about the true story of my own life and the life the way the people had to live in the mountains of Kentucky."[26]

Sarah's complex relationship to and with Molly shaped much of her life in New York City. Inevitably thrown together with her big sister, Sarah found it hard to escape. She resented and felt smothered by Molly's dominance, swagger, claims on songs, hogging of money—Sarah's list swelled. Her private anger occasionally trickled out to intimates—through biting sarcasm as she compared her own commitment to "truth" to Molly's exaggerations, and her own reserve with Molly's brashness and arrogance. On a visit to Ellen Stekert's class after Molly's death, Sarah finally felt free to publicly disclose smoldering resentment for her older sister, and to downplay her achievements. When a student confessed his admiration for Molly, Sarah sniffed, "She's an old Kentucky woman. She wasn't too much different from any of the others. Her life was a lot like other people. The only thing is that she got a chance to go to New York and tell people about it. She composed songs, too, about the Kentucky people and their lives. She got a little better chance to publicize than anybody else. Actually there is lots of people—they didn't just pick out our family to have all them hard times."[27]

When Ellen Stekert asked Sarah if Molly taught her songs, she swiftly responded: "No, she learned them from the same person I learned mine from except the ones she composed: my mother. [Elizabeth raised Molly from the age of six.] She couldn't have learned me very much if I already knew."[28] Sarah harbored resentment against Molly for not letting Barnicle know of her singing: "After I got to New York, I sang some songs for her [Barnicle] and she said [to Molly], 'Why didn't you tell me that Sarah could sing?' Molly said: 'I thought you know'd that she could sing. We all sing.' She didn't take me to New York because she . . . I think she thought she was doing Molly a favor by taking me."[29]

Sarah contrasted Molly's "ideological" reasons for writing songs with her own more diffuse ones. "The reason that she [Molly] composed her songs was to focus attention on the plight of the miners at the time. I composed mine because they were the truth about my own life and other people's at the time that I left there."[30]

The younger sister's self-image of directness and simplicity (always a subtext in Sarah's tellings about her life) diverged from Molly's pretensions. Before meeting Barnicle for the first time, Sarah recalled a conversation with herself to calm her nerves: "I was kind of worried, how should you act in front of a college professor and what should you do and so on and so forth. Should you put on an act or somethin' you know. I had a dream that night and it says to me, just be plain ol' corn bread, just be yourself and that's the way I am. I'm just me and that's always been the way I am and still am and I never change."[31]

Explaining to Archie Green why her older sister (rather than she) appeared at the Dreiser hearings, Sarah emphasized Molly's exhibitionism (compared to her own shyness): "I didn't push myself or get up and go to singin' in front of people. I sang at church and sang all kind of little funny songs with girls and things. I guess I was embarrassed to get up and go to singing in front of strange people and she wasn't."[32] (Of course, Sarah's youth could explain some of the reluctance.)

One of Sarah's stories illustrated how Molly made a public show of her rural innocence in the big city, when she herself would never stoop to this. Actor Will Geer invited Molly, Jim, and Sarah to a fancy dinner, as the guests of honor. "It was the first time I ever see'd caviar served in my life. They said 'Aunt Molly would you have some of this?' She said 'It don't make no difference to me because I never eat it before in my life.' I, of course, I didn't say nothin' you know. I just let them guess whether I had or I hadn't."[33]

On another occasion Sarah declared how Barnicle, who took her to a restaurant once, compared Sarah's refined manner to Molly's crude deportment: "I had gooder manners than anybody else and [Barnicle] said: 'You know something, I am surprised, you just act like anybody else and you never make a . . . in other words, go to talkin' loud and telling people 'you don't know this and you don't know that or you never did do this and you never did do that,' and she said 'Where Molly does the opposite. She draws attention to herself, no difference where she went by telling the people that.'"[34]

Sarah's fury with Molly peaked in 1936, during one of her first New York Christmases. Recall the "turkey" story, which inspired Sarah to publicly denounce Molly in song and needs further elaboration here. Tillman Cadle told me the following version:

> We used to have parties in New York, and Jim, Sarah, and Molly would come. People would ask about conditions in Kentucky, and one December, a group of patrons wanted to supply food for the Kentuckians' Christmas dinner. They asked how many families there were and sent three turkeys: one for Molly and Tom, one for the Garlands, and one for Sarah's family. They were delivered, with canned goods and other trimmings, to Molly's apartment because it was assumed that she was the center of the group. Since Tom was a "famous chef," Molly and Tom decided to prepare the turkeys and then distribute a cooked dinner to each family.

Hazel Garland, though, told me she never laid eyes on the turkeys, either raw or cooked, and felt that Molly obviously never intended to share them. The whole incident may not have surfaced but for a snoopy visiting cousin, who noticed cans of trimmings under Molly's bed. This selfishness infuriated Sarah (and the other Garlands), inspiring a nasty, funny song about her older sister that found its way to Barnicle's recording machine and ultimately (despite Tillman's protests) to the album Willie Smyth produced for the University of Tennessee. Sarah vents her anger toward Molly and her husbands, her lies and wiles—on one hand just a case of sibling rivalry, on the other, an outpouring of mistrust.

She had me taken off relief,
She's dirtier than a dirty thief.

Chorus:
She's mean I mean,
She's the dirtiest thing that ever you seen.

She stole the butter from my children's bread
And pretends to cry if I was dead,

Chorus

My husband's dead he had TB,
And little children I have three,
She wants to take them away from me,

Chorus

She wrote a lie and let her in,
and she pretends to be my friend,

Chorus

She thinks she's very wise and cute,
She told them I was a prostitute.

Chorus

I'm a decent mother but she's a louse,
When she runs over from a whore house,

Chorus

She lives with a Greek his name is Tom,
You better bet they're both agomb[?]

Chorus

I'll fight to send him back to Greece,
And have them both cut off relief,

Chorus

She has a husband down in Kentucky,
And if she ain't sent back she'll sure be lucky,

Chorus

She says he's dead but he's very much alive,
He carries two big forty fives.

Chorus

She said Bill dear don't do me no harm,
I'm going to buy you a lovely farm,

Chorus

He's a handsome guy about six foot two,
They call him Touch Hog and he's cock-eyed too,

Chorus

But poor Old Bill he wants her back,
When he cries the tears run down his back,

Chorus

There ain't no home that she won't wreck,
If I loved a skunk I'd hug her neck,

Chorus

I don't know why she's picked on me,
For I am her little sister tease,

Chorus

You may want to know how I know this,
Because I am her baby sis,
She's mean I mean,
She's the sneakinest thing that ever you seen.[35]

Disputes arising over song compositions furnished additional sources of strain in the sisters' relationship. Both sisters claimed "Dreadful Memories" as their own. In Sarah's words: "[I] composed [it] from the memories I had of the dreadful things that had happened to me and other people in the state of Kentucky."[36] When Ellen Stekert suggested to Sarah that Molly may have based her claim on some added verses, Sarah bristled: "She didn't add a word to that. Not a word. As a matter of fact, Molly was kind of selfish."[37] Sarah suspected that Molly glanced at her song notebooks (when she visited in 1941) and either recalled their contents (with photographic memory) or kept the books.[38]

The sisters squabbled over attention, money, and people. Sarah tells of a party in New York that she went to with Molly, Jim, and Earl Robinson. When people asked to hear Jim or Sarah more than they did Molly, the older woman grumbled. Sarah: "Why she didn't like it at all and she looked daggers through you."[39] But Molly, according to Sarah, invariably benefited, since she as the supposed "head of family" received the payment that was usually offered by wealthy hosts. Of course, Molly, feeling entitled, kept it for herself. Sarah also recounted stories of Molly's jealousy around Pete Seeger inviting her to sing with him.

Despite the sisters' tussles, Sarah claimed she was ready to come to Molly's defense, using the Dreiser inquiry at the Arjay Baptist church as an example: "The coal operators booed everything. When Molly got up and started to sing the company people tried to make fun. I was just sitting then and I was getting mad, more or less setting and waiting to see if anybody done anything to Molly so I could do something to them." When asked if she would protect Molly, Sarah responded she would.[40]

Sarah, in fact, shared many of Molly's reasons for writing songs. She told Archie and Ellen that she wanted to record a history of coal-mining people to leave a record for her grandchildren; to be somebody; because Jim and Molly composed songs; and because she needed the money. While Molly may have written songs long before the Communists came to Harlan and Bell, political associates certainly stimulated and shaped her output for years afterward. But Sarah, too, first encouraged by New York patrons, and then by Archie Green and Ellen Stekert in the early 1960s, realized she had something to give to the coal miners back home. Both Molly's and Sarah's desire to tell their truths motivated them to write songs. Sarah insisted, though, that *her* versions, and not Molly's, revealed the "real" truth.

In 1964 Sarah told eager folklore students in Ellen Stekert's class at Wayne State University, "I thought maybe that it [her own songs] would focus attention on the people that were still there and maybe somebody would help 'em. That was my intentions when I composed a song, was to sing the songs to somebody that would maybe, it would focus attention on them people what was still there that needed somebody to cure so badly." In response to a question from one of the students, "Do you think that writing a song was the best way to tell the world?" Sarah responded, "For me it was the best way because I was just, as I told you, a little green hillbilly. I didn't know nothing about getting up and making speeches or anything like that,"[41] working in a sly dig at Molly.

When Archie Green suggested that Sarah make a record, he fertilized seeds that others before had planted. It also gave the younger sister an opportunity to reestablish claims to authenticity. Sarah wanted people to know that despite TB and a missing lung she could still sing, that the songs "are a true history of my life and most of the other coal-mining people. I think they would probably be a benefit to the working class of people, to be able to hear them and play them and I could use the money."[42]

Archie encouraged Sarah to talk about her versions of the Appalachian traditional songs "Loving Nancy" and "Jack Frost," two of the singer's personal favorites. Archie: "What's your feeling about those songs? Why do you think they ought to be on a record?" Sarah: "Well, they are real old songs and a lot of the people, the ones that ever did know 'em are dead and I think they should be preserved and people should know 'em and they should go on and on. My mother, they was handed down to my mother from hundreds of years before and all them old people that lived then, the biggest part of 'em are gone now. A lot of those people, they don't know them songs, they never hear them and I think they should be able to hear 'em."[43]

Sarah's degenerating relationship with Molly and disappointment with others caused her to withdraw from New York's folk/political circles. She tried to disassociate herself from Communist radicals, not only to differentiate herself from her older sister, but because she professed no interest in its tenets. Record producer Moe Asch told Jim Garland that he thought Sarah's song "I Hate the Capitalist System" the most radical song he ever heard in his life. When Sarah was convinced to change the song's title to "I Hate the Company Bosses," she rationalized it like this: "because they said it sounded like I was a radical and I'm no radical. This thing that I did hate was the company bosses so it was better to change it to the real one I mean. At the time of the capitalist system I didn't even know what that meant. I had heard the word said in New York City but thought all the rich coal operators was the capitalist system."[44]

According to Ellen Stekert, Sarah's understanding of the phrase "capitalist system" remained vague, and she would interchange the phrases to suit her audience.[45]

> I hate the company bosses [capitalist system],
> I'll tell you the reason why.
> They cause me so much suffering
> And my dearest friends to die.
>
> Oh yes, I guess you wonder
> What they have done to me.

I'm going to tell you, mister,
My husband had T.B.

Brought on by hard work and low wages
And not enough to eat,
Going naked and hungry,
No shoes on his feet.

I guess you'll say he's lazy
And did not want to work.
But I must say you're crazy,
For work he did not shirk.

My husband was a coal miner,
He worked and risked his life
To try to support three children,
Himself, his mother, and wife.

I had a blue-eyed baby,
The darling of my heart.
But from my little darling
Her mother had to part.

These mighty company bosses,
They dress in jewels and silk.
But my darling blue-eyed baby
She starved to death for milk.

I had a darling mother,
For her I often cry.
But with them rotten conditions
My mother had to die.

Well, what killed your mother?
I heard these bosses say.
Dead of hard work and starvation,
My mother had to pay.

Well, what killed your mother?
Oh, tell us, if you please.
Excuse me, it was pellagra,
That starvation disease.

They call this land of plenty,
To them I guess it's true.

But that's to the company bosses,
Not workers like me and you.

Well, what can I do about it.
To these men of power and might?
I tell you, company bosses,
I'm going to fight, fight, fight.

What can we do about it,
To right this dreadful wrong?
We're all going to join the union,
For the union makes us strong.[46]

She talked about meetings she went to that she thought "silly because all they do is they jump up and you say 'upon our order' and one jumps up and out talks another and what they say don't make too much sense." But, Sarah, like Molly, also distrusted those who might record her songs without giving her credit or money. "If it was put on a record and anybody got any money out of it, it wasn't me. It was Pete or somebody else." She assured Archie Green that although she'd lived a poor life, she believed in America, religion, and God.[47]

Although Sarah's general suspicion of people threads through her taped interviews, Lomax and Barnicle, above others, seriously undermined the trust that she placed in them. In 1937, Barnicle invited Sarah to a party at her apartment. Alan Lomax, armed with his persistent recording machine, taped some of Sarah's songs, ostensibly for Barnicle's use in her New York University course. Sarah sang for them—"Come all you Coal Miners," "Picket Line," "I Am a Girl of Constant Sorrow," "I'm Going to Organize, Babe of Mine," "I Hate the Company Bosses" (or ". . . Capitalist System)." Several years later, while performing in Jim Garland's group at the 1939 World's Fair, Sarah discovered that the folklorists she thought her friends had used the tapes to make a record for the Library of Congress without telling or compensating her. Sarah later related this disillusioning experience: "I didn't make [records] for Alan Lomax . . . I never made a record for Alan Lomax in my life. I thought I was makin' them all for Barnicle and she was the one that turned 'em over to Lomax to take to the Library of Congress."[48] Although she never completely lost faith in the woman who rescued her from Kentucky, Barnicle, too, tumbled from Sarah's pedestal. Sarah bared, in interviews with Green and Stekert, her by then sophisticated understanding of scholarly ownership. "Other collectors . . . I guess they considered that . . . Barnicle is [our] sponsor . . . guess they considered us more or less her private property."[49]

But Sarah not only blamed (who she saw as) opportunistic folklorists. Woody Guthrie, too, tarnished in Sarah's estimation when she found out he recorded one of her songs, "Baby Mine," without telling her. "I went over to one of these hootenannies just after I got out of the hospital. Woody was there. I was kind of mad about the record. . . ." Sarah tells how Woody redeemed himself. He called her up to the stage and told everyone the song was Sarah's and "the reason he put it on the record was that he thought I was gonna die . . . he wanted the working class of people to have the song."[50] Others—Jim Garland, the Almanac Singers—recorded Sarah's songs with her blessing; all Sarah wanted was the acknowledgment, perhaps, that Molly had denied her.

Although Sarah attributed her withdrawal from the New York folk scene to illness, her disappointment with certain associates became increasingly obvious. Never paid for her recordings, she began to heed Joe Gunning's advice: "Well its nice to entertain your friends but you should stay home and raise your children."[51] Sarah became more private and rarely saw her former confidants. Despite her fondness for Pete Seeger, his politics too, gave her pause: "they was mixed up with the Communist business and I didn't want to be mixed up with it."[52]

Sarah lay claim to authenticity of style and content that, in her view, couldn't be replicated, reproduced by others, outsiders. She rejected ties with Communism and the organized Left and claimed to be the real tradition bearer. Her involvement, although marginal, in the sixties commercial folk revival as a "traditional singer" encouraged a very different representation from that of her older sister. Later, when she met newcomers at folk festivals, she couldn't help but be amused at their attempts to imitate her, and fall short of her authentic style. "Miss Baez was a nice young woman who hadn't learned to sing mountain music properly."[53] She readily offered her opinion of Bob Dylan: "He takes a couple of songs he mixed together for the melody. He hasn't lived 'em . . . I have nothing against him . . . he's alright."[54] For Pete Seeger, however, her praise remained strong: "I know him ever since he was sixteen years old and I feel like he's part of my family. He's improved so much over the years from what he was when I first knowed him. I think he's good."[55]

A sixty-six-year-old Sarah, ailing with tuberculosis, recalled her ordeals, but with some perspective: "When I get to thinking about the past

I get headaches and it makes me feel pretty miserable, but I smile and I try not to make other people miserable."[56] Her death came in a comfortable setting in 1983, while doing what she loved best, singing at a gathering with family and friends in Kentucky. Mimi Pickering's moving documentary film *Dreadful Memories* (Appalshop Film and Video, 1988), as testimony to Sarah's life and legacy, will endure for future generations and ironically allow Sarah's message to survive, while Molly's, which the latter so desperately desired to communicate, languishes.

So telling are Molly and Sarah's parallels and differences. Both of their repertoires were shaped by others' definitions and desires. Outsiders spurred their respective moves away from home—for Molly, the Dreiser visitors, for Sarah, Mary Elizabeth Barnicle-Cadle. Both women thoroughly believed their songs told the "truth" as they saw and lived it, and both felt disillusioned and exploited by political associates and folklorists they considered benefactors. But politics prompted Molly's move north in 1931, while personal reasons five years later influenced Sarah's decision. Though Molly claimed greater status and public recognition in the 1930s, the Garland family assured everyone that Sarah was the "real singer." The sisters' stories, relationships to each other and to others, and their contrasting constructions, urge me to explore some issues in the next chapter regarding authenticity and the politics of music.

PART 3

Music, Politics, and Women's Resistance

6

"White Pilgrims in the Foreign Heathen Country": Molly, Sarah, and the Politics of Folksong

Previous chapters followed Aunt Molly Jackson and Sarah Ogan Gunning from the mountains of Kentucky to the streets of New York. Here I shift to the musical and political contexts that defined the sisters' public lives. We begin to understand the various ways friends, acquaintances, and scholars viewed them as cultural brokers—transmitting Appalachian tradition to the world outside. Conventional stereotypes project an "authentic" Sarah and "radical" Molly, two Appalachian roles cast in historical stone. These differences derive not only from the accident of an era and contrasts in their ages and personalities, but also because the half sisters, responding to others' expectations and visions, consciously fashioned themselves as opposites. Molly and Sarah, who couldn't care less about academic scufflings, were thrust into a theater of intense debate, becoming exemplars of very different deeply held philosophical and political perspectives.

The Garland sisters' years spanned two cultural/political periods and two musical peaks in an ongoing amalgam of rural and urban musics: the first renaissance or revival in the 1930s centered on ideology; the second, beginning in the late 1950s, popularized and commercialized folksong. Each period, enclosing and enriching the sisters' stories, was rife with contested notions regarding the uses of folk music, style, aesthetics, tradition, and authenticity.

The idea of folk music revivals as awakenings or isolated musical periods deflects from the complex and continuous processes underlying peaks of activity. As John Cohen puts it, "Implicit in the concept of 'revival' is bringing to life something which is dying out. This ethnocentric concept—as applied to traditional music—was more a reflection on the revivalists than on what they were reviving, for . . . traditional music never dies out."[1] Song collecting in the nineteenth and early twentieth century (as heritage), the political left's use of song during the Great Depression, and American scholarly interests—all contributed to musical fusions climaxing in the popular folk revival beginning at the end of the 1950s and continuing through the middle 1960s. This "great boom," as folklorist Neil Rosenberg calls it, saw Joan Baez, Bob Dylan, and Peter, Paul, and Mary become household names.[2] Although the boom is now over, interest in folk music continues as a variety of musicians—professional and kitchen—discover, jam, debate the origins of old songs and tunes, and write new ones in "traditional" style. It's more accurate to say, then, traditional and tradition-like music, never defunct, experienced a number of public high points that have been thought of as "revivals" during the past decades.

My quotes around the term "traditional" serve to punctuate its problematic usage. Although analytically separating the political revival of the late 1930s and early 1940s from the popular one twenty years later, I am really interested in the processes and contested meanings surrounding people's music from the early 1930s through the middle 1970s. This forty-odd-year span in the Garland sisters' personal, political, and musical lives renders some of these ideological struggles visible. And of course, much of this took place in New York, not in the mountains and hollows of Appalachia.

With one and a half million people swarming its streets and neighborhoods, Manhattan in the 1930s sizzled with intellectual and political creativity. Tactical shifts in the American Communist Party during the 1930s and early 1940s saw it reach beyond its former narrowly sectarian position to Popular Front politics. With a sense of New York City as the hub and hotbed of the political universe, progressives joined forces to work for a new society. Small, ideologically committed enclaves embraced "people's" music as their rallying cry for social action and solidarity to create a better, more equal, world.

Molly Jackson and Jim Garland, plucked from Appalachia in 1931 to become miners' missionaries, formed the core of transplanted mountain folk in the urban North. Molly married a Greek immigrant, Tom (Gus) Stamos (I don't know if she divorced Bill Jackson), and settled near Jim and

Hazel on the Lower East Side. Several years later, with Professor Mary Barnicle's urging and the prospect of hospital care for her ailing husband Andrew Ogan, Sarah joined her siblings in New York. After Andrew's death in 1938, Sarah married Joe Gunning and remained in the city. Despite illnesses, poverty, and a longing for the mountains, the Garlands agreed about New York's advantages over Kentucky. Toward the end of the 1930s they became (with Leadbelly, Woody Guthrie, the Seegers, Alan Lomax, and Lee Hays) part of a folk-political hybrid community whose collective contributions culminated in a burst of musical creativity termed by sociologist Serge Denisoff the "proletarian renaissance."[3]

Aunt Molly Jackson's New York years spanned an extraordinary decade, from 1933 to 1943. This roughly divides into two periods: the early 1930s—as Appalachian transplant, ardent advocate of miners' rights, and darling of the Left; and the late 1930s and early 1940s—as part of a people's musical revival. Like Woody Guthrie and Huddie Ledbetter (Leadbelly), Molly inspired young singers such as Pete Seeger, who considered her one of his formative influences.[4] Although their music never had the society-wide impact they hoped for, the rural traditional singers and their urban counterparts gravitated toward one another, sang and composed worker songs, building morale and solidarity among the already committed. They sang about the masses, although not necessarily for them, articulating the values of political radicalism.

Many consider the "Grapes of Wrath" evening to be the wedding ritual in this early musical union. Activist and actor Will Geer arranged a benefit concert to support rural migrants on March 3, 1940, at the Forrest Theater, the home of John Steinbeck's play *Tobacco Road*. Aunt Molly, Leadbelly, Woody Guthrie, Bess and Alan Lomax, Burl Ives, and Pete Seeger shared the stage at the event Woody deemed a triumph for the "real folk": "'We showed 'em where singing started. We showed 'em how come songs come to be. And we showed 'em something different. We didn't have no fancy costumes, nor pretty legs, but we showed 'em old ragged overhalls, and cheaper cotton dress . . . shows [folk music] can be useful.'"[5]

The inspirational evening spurred Pete Seeger to launch a series of people's musical collectives during the 1940s—the Almanac Singers (1940–42), People's Songs (1946–49), and the Weavers (1949–52; 1955–63). With some alterations in personnel, and modifications for particular ideological environments, all composed and performed people's music for a new world. The Almanacs consisted of core members Seeger (then Pete

Bowers), Lee Hays, Millard Lampell, Woody Guthrie, Bess Lomax, and Pete Hawes, later joined by assorted others like Sis Cunningham and Gordon Friesen. Pete throws some light on the musical and social collective's name in a quote from Lee Hays: "'In the country a farmhouse would have two books in the house, a Bible and an Almanac. One helped us to the next world, the other helped us make it through this one.'"[6] The Almanacs—an eclectic group of intellectuals, activists, musical sophisticates—found a loft (Almanac House) in Greenwich Village in the fall of 1941, and hosted Sunday afternoon hootenannies (to pay the rent) that soon gained a reputation as a hot spot in New York City. Robert Cantwell, in an insightful analysis of the revival, speaks of the oneness between the way the Almanacs produced music and their everyday lives: "Fanatically democratic, virtually unregulated, youthful, collective, and, like their stage of life itself, temporary."[7] Their two performance years and repertoire paralleled the shift from an anti-war position to wartime solidarity (first, the Hitler-Stalin pact, then Hitler's invasion of the Soviet Union). The Almanac's vision stretched beyond ideology to fantasies of a world where lines blur between folk and intellectual, city and country, color and class. But their role as impersonators, *representatives of* and not *of* the working class, was somewhat problematic. In Cantwell's words, "surely among thoughtful people, and perhaps among the Almanacs themselves, there had been some uneasiness about the sheer fact of Leadbelly's or Aunt Molly Jackson's or even Woody Guthrie's presence in New York and about their appropriation by the left-wing community; surely there were some who saw exploitation in it, of the same old kind, along class and racial lines."[8] Moreover, Cantwell, as Richard Reuss before him, observed that the Almanacs (in constrast to Aunt Molly and Leadbelly) were *reliable* (my emphasis) ideologists.[9] While Molly Jackson (and later Sarah) rendered the miners' conditions accessible to limited audiences, the Almanacs made working-class life attractive for broader ones. Ironically, the popular folk music revival peaking in the 1960s, with its movement away from radical politics, encouraged the "real thing" to come out of their rural closets, either in the flesh or through some revivalists singing more "authentic" versions.

During the war, with Pete in the army, the group dispersed, reassembling in the middle 1940s as People's Songs, an organization that published the People's Song Bulletin, eventually to become *Sing Out!* magazine. Pete remarks about the limited appeal of labor songs to "real" people, revealing the gulf between intended and actual audience: "How our theories went astray! Most union leaders could not see any connection between music and pork chops. As the cold war deepened in '47 and '48 the split in the labor movement deepened. 'Which Side Are You On?' [by Florence Reece] was known in Greenwich Village but not in a single miner's union local."[10]

In the late 1940s a smaller Almanac core regrouped as the Weavers, with singer Ronnie Gilbert and guitarist Fred Hellerman joining Lee and Pete. Just when poverty began to discourage them, commercial success arrived, complete with manager, a Decca recording contract, night club gigs, and hits like "Tzena Tzena," "Goodnight Irene," and "Wimoweh." Although this kind of popularity was unanticipated—and maybe a little embarrassing—for a folk group with social consciousness and left-wing politics, Pete acknowledged the gains: "at that time [early 1950] millions of teen-agers first heard the words 'folk song.'"[11] Nineteen fifty, the year of the Korean War, arrest of Julius Rosenberg for his alleged spying, and the appearance of *Red Channels: Communist Influence on Radio and Television,* was a black one for progressive performers. Although Pete was the only one of the group "listed," the Weavers too would be targeted.[12] By 1953, despite vast public acclaim and number one records, the Weavers' radical associations piqued the curiosity of the FBI and the McCarran Committees: the group's work opportunities began to dry up. Lee Hay's pithy one-liner about a sabbatical turning into a Mondical and Tuesdical is now legendary in folk circles. Relentless pressure kept building, culminating in Seeger's House Un-American Activities Committee subpoena in 1955. Still, with the support of new manager Harold Leventhal, the Weavers reunited that year for a wildly successful concert at Carnegie Hall. Pete later appealed a prison sentence and never served time, but the blacklist dogged him into the 1960s. The Weavers, replacing Pete (who decided to go solo) with banjo player Erik Darling for a few years, and others after that, continued to perform until 1963.

Prior to all these events, during the early 1940s, the Appalachians—Jim, Hazel, Molly (and Tom Stamos), Sarah (and Joe Gunning) had already left New York City in search of wartime work in West Coast shipyards, airplane factories, and airfields. Molly and Tom followed Jim and Hazel to Washougal, Washington, then located a tiny house in Sacramento around the corner from Molly's niece, Lula Holcolm. Although Molly would never again return east or to the world of the 1930s, her thoughts still dwelt there. Rich and famous patrons in New York City and Washington, D.C., passionate political rallies and high-spirited parties, lingered in Molly's memory, which she regularly ransacked for anecdotes to regale scholars, journalists, and, as she aged, all too infrequent visitors.

Sarah, on the other hand, barely gave thought to her life in the decade that Molly most relished. She hated the Left's machinations and resented her sister's celebrity and humiliating stunts. Molly's sycophantic relationships with her stellar patrons confirmed Sarah's belief that Molly placed fame above family. And the lies—Molly, in Sarah's view, didn't know where to find the "truth" anymore! Sarah saw her own journey as different, private. After a brief sojourn with Jim and Hazel in Washington State, Joe Gunning secured work as an apartment building manager in Detroit, Michigan. Sarah retreated into a routine of housewife and churchgoer until the early 1960s, when after Molly's death, she experienced her own middle-aged renaissance.

For a short time traditional folk song, politically tainted, burrowed underground during the anti-Communist scare of the early 1950s, when kitchens, folk clubs, left-wing youth movements, and summer camps became its main venues. But by 1953 the seeds of the next revival, with a more commercial bent, started to sprout on American college campuses and in Greenwich Village. This period saw the rise of the Tarriers (Erik Darling, Alan Arkin, and Bob Carey), Harry Belafonte, who popularized versions of calypso songs, and other performers such as Cynthia Gooding, Theodore Bikel, Oscar Brand, Jean Ritchie, Sonny Terry and Brownie McGhee, Bob Gibson, Hillel and Aviva, the Clancy Brothers, Richard Dyer-Bennet, Burl Ives (I thank Cantwell for twigging my memory for some of these)—luminaries for us 1950s folkies.[13]

By the later 1950s and early 1960s a confluence of social and political conditions and crises—Fidel Castro in Cuba, Vietnam, the New Left, the Civil Rights and anti-nuclear movements—set the stage for a popular interest in folk music based partly on an interest in traditional song and partly on entirely new creations. Electronic media, critical for diffusing and homogenizing musical preference, burgeoned, spawning a new kind of cultural hybrid, the "folk scene,"[14] or "great boom."[15]

Many deem the Kingston Trio's 1958 hit version of "Tom Dooley" (based on Frank Proffitt's "Tom Dula") the kickoff recording for this second folk music renaissance and what is usually referred to as "the revival." The Trio's (Dave Guard, Bob Shane, Nick Reynolds) astonishing commercial success spurred admirers of Seeger and Guthrie to create their own versions of traditional songs, and adopt dress and manners of the workers not only for stage performance, but as conscious life-style choices. A new kind of singer-songwriter—Joan Baez, Phil Ochs, and Bob Dylan—became media celebrities.[16] Baez's pure American tones rendered multiversed English ballads emotionally accessible; Och's lyrics engaged politically disfranchised youth (although he never reached the popular audiences of the others); and a generation yearning for anchors in a choppy social sea elevated Dylan to a kind of mystical Poet Laureate.

The 1963 Newport Folk Festival served, like the "Grapes of Wrath" benefit for the proletarian renaissance twenty years earlier, as a symbolic peak in the ongoing rural-urban musical interweavings. In 1964, Sarah Ogan Gunning joined the Newport melange of other "folkniks" who assembled to celebrate the music of the people. Confronted by strange faces in a formal concert setting, Sarah marshaled courage (as she went onstage clutching her purse) for a traditional rendition of her "Girl of Constant Sorrow." Despite the artificial setting, she knew the audience would be exposed to the "real" thing, not the stylized simulations of city kids.

Revivalist folk singers during these years spanned the interest spectrum from traditional American music (New Lost City Ramblers, Joan Baez), internationalism (Cynthia Gooding and Theodore Bikel) to singer-songwriters like Bob Dylan and Phil Ochs, whose personal/political identity probings characterized the cultural politics of the 1960s.

In the broadest sense, the trend from the late 1950s through the 1960s shifted away from collective politics and socially conscious radicalism toward explorations of personal alienation. The second, more popular revival diverged from its earlier counterpart of the 1930s by tending to reflect individual rather than collective resistance, homogeneity rather than regionalism or class diversity. It targeted a concert and record-buying market as opposed to the politically committed audiences played to by Aunt Molly, Woody Guthrie, or the Almanacs. Revivalists performing traditional or newly composed tradition-like songs, added smooth vocal harmonies and instrumental accompaniment, softening and popularizing people's music for a mass audience. For Cantwell, the folk revival of the 1960s reflects, in part, privileged elites' romantic reaction to and reclaiming of a world lost, transformed by postwar consumerism, technology, and suburban conformity.[17] Lacking the hard-core politics of the earlier musical marriage, the revival was, he believes, "neither reactionary nor revolutionary."[18] But commitment to social and political ideals remained and still remains, for many, the reason for singing. Of course, modes of expression, vehicles, and styles change to appeal to different audiences, to suit new political times.

Leaving the "what happened" for now, I turn to some conceptual issues: ideological-musical blendings culminating in revivals throw certain themes regarding tradition and authenticity into relief. Most folklorists and anthropologists today agree with Handler and Linnekin's notion of tradition as active, arbitrary, negotiable, invented in the present to devise the past. Not only do class and power interests shape memory and thus historical recording, but our own scholarly representations mediate and define our subjects.[19] We are refocusing questions from *What* is traditional, and thus, for many, authentic, to *Why* does tradition become valued or contested? How do people use these notions to construct their identities?

Rural folk invest in their histories and cultural selves, reweaving stories of the better times, before industry invaded their countryside. The past becomes a battleground on which claims to ownership, ideological purity, authenticity, and the "truth" lock horns. The questions—Whose version was first? Whose testimony preceded the others?—are really about whose version is "realer." "Truth" surrenders its potency to the dynamic interplay, relationships, and motivations among various stakeholders.

What do we mean by "folk" and "traditional" music and why did it attract the American Left? How were the Garlands involved in struggles over meaning and style? What were the various interests at play in defining authenticity?

While I hesitate to enter definitional lions' dens, I'll offer some working ideas. "Folk music" can run the gamut from including all people's songs—whether old or new, written or orally transmitted—to only those anonymously and aurally received. The more restrictive term "traditional" is often used to distinguish old songs or tunes emerging out of a cultural group, with original authorship lost, from those newly composed. Some think it refers to the type of music rather than who plays or sings it, and others would argue that songs that just sound old (and aren't) should be called "tradition-like." Archie Green contrasts true folksongs, which have entered tradition, and folk-like songs, that is, occupational or labor songs.[20] But I've heard arguments—which reach beyond my fairly flexible umbrella of folk music—that Beatles songs could qualify for the category, since everyone knows them and despite their authors' distinctive stamp, we have imprinted them on our North American psyches.

"Folk music" communities share definite ideas about what is or is not traditional. I was recently at a St. Patrick's eve Irish session where a woman sang her own feminist song—something about a woman warrior—in a traditional style. The session leader drolly remarked that the house rules require that songs sung must be "traditional"—meaning "we only sing songs written by others."

Authenticity, though, enters a deeper level of contested terrain. The notion of an "authentic" Appalachian ballad owes much to the efforts of English folklorist Cecil Sharp early in the twentieth century. Ferreting out cultural survivals, Sharp urged mountain informants to dredge up "pure" old family songs, dismissing newer hybrids or commercial creations. In the 1930s, John and Alan Lomax, well-intentioned advocates of "real folk," packaged and marketed their own conceptions of Appalachian traditional style. Yet, Jim Garland asserted, Kentucky mountaineers, neither cut off from larger North American society, nor a "strange culture," continually experienced commerce, visitors, and migration. Appalachia's isolated image was, for Jim, "hogwash pure and simple!"[21] Mountain people, even before curious collectors, ubiquitous radios, and phonograph records, listened to and incorporated a mixture of musics. Traveling entertainers like Swedish Songbird Jenny Lind, performed in mountain outposts in the nineteenth century. Music of blacks, whites, elites, and the folk mingled. Later, mountain music, a traditional-commercial brew known as "hillbilly," in Green's view, embodied national ambivalence: "We flee the eroded land with its rotting cabin; at the same time we cover it in rose vines of memory."[22] This popular "country" music, loved by the mountain folk, became too inauthentic for academic folklorists and too tacky for progressive southerners.[23]

The Garlands scoffed at scholarly hairsplitting. For Aunt Molly, folksongs were simply what folks sang. "People just opened their mouths like the birds in the trees and whatever melody come to them and whatever was on their minds, they just sang it out and that's a folksong. If anybody tells you that anything else is a folksong, well you just say 'don't kid yourself, because I know different.'"[24] If she sang an old song or penned a new one, it became by virtue of her being "folk," a folksong. Sarah Gunning also dismissed definitional discussions and never heard the term "folksong" until she came to New York City: the mountain people just called them "songs."

To sum then, most scholars agree on some basic characteristics of "folksong": oral/aural transmission, communal ownership or rootedness, and cultural longevity. The category of folk music in its broadest sense includes old songs or tunes in any culture (traditional), new ones written in the old style (tradition-like), and new ones written for, by, or about, and accessible to ordinary people, and not necessarily for commercial reasons. The key, as Greenway put it, is not in who composes the music but whether she/he speaks for the group: "It is impersonality of authorship, not anonymity of authorship, that is a requisite of genuine folksong."[25]

In popular imagination, folk music, either a capella or accompanied with acoustic rather than electric instruments, remains hinged to nostalgic remnants of a simpler past, or expresses leftish anti-establishment, political sentiments. This linking of folk music to left politics has been the bane of some folks' existences, for others the very reason to sing. In my story of Molly and Sarah, the marriage of folk music to politics, particularly those of the American Left, played a critical role.

Political music—"lyrics or melody [that] evoke[s] or reflect[s] a political judgment by the listener"[26]—ranges from eighteenth-century class-conscious verse, slave laments, and union solidarity chants to blues, women's songs, and contemporary punk-rock styled critiques. Aphorisms like John L. Lewis's "A singing army is a winning army," or an oft-quoted seventeenth-century Scot's "Give me the making of the songs of a nation, and I care not who makes its laws," recognize songs' evocative force in historical and contemporary political movements.

Songs with overt political content became "protest" songs, a term that folklorist John Greenway adopted for the title of his 1953 book, *American Folksongs of Protest.* He defined them as community-based "struggle songs of the people. They are outbursts of bitterness, of hatred for the oppressor, of determination to endure hardships together and to fight for a better life."[27] Fine tuning varieties of protest song, sociologist Serge Denisoff differentiated "magnetic songs" (which attract with organizational aims) from "rhetorical" songs (which dissent without solution—the Dylan, Baez type).[28] Today "protest" music connotes recent social movements—feminist, anti-nuclear, peace, environmental.

The Industrial Workers of the World (Wobblies) was one of the earliest organizations to harness people's music for political purposes. Distributing "Little Red Songbooks" in 1909 along with union cards, the Wobblies became the "singingest union of them all."[29] In 1915, labor organizer

Elizabeth Gurley Flynn hinged the term "folk music" to politics when she lauded Joe Hill's compositions that "sing, that lilt and laugh and sparkle, that kindle the fires of revolt in the most crushed spirit and quicken the desire for fuller life in the most humble slave. . . . He has crystallized the organization's [IWW] spirit into imperishable forms, songs of the people—folk songs."[30] Flynn's statement, anticipating the American Left's co-optation and incorporation of folksong as a weapon for social change, helps to position the lives and careers of Molly Jackson, Sarah Gunning, and Jim Garland.

During the 1920s the International Communists' Third Period policy fashioned culture in its own sectarian image. (I rely on Richard Reuss's work for the following discussion.) European workers' choruses with rousing marching songs embodied proletarian cultural expression. New York intellectual radicals, attracted to these formal versions of worker culture, gathered to write and perform their concepts of people's music. In 1931 they founded the Workers Music League, an association of choral and orchestral groups, which spawned the Composers Collective of the Pierre Degeyter Club. About thirty classically trained musicians, including notables Charles Seeger, Henry Cowell, Elie Siegmeister, Mark Blitzstein, Aaron Copland, and Earl Robinson, chewed over issues, composed, and performed radical music committed to social change. For three years, from 1932 to 1935, using the name Carl Sands, Charles Seeger headed the collective and inspired the group to invent avant-garde works. He rejected people's music or folksongs as conservative, complacent, and defeatist.[31] The collective's members prided themselves on their talents to create music "so unique in its essence that it could never be borrowed, stolen, or imitated by their capitalist enemies."[32]

Recall that Aunt Molly's two visits to the Composer's Collective in the early 1930s captured the critical dilemma confronting the musical experts. The members winced at Molly's raspy delivery of "I Am a Union Woman," which grated on their sensitive high-culture ears. With their snobbish disdain for unschooled "people's music," the intellectuals' initial encounters with the earthy mountain woman became a metaphoric collision of formal and folk aesthetics.[33] In the first volume of a Workers' Music League publication, *Worker Musician,* a reviewer attributed the so-called immaturity and arrested development of American folk melodies to years of exploitation by coal barons. Folklore collector and singer Margaret Larkin, in her *New Masses* review in February 1933, rebutting this argument, praised the publication of the "Red Song Book" and its inclusion of songs by proletarian poets Aunt Molly and Ella May Wiggins.

Political winds would soon reverse the collective's attitude toward Aunt Molly's music. By the middle 1930s, the Communists' Third Period rigidity softened in the direction of increasing mass support with Popular Front outreach policies. The party's formalism and experimentation yielded to an appreciation of the appeal of "real folks" music. Cultural political changes during the latter years of the decade sealed the relationship between the Left and traditional artists, promoting folk music as a democratic mode of expression for a broader-based audience. Franklin Roosevelt's New Deal spawned opportunities by funding folklore activites, not only providing work for unemployed intellectual and white-collar workers but encouraging cultural unity or "thinking American."[34] John Lomax's son, Alan, became head of the Archive of American Folksong, a unit that they established within the Library of Congress. A champion of people's music, the younger Lomax brought rural singers to perform for urban audiences. Real people's music, emerging out of the folk (via the guidance of intellectuals), would replace the professionally driven proletarian music as the "great weapon for the Left."[35]

As party policies shifted, widening social circles embraced Molly and her cohorts, with the Kentuckians quickly reciprocating. Instead of specific speeches and songs about Harlan County travails, their repertoires began to reflect a discourse of universal class oppression. In the late 1930s the now-established Appalachian transplant Molly Jackson turned up at all manner of conferences, panels, parties, and rallies. She hobnobbed with scholars and writers, sharing stages and panel tables with Alan Lomax, Earl Robinson, and Ben Botkin. Aunt Molly evolved from miner's canary at the beginning of the 1930s to mouthpiece for America's disenfranchised proletariat by the end of the decade.

Members of the Composers Collective, reevaluating Molly Jackson's initial impact, sought to locate and incorporate grassroots music. Charles Seeger (as Carl Sands) especially, came to appreciate its "greater recruiting and agitating effects . . . [as opposed to] the doctrinaire slogans and pamphlets formulated by northern Communist bureaucrats."[36] When Seeger moved to Washington, D.C., to head the music program in the Technical Skills division in Roosevelt's Resettlement Administration, which assisted relocation during the Depression, he became even more firmly persuaded of the mobilizing power of traditional music.[37] Seeger understood that his early radicalism laid the foundation for this epiphany. Years later, in a 1971 letter to Richard Reuss, he credited his struggles with Marxism for his eventual realization that tradition, people's music, rather than elitist creations, were the ultimate resistance tools.[38] For Seeger, progressive politics were bound to music but birthright ultimately held the key to authenticity. In an obituary in honor of Seeger, Green noted that the influential composer and musicologist remained faithful to the idea of survival of tradition as resistance to elite art's hegemonic power.[39] Seeger's conversion parallels those of fellow composers Elie Siegmeister and Earl Robinson. In the early 1940s, Siegmeister acknowledged Aunt Molly's considerable impact on his own rethinkings:

> Like Mahomet [*sic*] and the mountain, I didn't come to folk music: it came to me. Walked up to me one day, as it were, in the person of Aunt Molly Jackson. It was after one of our downtown concerts that she cornered me and began forthwith to sing some of her Harlan (Kentucky) miners' songs. Then followed a whole series of blues, songs, ditties, and ballads that she garnered from her rich memory and imagination. I liked Aunt Molly and her music. It seemed fresh and alive.[40]

Earl Robinson, who enountered the gregarious Molly at Greenwich Village hoots, told me (when I visited him in Seattle in 1990) how the mountain woman's talents impressed him. As a "natural, gutsy woman [she] never sang the same song twice the same way." He loved Molly's penchant for one-liners and ribald stories: "With a sly look in her eye she would sing at the drop of a hat, and then, if you were relaxed with her, she'd go to town on some of the folk songs. Aunt Molly had her own verse to 'Old Joe Clark.' 'Went down to Old Joe Clark's house, Joe Clark was in bed, stuck my finger up Joe Clark's ass and pulled out meat and bread.'"[41]

Although the "Grapes of Wrath" benefit's success and critical symbolic value cannot be underestimated, by the time it occurred another cultural (and political) aesthetic superseded Molly's and Leadbelly's rough-hewn styles. In his biography of Woody Guthrie, Joe Klein suggests that the fantasy of the folk overshadowed the reality: "They were museum pieces, priceless and rare, but not quite marketable in the mass culture."[42] Robbie Lieberman, in her account of Communist and movement culture in the 1930s, agrees that left aesthetics shifted along with political ideology: in time, Leadbelly and Aunt Molly were less attractive than the more polished interpreters, Josh White and Burl Ives.[43] The interpreters, or impersonators, as Cantwell terms them, were "more real than real."[44] Despite declining public interest in listening to the real thing (like Aunt Molly), the Garlands, Leadbelly, and Woody played pivotal roles as transformers of musical taste and performance. When I spoke to Henrietta Yurchenco (host of a New York radio show in the early 1940s), she emphasized the rural singers' impact on New York musical and political circles. "They taught us a particular style. No longer could you play blues without regard to accompaniment. You had to learn style. It was a completely different sound and way of phrasing." Richard Reuss, too, wrote of the singers' extraordinary effect on musical taste. Although failing to create culture along class lines they succeeded in "laying the groundwork for the popularization of traditional music on a scale hitherto unknown in American society and the interweaving of folksongs and the folk idiom into the entire fabric of American music and cultural life. As such, their contribution cannot be underestimated."[45]

The Garlands introduced urban northerners to southern mountain cultural life and song style. In 1939, Jim Garland gathered a small group of singers (including Sarah but not Molly), replete with gingham dresses, bonnets, miners' caps, and lamps to represent Kentucky at the World's Fair. A few years later, Gordon Friesen wrote in the *Daily Worker* on January 10, 1942: "When Aunt Molly sang her generic folk ballads they heard the 'real living song.'" Molly, Jim, and later, Sarah, articulated an emotional rural experience for consumption by the urban middle class. Politically disaffected intellectuals and artists, sensitive to disparities in an industrializing world, identified with the rural marginals. The Harlan and Bell County coal struggles became a metaphor for dominant bosses and oppressed workers, haves and have-nots. New York intellectual radicals and Appalachian exiles were not only attracted to each other, but became "compatriots," merging traditional music and speech patterns with class consciousness and union politics.[46]

Father and son, John and Alan Lomax—who, like the Seegers, exerted a far-reaching influence—brought together radical politics and folklore scholarship in the 1930s, with their particular slant on the "real." Their discovery of Huddie Ledbetter (Leadbelly) illustrates how their ends (advocacy) justified the means (shaping authenticity). In the well-circulated story, the Lomaxes found Leadbelly in a Texas prison (serving a murder sentence), wangled his reprieve, brought him to the East, and coached him on how to adapt his repertoire for urban audiences. They urged the singer to appear in prison garb and perform "authentic" songs instead of popular items like "Silver Haired Daddy of Mine." The Lomaxes marketed Leadbelly's "savage," wild child image.[47]

Alan Lomax's idealism and fervent desire to preserve folk culture spurred him to create his own renderings of "traditional," which seemed to prevail, at times—even if unintentionally—over other concerns. Molly and Sarah seethed when they discovered that Lomax gave to the Library of Congress songs that they and Jim recorded in Mary Barnicle's New York apartment and Greenwich, Connecticut, home—supposedly for Barnicle's NYU folklore class—while never informing or compensating them. Moreover, to apparently heighten the songs' authenticity, Lomax claimed they were recorded in Pineville, Kentucky. This wasn't the only time the Garlands felt violated. According to Sarah, without her knowing it at the time, a recording she made with Leadbelly met the same fate.[48] Alan Lomax shaped authenticity in his role as an advocate—for him the ends—the positive social consequences—justified the means. He coached traditional performers, placed them on pedestals as ideal types, pressed "citybillies" to learn authentic rural style.[49] Charles Seeger, acknowledging Lomax's contouring of tradition, forgave his maneuverings in print in his first review for the *Journal of American Folklore:* "This reviewer may as well confess to an almost parental solicitude also for Alan Lomax and his doings that may impede strict application of critical principles." Seeger also saw "a distinct weakness in his valiant championship of folk music in the modern world—a tendency to sentimentalization of 'The Folk' and of the social and cultural role he believes it is playing."[50] In a 1993 "author's introduction" to an article she wrote in the 1960s, Ellen Stekert reflected on some of her earlier judgments about the urban folksong movement. She was critical of "benevolent paternalism: the moving of traditional singers to places like New York City (where they often wished to go), having them sing for the well-meant causes of the Progressive Movement, and then leaving them to wander unprepared in the strange landscape of urban poverty."[51] Implicitly, Stekert contrasts her own close and caring relationship with Sarah Gunning, whose life history and repertoire she recorded from 1964 through much of the 1970s.[52]

Cultural transfers traveled in both directions, with city folk and traditional folk influencing each other's styles, tailoring their performances to approximate the other's expectations. Charles Seeger recognized that Lomax and other folklorists cobbled together "tradition" with only part

of the ingredients. The rural singers came to model themselves as workers of the world with a new consciousness, not only of regional but of class
difference, adopting styles for their middle-class audiences to emulate.

While Molly saw herself as "political" and Sarah as "traditional," the
politics that shaped both their musical repertoires and in turn how these
repertoires reflected their politics becomes central to their (and my) story. Just as Charles and Pete Seeger renovated the past for a purpose, Molly
and Sarah forged a role for their own traditions within an urban context.
Charles Seeger stressed the showbiz creativity, rather than the victimization of the folk:

> Put, for example, any good "authentic" traditional singer before a
> microphone or on a platform before an audience not of its own kind
> and soon the peculiar requirements of the situation produce the typ-
> ical traits of exhibitionism. To my personal observation, it took Molly
> Jackson only a few months to convert herself, when expedient, from
> a traditional singer, who seemed never to have given any particular
> thought to whether anyone liked or disliked her singing, into a shrewd
> observer of audience reaction, fixing individual listeners one after
> another with her gaze, smiling ingratiatingly, gesturing, dramatizing
> her performance.[53]

Seeger saw Leadbelly, too, as an "astute handler of the non-folk." Here
the rural singer becomes the shaper of oral tradition, no longer in the
context of her/his home community, but representing it to and changing
it for outsiders.

Molly's compositions and renditions of traditional ballads imparted
genuine Appalachian cultural tradition. Her versions, whether molded to
suit audiences or sung by herself in her kitchen, remained "authentic."
She claimed songs as her own when she added verses or changed text but
did object, though, when *others* changed what *she* understood as tradition:
"I think they should be left just like our ancestors composed them."[54]
Molly also carefully policed her own image. When she read parts of Mary
Barnicle's planned biography of her life she took umbrage at expressions
that fine-tuned her speech, rendering her less authentic, more uppity. Her
dislike of Barnicle's prose was apparently one of the reasons that the English professor decided to abandon her project—but the subtexts of the
story are unknown to me. Molly clearly felt her image threatened by Barnicle's language transformations:

[Barnicle] had an educated secretary and she thought I spoke with a different accent . . . which of course it's no high language. It's just an old Kentucky mountain dialect. . . . Where you folk says "tobacco" I say "backer" and where you folks say "tomato" I say "mater." . . . If I'd went around there, I knowed a better way to speak . . . they [mountain folk] would have said I had a big head and kicked me out of the house. . . . So she put down big high-fallutin' words. I said why they mountain people they wouldn't accept that a bit more to be my story . . . you can do anything you want but don't tack my name to that. . . . I demanded my material be brought to me pronto.[55]

Charles Seeger understood that those with access to the media controlled the power to shape music in a way no traditional performer could. Commercial recording operated by its own set of conventions, creating popular musical tastes and expectations. In the process, it altered traditional music through stanza editing, instrumental improvisation, and accompaniment. Performers needed to entertain urban audiences. "Almost inevitably the folk singer comes to sing 'with expression,' to aim for 'lovely tone' and to dramatize for special effect. Or, he fears (and with reason), that he may not be reengaged."[56] In his second record review for the *Journal of American Folklore* in 1949, Seeger criticized revivalist singers' fundamental distortions. Referring specifically to albums by singers Burl Ives, Josh White, and Richard Dyer-Bennet, he wrote:

[They] represent one of the most potent means for the artful re-insemination of vast sections of the American people with a heritage of their own dominant majority, a process that cannot but affect profoundly the nature of what the folklorists of tomorrow will call "folklore" upon the North American continent. . . . One's disgust at these all-too-frequent breaches of good taste make one ashamed not so much of the artist, who is floundering in a commercial maze, as of the public that acclaims him and the record manufacturers who fatten on this acclaim.[57]

With sophisticated insight into the relationship between performance and context, Seeger concluded that the only route to authenticity is through birthright: "as a rule, a performance representative of one direction can be clearly distinguished from a performance representative of the other. It would seem that inheritance always shows, no matter how extreme the adaptation to environment."[58]

Although folk music as commodity played a clearer role in the second revival than it did in the first, kernels of strife over ownership and compensation germinated even before the 1930s with northern record companies interested in "race records." Alan Lomax seemed a locus of controversy over collection and payment, probably because he took so active a role. Obsessed over not receiving payment for her recordings in the 1930s, Molly bombarded Lomax with letters alternately angry or ignominiously pleading for money (I quote some of these in chapter 4).

Alan Lomax loomed large in Molly's hierarchy of offenders, but he was hardly alone. During interviews with Archie Green in the last years of her life she listed a litany of violations. "Material thief" Burl Ives recorded Molly's and Jim Garland's songs, "and he's not by his self, there's a lot of them. But they got hundreds of dollars worth of material from me before I ever know'd that a story from the hills of folk songs was worth a cent."[59] Appalachian singer Jean Ritchie also became the butt of her criticism: "poor kid, she may mean well but she don't have the original nothing." In her self-centeredness and absorption, which inflated with age, even Molly's siblings were not spared her tongue: "they don't know a thing in the world about these here real old old songs. . . . No, Sarah Ogan and Jim Garland, they don't know from Adam . . . all the old songs they know just what they learn from me."[60]

Within the community of rural singers in the city the stakes for authorship intensified: not necessarily because of potential economic rewards, but for prestige and recognition. Sarah's anger with Molly for claiming her songs, and with Woody for recording her "Babe of Mine," stemmed from her fresh understanding that her own authenticity mattered. Songs, newly commodified and infused with new symbolic value, became even more important to own.

Tensions linking money, authenticity, and contemporary revival music are still simmering in the 1990s. Contests over tradition and its economic consequences have engaged scholars in academic journals, folkies in the pages of *Sing Out!* and the *Old Time Herald,* and become the stuff of panels at folklore and anthropology meetings. In 1989, banjoist Mac Benford spelled out one position in the *Old Time Herald,* taking Bess Hawes (as head of the National Endowment for the Humanities at the time) to task for withdrawing funding from revival (middle-class white) performers of traditional music, undermining their efforts to keep that music alive.[61] Hawes felt that the limited pools of money should go to the "real" traditional artists rather than advantaged imitators, regardless of how well-meaning and orthodox their treatments of the music.

Some critics argue that the urban Left's adoption of folk style was not only exploitative but politically naive in both revivals. The Composers Collective, in Ron Davis's view, took the wrong turn in the 1930s, toward the popular, grass roots, "feelgood" music of Charles and Pete Seeger, rather than the intellectually stimulating, purist route aimed at raising the workers' sights, spearheaded by Bertolt Brecht and Hans Eisler.[62] Archie Green told me he would contrast Charles and Pete Seeger, believing the father's concern with authenticity distinguished him from his son, who homogenizes for audience appeal. "Hokey" left-wing aesthetics remains a continual sore point for some. I spoke to Hedy West, daughter of the late radical activist Don West, who disparages middle-class identification with the workers. A singer herself, hailing from rural roots in Cartersville, Georgia (her father a generation away from dirt farming), Hedy denounces the second revival as an anti-intellectual denial of the past. She believes it romanticizes poverty and working-class images, with the notion of fostering creativity, "an indulgence in ideologizing want." Hedy West credits Pete Seeger for being the real thrust to the revival, "as builder of public image and spinner of myth, a fantastic performer and great falsifier."[63]

The Left's invention of authenticity through working-class style was also the focus of a debate in *The Nation* in 1986. For author Jessie Lemisch, contemporary singer-songwriter Si Kahn represents a genre of popular radicalism in the Seeger tradition that manipulates, or exploits, the "real" through documentary and song.[64] Angry response letters flooded in to defend folk artists like Kahn, whose work, they argued, serves to raise consciousness of historical struggle, infusing traditional music with new energy and generating alternatives to popular culture. The consequences of imitation and impersonation of rural poor by middle-class revival singers remains controversial since the middle-class singers themselves are divided on overlapping political/ traditional/commercial lines. John Cohen of the New Lost City Ramblers (NLCR), a trio with Mike Seeger and Tom Paley formed in the late 1950s, zeroes in on this issue in Ronald D. Cohen's collection *Wasn't That a Time*. Cohen (John) tells how the NLCR distinguished themselves from commercial and/or political groups. When ABC-TV's *Hootenanny* blacklisted Pete Seeger in 1963, the folk community split, with supporters of Seeger refusing to appear on the show. After much "soul searching," NLCR accepted *Hootenanny's* invitation, attempting (as Cohen rationalizes) "to balance our repugnance at the blacklist industry with the opportunity to bring traditional music, played in a traditional style, to the widest possible audience." Representing themselves as embodiments of pure tradition despite their lack of birthright, the New Lost City Ramblers considered "commercial folk singers, their driving desire for exposure, and their total disinterest in traditional music or traditional musicians . . . [as] our enemies."[65] For Cohen, revivalists of the 1960s spring from two main sources: the Weavers with jazzy, pop-crafted arrangements and "political optimism," giving birth to a Joan Baez or Judy Collins; and country traditionalists (NLCR) or urban blues singers (Dave Van Ronk, John Hammond), using old recordings as teachers and inspiring the likes of the Highwoods Stringband and the Red Clay Ramblers. Cohen points out important divisions tending to polarize discussions of folk music. Traditional music (often associated with authenticity, preservation, whiteness, and political conservatism) pits itself against folk music (often associated with radical or at least left-wing political ideology and internationalism), placing more importance on the solidarity function than the content or "purity" of the music. These divisions, although far from being mutually exclusive—and either can fall into commercial or noncommercial realms—fossilize and divide advocates.

Although the focused, collective, radical renaissance that involved Molly and Jim in the 1930s contrasted with the blander middle-class, commercial embrace of people's musical style in the 1960s, their commonalities ring out. In a number of respects, the earlier and later folk revivals linked Aunt Molly to the Weavers and Joan Baez. When Aunt Molly Jackson, and later Sarah Ogan Gunning, performed for urban audiences, they touched a deep chord in their listeners. Musical revival allows participants to reach across regional, class, and gender lines to a time and place—regardless of how mythical—in which humanity counted. Romantic visions of an egalitarian, caring world cut through both earlier and later revivals. Performer-participants in each movement, from Woody to Dylan, considered themselves resisters, anti-elitists. In both peak periods of fusing, urban singers adopted people's musics as alternatives to mainstream bubble-gum culture; and in both, performers saw opportunities to communicate simpler rural life to city folk. Revivalists produced a version of the "real" (even though the definition of that term remained contested), opposed it to the artificial, and bound it to a politic. Though singers and players defined, played with, and stretched the "real" for audience appeal, and though they might achieve commercial success, they nevertheless saw themselves expressing values in opposition to mass-market profitability. Positive values emerging from revivalists' adoption of style, regardless of whether participants consider themselves "political," emphasize common desires for connection, resistance, and optimism. Ben Botkin's quoting of Charles Hayward is decades old, but still seems relevant: "[The youth] are harnessing their critical and creative faculties in their demands for a say in the world they never made, and using song as a weapon and moral force to help remake it. . . . It involves psychological and imaginative identification with the folk and a community of interest based on the continuity of a living tradition rather than the impulse of a nostalgic wish."[66]

Folk festivals in the 1990s suffer from declining crowds, technological foul-ups, volunteer coordination problems, "bigger is better" notions, and that greatest bugaboo, inclement weather, which is likely to drive all but the hard core away. Still, the best of them offer occasions for musical sharings, crossovers and fusions, whether traditional music or singer songwriter-driven, and are inspired by an alternative politic. Singer Hazel Dickens, in a story she told me about her first meeting with Sarah Gunning, underscores the notion of festival as opportunity for lateral cultural dispersion, and respect for the other.

> When I started going on those tours, when I first met Sarah, there were lots of different people from different ethnic backgrounds. They had the Appalachians, an old banjo picker, Cajuns, black blues singers, [Georgia] Sea Island singers. We'd all get to talking in the back of the van while on the way to do our concert. This one conversation we had was just incredible. It was all of us, from all different places. "I'm trying to think about your mountains," "Well I'm trying to think about your bayou." We would start talking about how we grew up and had to go to work to earn a living. We found that all of us were coming from the same place, although we'd never seen each other before or each other's territory. We were all working-class people—there wasn't a college grad in the bunch. I tell you, there were plenty of tears when we got done talking.[67]

For Dickens, the value of revival emerges from new communities born out of folk festivals, ones based on interests and shared life experience rather than region, with rural singers from a variety of traditions coming to appreciate their common humanity. Folk festivals are not the sole way of perpetuating traditional/folk music. Appreciators of traditional and folk music proliferate in kitchens, living rooms, church basements, and community centers, shaping old and inventing new traditions, considering doing music together an opportunity for discovering, sharing, communicating identity.[68] In a wide range of grass-roots music groups and events—family music camps in the Mendocino Woodlands, Scottish fiddle club meetings in San Francisco, song circles, international dances, New England Contra backed by Celtic fusion bands, weekly Irish sessions, Balkan women's choruses, Cape Breton style fiddlers in Toronto—participants identify through empathy and a common aesthetic more often than common ancestry.

In my own Toronto experience, a song circle provides one such context. Overwhelmingly middle-class, white, and mature (except for a few daughters of veterans), our diversity lies in our genders and (varied) musical interests and talents. We are building a repertoire of music from members' recollections, old sheet music or vinyls, the blue songbook (or "bible") published by *Sing Out!* magazine, and new compositions by members. Swelling at times to more than thirty bodies on Friday nights, the song circle meets in members' homes, prefers participatory chorus songs to performance pieces, and lends particular support to those with weaker voices and less confidence. We look askance at those doggedly following written text rather than committing songs to memory. There is an informal understanding that regulars "own" songs if they introduce them to the circle; if a newcomer unwittingly sings one of these, we old-timers roll our eyes and smile knowingly at other veterans. Resistance to popular culture becomes one of the song circle's subtexts: we eschew popular versions except when we break out in a raucous send-up, signifying our love/hate relationship to commercial music. Political protest becomes another subtext, as members sing old labor songs, write and perform feminist and environmental songs, to remind us of our progressive roots. We see ourselves as an alternative cultural group, born of common interests, sharing and carefully nurturing our dislike for commercial, electronic, second-hand, slickly packaged music, and desire to create community.

In this chapter I have located Aunt Molly and Sarah Ogan Gunning in the broad framework of the politics of culture. Although my account of their lives has focused primarily on their places in labor history and the politics of resistance to big-business control of Appalachian coal economy, their vast repertoires spanned both "traditional" and "protest" song. Differences in the sisters' ages, personalities, and experiences affected the way each related to their social milieus. The cultural-political periods that framed each woman's life contrasted as well: Molly during the radical days of the early 1930s and Sarah during another wave of interest in tradition in the 1960s. Their personal and political profiles raised central questions about the molding of tradition and authenticity, which I have considered both in the context of their lives and after, as a continuing debate in folklore studies. Some, like Charles Seeger and Archie Green, see authenticity in birthright and true resistance in tradition. But there are also good reasons to focus on tradition as fluid, malleable, shaped by audience and market expectations, and to enjoy the search for new and reinvented identities.

The Left used tradition for particular political reasons, but it continues to serve a multitude of purposes: to valorize the past, to make sense of and enrich the present, to emphasize or bridge differences. In the next chapter, I will speak of another context of resistance that grounds my story of Molly and Sarah. The "Girls of Constant Sorrow" rewrite themselves (as I rewrite them) as gendered people, women. Aware of the constraining forces, they tug at the ropes that bind them to tradition as much as they honor it.

7

"Dreadful Memories":
Class-Conscious Wives, Radical Mothers

As we follow Molly and Sarah from their Kentucky mining towns to the tenements of New York, we can imagine the startling cultural shifts these travels involved. How strange their first encounters and experiences: cold-water flats, thronged pavements, bellowing hot dog vendors, rich society patrons, Communists, folklorists, and professors.

My story of the Garland sisters hinges them as individuals to a politics of history with contests of scholarly interests, ideologies, aesthetics. While I render Molly and Sarah special by writing about them, the backdrop of resistant women in coal-mining and other kinds of communities places them in further perspective. Molly's and Sarah's emotional songs voiced their struggles as miners' wives, workers, the rural poor, as mothers with hungry mouths to feed—but served equally as narratives of resistance, rallying cries and strategies for social action. The Garland sisters have much in common with resistant women in coal mining and textile communities in Appalachia and with others far removed—in Britain, Latin America, Europe, Africa.

Since my own discipline, anthropology, inspired my immersion in Molly's and Sarah's worlds, I'll share some intellectual grapplings. Although anthropologists are thoroughly socialized cultural relativists, appreciators of diversity, champions of "common people," until recently we reflected little on how we as privileged scholars influence our work. Since the late 1960s, critical recastings have encouraged examination of the ethnographic enterprise. Objective fieldworkers became interpreters of meaning and authors of cultural text.[1] The anthropological trust in data collection and "fact" finding was replaced with an attempt to include voices of "others," or at least consider how we speak for them. The pride in "value freedom" and social scientific "objectivity"—our faith in our entire canon diminished in light of new analyses of how ethnocentric notions permeate our research.

For me and many female colleagues, the early 1970s saw a particular kind of reevaluation. We noticed how male bias permeated the literature on which we cut our scholarly teeth, of the way "serious" scholars devalued softer, more trivial research on women. With this new awareness, we searched for structural and economic reasons to explain women's seemingly universal lower status. Debates ensued regarding the sources of social heirarchy. Was it women's embeddedness in the domestic[2] or historical circumstances—colonialism and capitalism?[3] "Historians" accused "universalists" of ethnocentrism or biological reductionism; universalists reproved historians for romantic reconstructions of gender role egalitarianism.

Throughout the 1970s and 1980s, simple explanations of women's status evolved into multilayered explorations of relationships and meanings. Some academics considered women's worlds as separate cultures or meaning systems, often inaccessible to male ethnographers. Others looked at how women develop alternative symbolic codes or behavior in response to larger political realities, generally shaped by male institutions.[4] Although intellectually divided, feminist scholars have generally understood gender differences as social and cultural constructs and not biological givens.

Feminist scholarship during the past twenty years constitutes nothing less than an epistemological revolution. Historians and anthropologists have focused on events, structures, processes important to women, highlighting women as creative social and political actors rather than victims. Oral histories, testimonials of poor women, and life writing—incorporating diaries and letters—in which a self-reflexive author remains present in the text, weave narratives of experience that have become the currency of contemporary feminist critique.[5]

A feminism valuing sentiment, partial truth, and self-reflection sees itself in opposition to scientific objectivity. Gender identity is problematic, socially constructed, negotiated. Some academic feminists seek sources of essential womanhood, but most prefer to think of differences like class, culture, race, ethnicity, history, and sexual preference, that bring both unity and separation. For me, as for other feminist scholars, one of the crucial aspects of gender is its political dimension: knowledge produced about gender difference in historically shifting contexts and how this knowledge is used. The way that societies think about gender becomes a window into a critical politics of history.[6]

Much resistance or protest, taking non-dramatic, non-collective forms, attracts scant notice. Women's resistance, doubly muted, tends to suffer even greater invisibility.[7] Small-scale resistances can be, nevertheless in James C. Scott's view "the stuff of revolution," as minor subversions—worker slowdowns, lying, cheating, slaves poisoning masters—serve to undermine those in power.[8] Abu Lughod tells of Bedouin women's creative resistance through secrets, silences, avoidance of arranged marriages, sexually irreverent discourses.[9] Some scholars regard women's protest or resistance, generally revolving around home and family, as a shelter for traditional gender relations. Moral reform campaigns or food riots become another way of reaffirming, rather than challenging, gender hierarchy. Others see radicalizing potential in women's collective action. Analyzing a case of women's protest in Barcelona, Spain, from 1910 to 1918, Temma Kaplan discusses how women, newly aware of their critical role in the family's survival, learned effective political strategies. She proposes an analytical distinction between "feminist" and "female" consciousness. Feminism focuses on power relationships and unequal access to institutions; female consciousness underscores gender rights, survival, and social concerns. But rather than being bounded and conservative, Kaplan argues that the latter has revolutionary consequences, as it "politicizes the networks of everyday life."[10]

The women of Greenham Common Peace Camp in Berkshire, England, motivated at first by desires for a safe, non-nuclear world for their children, became sophisticated analysts of the government and military. For about ten years, beginning in 1981, they fixed themselves outside the perimeter of an American air base located an hour from London that housed and tested cruise missiles. Pitching tents at various gates, they stood watch as truck convoys crept out at night, organized mass vigils, snipped away the green wire fence with bolt cutters, and plagued the guards by dancing on the sacred silos housing the missiles. Greenham women painted their faces, chanted and sang, planted flower gardens, and wove colorful spider webs through the fence links. Clothed in mourning black, they appeared in London train stations hauling coffins and outside government buildings carrying placards. When arrested, their false names confused and provoked officials. With nonviolent but stubborn torments geared to drawing attention to surreptitious maneuvers in the inner sanctum, they managed to sidetrack, render more difficult, certain military plans. Although the media would often dismiss them as lesbians and nuisances rather than considering them dangerous intruders, Greenham women's symbolic acts were effective political strategies—instrumental in altering military decisions.

Greenham Common magnetically drew "ordinary" wives and mothers, who either established permanent camp sites or visited the color-coded gates on weekends. Romantic statements about a better world soon transformed into angry and profound distrust for systems of authority. As links between militarism, poverty, and gender disadvantage became visible, the line between "female" consciousness and "feminist" consciousness blurred. Private reproductive interests converted into public political action.[11]

An example from colonial West Africa earlier in this century illustrates how family interests can kindle gendered protest. Women of the patrilineal, patrilocal Igbo of southeastern Nigeria relocated to husbands' communities after marriage, but maintained ties to their natal villages. Crosscutting alliances allowed the women opportunities to meet regularly, exchange news, disperse information, and share problems with a wide social network. If one felt violated or insulted, she could access support from this network, who would retaliate by "sitting on a man," instituting a variety of harassments, fines, and boycotts.[12] While British rule in Africa weakened indigenous power balances, legitimized male leadership, and undermined traditional processes for redress, Igbo women continued to draw on their collective power into the twentieth century. In the early twentieth century, when the mechanization of palm oil production threatened to erode women's economic independence from men, they staged a revolt.[13] Another instance of female/feminist consciousness converted into action occurred when the British levied a 1929 education tax on each family. This sparked the "women's war," in which thousands marched and destroyed property, not only in protest as wives, but as individuals suffering a loss of economic independence and political power.

Motherhood discourses also underlie Latin American women's resistance and North American women's environmental movements. The Argentinian "Madres De Plaza de Mayo," searching for disappeared children and grandchildren under a military regime, took personal grief and outrage to a public space, urging others to confront state terrorism.[14] In recent examples from the United States and Canada, housewife activists in the environmental protection movement have mobilized against toxic wastes in the non-negotiable health of children.[15] In all these cases, distinctions between female and feminist consciousness deflect from the strength of the women's political interests and impact outside domestic concerns.

Closer to the site of Molly and Sarah's story, women textile mill workers were at the core of 1920s labor unrest in the Piedmont region of Appalachia. In the early days of cotton production, workers, many of them women, could change jobs when dissatisfied. After World War I, competition from other producers, shrinking hemlines and markets upset the southern textile industry. New machinery reduced the size of the work force, while employees worked faster, for longer hours and less money. By the 1920s, the effects of the Depression reverberated through the mill towns.[16] Mill workers, like miners in Southern Appalachia, spurned the conservative anti-strike position of the resident United Textile Union (a branch of the American Federation of Labor) and swung to the alternative Communist-created National Textile Workers Union. The series of strikes erupting in mill towns of North and South Carolina and Tennessee involved young women—a substantial proportion of the labor force—with fewer dependents, as active supporters.[17]

Ella May Wiggins, born in Tennessee in 1900, twenty years after Molly Jackson, affords an interesting comparison. Ella May moved in the early 1920s to the Piedmont textile area in Gaston County, North Carolina, with her husband, John Wiggins, and their nine children. When John was injured in a logging camp or refused to work (depending on whose version of the story), Ella May became the sole support for her family as spinner on the night shift in the American Textile Mill in Bessemer City, North Carolina. Communist strike organizers, gravitating to the textile region as they had to the coal areas, took note of Ella May's magnetic speech and songmaking gifts. They sent her to training classes for local leaders, then to Washington, D.C., to represent textile workers before a Senate committee investigating mill conditions. So perfectly did Ella May's "ballets" capture the workers' wretched plight that they became her trademark. One observer remarked on her charismatic quality at worker "speakings": "in a deep resonant voice she would give us a simple ballad . . . the crowd would join in with an old refrain and Ella May would add verse after verse to her song."[18]

The boss man wants our labor,
And money to pack away,
The workers wants a union
And the eight hour day.

The boss man hates the workers,
The workers hates the boss.
The boss man rides in a big fine car
And the workers has to walk.

The boss man sleeps in a big fine bed
And dreams of his silver and gold.
The workers sleeps in an old straw bed
And shivers from the cold.

Fred Beal he is in prison
A-sleeping on the floor,
But he will soon be free again
And speak to us some more.

The union is a-growing,
The I.L.D. [International Labor Defense] is strong,
We're going to show the bosses
That we have starved too long.[19]

Although Ella May wrote a variety of songs about community events and people, her primary political message rang out: multiple responsibilities of working and family care intensified women's burdens. They could be neither good mothers nor workers with pittance wages, long hours, and wretched mill conditions. Using her own experience, Ella May appealed directly to women: "'I'm the mother of nine,' she said. 'Four of them died with whooping cough, all at once. I was working nights and nobody to do for them. . . . I asked the super to put me on day shift so's I could tend 'em, but he wouldn't. . . . So I had to quit my job and then there wasn't any money for medicine, so they just died. I never could do anything for my children, not even to keep 'em alive, it seems. That's why I'm for the union, so's I can do better for them.'"[20]

"Mill Mother's Lament," Ella May's best-known song, captures these sentiments.

We leave our home in the morning,
We kiss our children goodby,

While we slave for the bosses
Our children scream and cry.

And when we draw our money
Our grocery bills to pay,
Not a cent to spend for clothing,
Not a cent to lay away.

And on that very evening,
Our little son will say:
"I need some shoes, dear mother,
And so does sister May."

How it grieves the heart of a mother,
You every one must know,
But we can't buy for our children,
Our wages are too low.

It is for our little children
That seems to us so dear,
But for us nor them, dear workers,
The bosses do not care.

But understand, all workers,
Our union they do fear.
Let's stand together, workers,
And have a union here.[21]

In September 1929, diggers and mourners sang Ella May's song as they lowered her young body into its grave. Murdered by gun thugs while on her way to a union meeting, Ella May hadn't yet reached her thirtieth birthday. Playwright and song collector Margaret Larkin, who met Ella May in Gastonia mere weeks before her death, was so taken with the activist's courage that she eulogized her in *The Nation* and *New Masses* and introduced her songs to New York audiences. Larkin wrote of a "'sightly' woman, rather short and round, with bobbed brown hair and fine eyes. She was only twenty-nine years old, but Southern mill workers age early. Her face was lined with fine wrinkles; her cheeks were sunken, but her chin was firm and determined."[22]

Ella May's reputation in her community, though, was that of a hard-boiled nonconformist and neglectful mother, disclosed in this eulogy from a local newspaper: "The poor woman is dead and gone, and it is not for anyone to say much about her now, but if some of these sob sisters who are writing about her 'riding into the West' and all that sort of ridiculous tommyrot, knew the real life story of Ella May, there would be a different story. Her children, motherless and nameless, are far better off where they are (in an orphanage) than if their mother were living."[23]

How similar were reactions to Ella May and Molly! They were "bad" and deviant, in contrast to "good" wives and mothers. Outspoken, independent, unconventional, they defied notions of appropriate gender behavior. Hall's term "disorderly women" would suit both Ella May and Aunt Molly, as "women who, in times of political upheaval, embody tensions that are half-conscious or only dimly understood."[24] Ella May dropped her husband's name, "Wiggins," after she had a child with her lover, Charley Shope. She lived in Stumptown, an area outside Bessemer City populated largely by black workers, a significant proportion of the American Mills labor force. Her children, accustomed to their mother's absence during her night shift, scrounged, foraged, and stole chickens.[25]

Molly Jackson married several times, in itself not unusual because of mining deaths. Many in the community considered her a troublesome, domineering woman who frequently "stretched her blanket" (exaggerated or lied). As we know, Molly cultivated this wild, "pistol-packin'" image, reveling in others' shock. For both Aunt Molly and Ella May, as well as Sarah, various facets of their gender identities—wife, worker, mother, sexual person—were not incompatible. Although neither of the women drew on a feminist political framework as articulated discourse, both were aware of the contradictions in and constraints on their lives as women. Ella May's, Molly's, and Sarah's songs—resistance narratives—explicitly depicting class oppositions, revealed a consciousness of gender as political text. Maternalist discourse became a useful strategy to link domestic interests to social and political action.

Unlike textile mills, coal mining excluded women as underground workers for the first half of the century. But the whole system of mining hinged on women's domestic management, everyday chores, keeping boarders, and service jobs. Often barely out of their own girlhoods, they bore and cared for children, tended husbands and animals, hauled water, chopped wood, scrubbed grime, scrounged scraps, and anxiously awaited their men's emergence from treacherous black tunnels. Recall Jim Garland's account of women's arduous days, of survival struggles that ground them down, even killed them earlier than husbands with dangerous underground jobs.[26] Frequent mine accidents, though, often meant serial marriages, widowhood, or a lifetime of sustaining maimed men and hungry dependents. Women like Molly and Sarah suffered the consequences of men's work conditions, paltry wages, and debt relationships. When the Depression clobbered the coal industry, they joined their husbands at union meetings, on picket lines, confronting evictions, scabs, and violence. Although they didn't enter the mines as workers, family and worker were one: the oppressed.

Barbara Kopple's remarkable film *Harlan County USA* (Cabin Creek Films, 1990) visually documents the 1973 strike in which women's actions determined it's success. Historical examples of disorderly (activist) women stuff Philip Foner's two-volume *Women and the American Labor Movement.* In 1921, two thousand West Virginian miners' wives and daughters drove strike breakers out of eight mines. In 1927, women in Western Pennsylvania, Ohio, Indiana, and Illinois, the core of the United Mine Workers of America resistance, showed "heroic endurance" during a mine lockout, organizing auxiliaries and picketing. One reporter noted: "'The women are right in the front-line of the struggle . . . coming back to the fight with cool courage again and again after they have been beaten up.'"[27] The chaotic style of women's strike actions proved a useful tactic—egg throwing, club wielding, and shrieking caused some apprehension for officials who considered out-of-control behavior at best dangerous and unpredictable. Hall tells how women strikers in Elizabethton, Tennessee, made much use of laughter and playfulness, disconcerting authorities.[28]

One of the most legendary strike leaders, Mother Jones, bears discussion here, since her case compares like Ella May's, to Molly Jackson. Irish-born Mary Harris Jones lost her husband and four children to Yellow Fever in 1867. She joined the Knights of Labor and remained an active organizer until her death in 1930 when almost one hundred years old (or eighty-seven depending on whose account one believes).[29] Mother Jones's name remains linked to major strikes in the late nineteenth and early twentieth century—Chicago Haymarket Riot, 1886; Pennsylvania Anthracite strike, 1902; Ludlow Massacre, Colorado, 1913.

The contrast between Jones's prim clothing and spunky behavior never failed to shock. Archie Green tells how a young reporter described the seventy-year-old white-haired activist: "'Sometimes a torrent of harsh language would flow from the mouth of this old woman, in strange contrast to her general appearance which was that of a grandmother, wearing a shabby watered-silk dress to which bits of lace were pinned, with a tiny black bonnet stuck up the back of her head. Mother Jones was intelligent, but in speaking to a crowd would often spoil her argument by raving.'"[30]

Green also reported a miner's recollection of the feisty union organizer: "'She came down Pike Street in a buggy and horse. Two company thugs grabbed the horse by the bridle and told her to turn around and get back down the road. She wore a gingham apron, and she reached under it and pulled out a .38 special pistol and told them to turn her horse loose, and they sure did. She continued on to the park, and spoke to a large bunch of miners. She wasn't afraid of the devil.'"[31]

Although Mother Jones couldn't draw on personal experience as a coal miner's wife, like Aunt Molly she appealed to high society for money with graphic images of poor, hungry children, testimonies about suffering and devastation in mining towns. Like Molly too, Mother Jones sang her own praises, believing herself a born leader. She elaborated her own triumphs in rallying speeches, and as Ronnie Gilbert (author, singer, and one of the Weavers), who wrote a musical play about the activist puts it, she "never let the absolute truth spoil a good yarn."[32] In Green's account, one wealthy patron to whom Jones appealed for money understood her motivation: "'Are her tales all true? In a sense, yes; undoubtedly she believes every word she speaks. But upon reflection you conclude that life can never have moved so dramatically as in her narration. These stories have been told by her again and again with propagandist intent.'"[33]

Mother Jones's strategic grab bag depended, in Green's view, on her "use of song and trickster's bluff as organizational tools [that] seems to have been a highly conscious mastery of rhetorical forms in trade-union society."[34] These tactics deserve a closer look, since Jones so expertly manipulated gender symbolism. Urging women to dress in rags to underscore poverty, she felt they often made more stalwart, effective strikers than men. In her autobiography, Mother Jones recalls her advice to strikers in Arnot, Pennsylvania, in 1899 and the different reactions of men and women: "'You've got to take the pledge,' I said. 'Rise and pledge to stick to your brothers and the union till the strike's won!' The men shuffled their feet but the women rose, their babies in their arms, and pledged themselves to see that no one went to work in the morning."[35]

Mother Jones's confidence in the effectiveness of women's, particularly mothers' demonstration was legendary. "I told the men to stay home with the children for a change and let the women attend to the scabs. I organized an army of women housekeepers. On a given day they were to bring their mops and brooms and 'the army' would charge the scabs up at the mines."[36] In Jones's eyes, the heroism of this unruly lot, brandishing kitchen utensils, was in large part responsible for the Arnot strike's victory. In Hazelton, Pennsylvania, she summoned the women again and staged a theatrical action. "We marched over the mountains fifteen miles, beating on the tin pans as if they were cymbals. . . . [When meeting the militia, Jones said,] 'We are not enemies. . . . We are just a band of working women whose brothers and husbands are in a battle for bread. . . . We are here on the mountain road for our children's sake, for the nation's sake.' . . . When they saw the army of women in kitchen aprons, with dishpans and mops, they laughed and let us pass. An army of strong mining women makes a wonderfully spectacular picture."[37] Housewives who mobilized in Greensburg, Pennsylvania, were arrested and sentenced to thirty days in jail for provoking scabs. When the judge asked if the women could leave their children, Mother Jones told them to inform him that "miners' wives didn't keep nurse girls; that God gave the children to their mothers and He held them responsible for their care." On their way to jail, singing, carrying their babies, the women also roughed up some scabs who joined them in the transport car. "'Mother,' [the sheriff pleaded to Jones,] 'I would rather you brought me a hundred men than those women. Women are fierce!'" Mother Jones advised the women to continue their song through the night: "'Say you're singing to the babies.'" After complaints about the cat howls, Mother Jones retorted "'That's no way to speak of women who are singing patriotic songs and lullabies to their little ones.'" The women "no one could muzzle" were dismissed after five days.[38]

Empowered by symbolic motherhood, Mother Jones also involved children as strategic protesters. In 1903 she organized a parade of disabled youngsters—The March of the Mill Children—to highlight the tragedies of child labor: "I put the little boys with their fingers off and hands crushed and maimed on a platform. I held up their mutilated hands and showed them to the crowd and made the statement that Philadelphia's mansions were built on the broken bones, the quivering hearts and drooping heads of these children."[39]

Mother Jones has been a problematic figure for contemporary feminists, since she placed socialism and class interests above all else. Jones once told a meeting of suffragists, "'You don't need a vote to raise hell! You need convictions and a voice!'" When accused of being anti-suffragist, she responded, "'I am not an anti to anything which will bring freedom to my class.'"[40] She insisted that it was human rights rather than those of women or men that concerned her, feeling that vote pursual and charity deflected women's energies.[41] Mother Jones took a leading role in the United Mine Workers of America's fifteen-month-long Colorado Fuel and Iron Strike in 1913–14. Women, who weren't themselves members of the union, bore the brunt of high rent, soaring company store prices, harassment, and rape. Priscilla Long argues that despite Jones's recognition of gender power and women's militancy, she was "virulently anti-feminist." Although women, in Long's view, may have been radicalized in some respects as a result of strike involvement, traditional domestic divisions and long-term gender arrangements remained unchallenged.[42] More optimistic about union auxiliaries' radicalizing impact on women's political lives, Marjorie Lasky claims that they nevertheless "were constrained by the conservative nature of the very ideology that had enabled them to organize."[43]

To box the sophisticated maneuverings of Mother Jones into an "anti-feminist" corner because she didn't challenge gender inequality nor support suffrage, is to see the perennial half-empty glass. It is more useful to focus on how Jones, like Greenham and Igbo women, manipulated gender symbols toward radical ends. Gilbert points to how her artful costuming in long black skirt consciously milked the "mother" persona, which "not only got her down into the mines past a lot of murderous guards, but onto the stages of a hundred theaters and hallowed auditoriums, into the White House and the presence of forty years' worth of chief executives."[44] Strategic attire to manage impression reminds me of peace activist Helen Caldicott's urgings at public lectures for women to turn up at demonstrations wearing their pearls.

Although the impact of women's involvement in radical actions may not be immediate or apparent, in the longer run it can subvert traditional power hierarchies. Women tend to perform gender typed functions such as cooking food and running messages during strikes, but also offer perspectives and opportunities for evaluating gender-based roles. A writer in 1927 quoted one wife who became aware of the oppressive nature of her household responsibilities: "'the less work fer the men, the more we work. It's us has to put the children off till next day without food. It's us has to hold rags together to cover our bodies and our men's and babies. It's us has to cook meals with nothin' fit to cook, an' make bread with

water an' salt an' moldy flour. The men set an' jaw while we work our arms
loose: that's what a strike means.'"[45]

For some women housework during strikes becomes less routine and
life more precarious and precious. For others, strikes pave a route to shed-
ding traditional domestic patterns. How easily sixty-three-year-old Ma
Guynn from Lansing, Ohio, transformed herself from housewife to public protester, while her husband carried out her duties!

> "I was always a fighter. But somehow I never got right out into the
> thing as I did in this strike. I used to always stick in the house and sew
> patch-work quilts. And my lands, I was sick all the time! But now that
> I've got out fightin' and organizin' like this, I don't know a sick day.
> And I don't spend time cleanin' my house either, the way I used to. I
> used to think if I don't mop up that kitchen every day, something ter-
> rible would happen. But now I just leave everything and go out and
> fight. Pappy, he cleans up the place and washes the dishes. My boys
> don't have a clean shirt to their backs half the time, but they don't care.
> I just want to go out and FIGHT all the time."[46]

We don't know whether Ma Guynn assumed her "normal" household
role after the strike, but note that she realized that gender identity and
behavior were neither natural nor immutable. Women may accept traditional gender divisions to "keep the peace," fulfill reciprocal obligations
to husbands and children, but recognize that they are not bound by un-
alterable roles. While structural change may not immediately result from
strikes, the spectrum of possibilities enlarges. Priscilla Long tells how after the Ludlow Massacre in the Colorado Fuel and Iron strike, wives traveled the country speaking about conditions from a gendered perspective.
Mary Petrucci shared a class consciousness with her husband, but not
perceptions or experience. "Her consciousness was that of a miner's *wife;*
her experience of class oppression was a particularly female one; and her
class-conscious view of the world took a female form."[47] While Long concludes, as cited above, that oppression didn't produce a split between the
sexes, she admitted to some "new ideas under discussion."

Mother Jones, Ella May, Aunt Molly, Sarah, Ma Guynn, and Mary
Petrucci intertwined class and gender issues. Mother Jones's rhetoric, for
example, which included much about the position of women as wives,
didn't vary much from that of contemporary feminists. Although her
women's armies promoted the discourse of family and traditional role

divisions, as did union women's auxiliaries, they presented openings for disengagement from expected behavior, opportunities for self-esteem.

In this chapter I have looked at relationships among female consciousness and feminism, work, wifehood, and female militancy. I want now to consider the way women used song with maternalist discourse as a resistance tool. Songs integral to people's lives in Southern Appalachia, became, during hard times and strikes, organic vehicles for telling new stories. Although women and men both sang traditional and composed songs, women tended to highlight domestic concerns, family, and children's welfare. Transforming traditional texts into new stories became a way of writing people's history, recounting oppression and appeal for worker solidarity. Women songwriters like Odell Corley (a mere eleven years old!), Daisy McDonald, and Ella May moved beyond voicing powerlessness to persuading others of the benefits of union solidarity. Stephen Wiley believes that the significance of mill mothers' compositions (and this also applies to mining women's songs) "lies most basically in the extent . . . to which the singers in their participation in the strike through their art, made the raw experience of socioeconomic and gender exploitation over into a shared justification for withdrawal from an evil system and organized resistance to it. Their singing was both a public articulation and a strengthening of the resolve beneath their actions."[48]

In coal-mining communities, Molly's and Sarah's songs verbalized anger against the bosses and pleaded for union support. Florence Reece's "Which Side Are You On?" became an anthem, exemplifying the fusing of domestic concerns with ideological issues. What could be a more penetrating image than Florence scrawling words on the kitchen wall calendar to record her anguish!

Eleanor Kellogg, a miner's wife, wrote this to the tune of "My Bonnie Lies Over the Ocean."

> My children are seven in number,
> We have to sleep four in a bed;
> I'm striking with my fellow workers,
> To get them more clothes and more bread.
>
> *Refrain:*
> Shoes, shoes, we're striking for pairs of shoes,
> Shoes, shoes, we're striking for pairs of shoes.

Then, in an intriguing turnabout, Eleanor uses the male voice:

Pellagra is cramping my stomach,
My wife is sick with T.B;
My babies are starving for sweet milk,
Oh, there's so much sickness for me.
Milk, milk, we're striking for gallons of milk.[49]

For women in mining camps and mill towns, wife and motherhood was a key source of empowerment. Class and gender mingle in songs of resistance to the bosses. The Garland sisters, with very different personalities, were both clear about their primary caretaking obligations. They walked the picket lines as wives and mothers, capturing these experiences in songs they hoped would make a difference. Singer and songwriter Hazel Dickens portrays today, as Molly and Sarah did in their times, the lives of coal-mining men and women, recording their history, confirming their identity.[50] While Dickens's music comes to us through technologically sophisticated recordings and movie sound tracks, thus infinitely more accessible than Molly's or Sarah's, she joins the Garlands as part of a powerful historical conversation. They use women's songs as "weapons of the weak," the "stuff of revolution."

Although Molly wasn't reluctant, and was even proud, to report her facility with physical violence, she resisted largely through her songs. She told John Greenway "the truth" about how she wrote "Hungry Ragged Blues":

On the 17th morning in October my sister's little girl waked me up early. She had 15 little ragged children and she was taking them around to the soup kitchen to try to get them a bowl of soup. She told me some of them children had not eat anything in two days. It was a cold rainy morning; the little children was all bare-footed, and the blood was running out of the tops of their little feet and dripping down between their little toes onto the ground. You could track them to the soup kitchen by the blood. After they had passed by I just set down by the table and began to wonder what to try to do next. Then I began to sing out my blues to express my feeling. This song comes from the heart and not just from the point of a pen.[51]

Molly told Archie Green how she assembled a group of women to go into the mines, while singing her blues, confident about the power of her song: "I urged the eighteen men out on strike and threatened not to leave until they left. . . . They throwed their tools down and poured the water out of the bucket all together. I marched them all through the hills and me yelling, 'Sad and weary'. . . they didn't go back no more either. . . . It was a song that actually helped the miners win."[52]

While Molly's version of "Poor Miner's Farewell" varied from others by depicting herself as savior, it also inspires action rather than resignation. The following text is from the *Red Song Book,* compiled in 1932 by the Workers Music League (including Charles Seeger and Elie Siegmeister), and is, according to Archie Green, the first of Molly's songs to be published. The song's first two verses and chorus are traditional:

Poor hard working miners, their troubles are great,
So often while mining they meet their sad fate.
Killed by some accident, there's no one can tell,
Their mining's all over, poor miners farewell!
Chorus:
Only a miner, killed under the ground,
Only a miner but one more is gone.
Only a miner but one more is gone,
Leaving his wife and dear children alone.

They leave their dear wives and little ones, too,
To earn them a living as miners all do.
Killed by some accident, there's no one can tell,
Their mining's all over, poor miners farewell!

Chorus

Molly's own three added verses not only refer to hungry orphans, but inevitably credit her role in helping them:

Leaving his children thrown out on the street,
Barefooted and ragged and nothing to eat,
Mother is jobless, my father is dead,
I am a poor orphan, begging for bread.

Chorus

When I am in Kentucky so often I meet,
Poor coal miners' children out on the street.
"What are you doing?" to them I have said,
"We are hungry, Aunt Molly, and we're begging for bread."

Chorus

"Will you please help us to get something to eat?
We are ragged and hungry, thrown out on the street."
"Yes, I will help you," to them I have said,
"To beg food and clothing, I will help you to get bread."

Chorus[53]

Molly and Sarah claimed a special version of history, legitimized, authenticated by having lived as coal-mining wives and mothers. Aunt Molly proferred her talents to the Communists, cognizant of how they valued her as a prototypical Appalachian miner's wife. Sarah rejected an overtly "political" identification, clinging instead to her image of herself as simply a tradition bearer. But both understood how coal mining shaped the lives of women, how it kept them poor and exploited, how motherhood affected their perceptions of the world, and how telling those stories—their maternalist narratives of resistance—would appeal to others. "Dreadful Memories," which both sisters claimed to write first, illustrates this.

Molly tells the story of her version: "Thirty-seven babies died in my arms in the last three months of 1931. Their little stomach busted open; they was mortified inside. Oh, what an awful way for a baby to die. . . . Then four years later I still had such sad memories of these babies that I wrote this song."

Dreadful memories! How they linger;
How they pain my precious soul.
Little children, sick and hungry,
Sick and hungry, weak and cold.

Little children, cold and hungry,
Without any food at all to eat.
They had no clothes to put on their bodies;
They had no shoes to put on their feet.

Refrain:
Dreadful memories! How they linger;
How they fill my heart with pain.
Oh, how hard I've tried to forget them
But I find it all in vain.

I can't forget them, little babies,
With golden hair as soft as silk;
Slowly dying from starvation,
Their parents could not give them milk.

I can't forget them, coal miners' children,
That starved to death without one drop of milk,
While the coal operators and their wives and children
Were all dressed in jewels and silk.

Refrain:
Dreadful memories! How they haunt me
As the lonely moments fly.
Oh, how them little babies suffered!
I saw them starve to death and die.[54]

Although Sarah's words may differ from Molly's, her message is similar: that she, as other women (and men) in coal-mining communities, lived with fear of harassment, and haunting images of hungry and dying children. Ironically, Sarah concludes her version with optimism that resistance, political action will pay off:

Dreadful memories, how they linger,
How they ever flood my soul,
How the workers and their children,
Die from hunger and from cold.

Hungry fathers, worried mothers,
Living in those dreadful shacks.
Little children, cold and hungry,
With no clothing on their backs.

Dreadful gun-thugs and stool-pigeons,
Always flock around our door.
What is the crime that we committed?
Nothing, only that we poor.

When I think of all the heartaches,
And all the things that we've been through,
Then I wonder, how much longer,
And what a working man can do.

Really friends it doesn't matter
Whether you are black or white
The only way you'll ever change things
Is to fight and fight and fight

We will have to join the union,
They will help you find a way.
And to get a better living,
And for your work get better pay.[55]

Reflections: "Be a Grievin' after Me"

Cast your mind back to that fateful November day in 1931 when the Arjay Baptist Church bulged with witnesses and onlookers as Aunt Molly, the midwife, sang her "blues" about hunger and oppression. Instantly recognizing the answer to their ideological prayers, the panel of northern writers lured "Kentucky herself," in the body and soul of one mountain woman, to New York City to carry the torch for the striking miners. This began for Molly and later for her younger half sister, Sarah, a journey across multiple boundaries of region, music, and politics.

During the 1930s and early 1940s in New York, Aunt Molly Jackson and her family personified Southern Appalachia for the urban elite. Together with other singers, Leadbelly, and Woody Guthrie, they represented the rural poor, now on tenement steps, guests at society parties, hootenannies, and political rallies, testimony to another America.

Molly's historical moment, alas, was brief: her luster tarnished for the intellectuals who courted and befriended her; self-centeredness exasperated her family; she "stretched her blanket" once too often. Still, personality factors only partly accounted for the waning of her popularity. Broader causes had to do with the commercial homogenization of American aesthetic tastes, as well as the Left's swing to popular politics; interest in Molly as a symbol outlasted that in Molly as singer. Richard Reuss writes:

> Aunt Molly Jackson . . . was revered as a militant example of the Kentucky proletariat, admired for her ability to blend class sentiments with old mountain tunes, yet few radicals other than some of the Lomax

singers really enjoyed the harsh, tense sound of her voice, or the modal or minor-key tunes of many of her songs. In spite of later occasional publicity in the left-wing press, she seldom was asked to perform at progressive functions once the Dreiser hearings and the Harlan County coal struggles of the early thirties receded from public attention.[1]

Tracking Aunt Molly's life through contextual lenses magnifies her portrait: a young girl suffering the loss of her mother and cruelty of her teenaged stepmother, her attachment to preacher and coal miner father Oliver Garland, and early introduction to union activities. Molly's family's transient life in assorted coal towns, her touching loneliness, loves and marriages, the loss of her own babies, and subsequent mothering of her husbands' children, her midwifery experiences, her endurance through the coal depression. The entry of the Communist-run National Miners Union and strike in "Bloody Harlan" and Bell Counties. The invitation to New York City, comrades, admirers, and detractors in political/intellectual circles. Then, after Sarah comes to New York, the two women compared with one another.

Journeying through the Garland sisters' stories, I am struck by their similarities. Strong Appalachian women, they survived and resisted through their music. For both women, traditional song and their newly made protest songs became a way to remember, to communicate the remembering to others, to name injustices, to identify their place in the world. Molly and Sarah, distinctly different in personality, political orientation, and era—one brazenly sallying beyond the image of traditional singer and the other tenaciously clinging to it—yet both sang and wrote traditional and political songs. Aunt Molly cultivated her talents with the Communists, who delighted in and embraced them, while Sarah rejected ideological pigeonholes. But both sisters turned to the domestic sphere, to what they knew, as a microcosm to capture the way coal, capitalism, and industrialism curtailed human freedom and dignity.

The Garland sisters' songs, emblematic of particular class struggles in the early 1930s, and later of class, power, and regional differences on a global stage, take on new significance with today's resurgence of women's resistance music. Although neither sister's new compositions "entered tradition," some contemporary singers in the folk tradition know their names and their songs. Magpie (Terry Leonino and Greg Artzner), a Washington, D.C., based duo who perform socially conscious music, often include Molly's "I Am a Union Woman" in their sets, as a tribute to her courage and contributions. Song texts of both women (Molly's "I Am a Union Woman," and Sarah's "I Hate the Company Bosses") were reprinted in a book of women's poetry published in the 1970s.[2] Folklorist Ronald Cohen recently co-produced a comprehensive set of labor songs including Molly's and Sarah's.

Rooted in strategic identities as coal miners' wives and mothers, the women's songs connect to other women's experiences across time and place, and assume new meaning with contemporary feminist revision.

The two Garland sisters' lives, as we know, spanned a century, with the women inhabiting overlapping but diverse historical and political spaces. By the time Sarah left Kentucky, the radicalisms that inspired Molly began to fade, as did others' interest in her ideological message.

Molly and Sarah, paradigms of the radical and traditional, both migrated north, five years apart, through changing contexts of regionalism, radical politics, musical aesthetics and markets, scholarly inquiries, feminism—filters or magnifying glasses for our images of them. After her death in 1960, memory of Molly's iconoclasm dimmed for all but a few, while Sarah's personal renaissance paralleled the folk revival of the later 1950s through the 1960s.

As you know, Aunt Molly Jackson's urgency to tell her story, her intricate alliances with people, and the problematics of her "truths" inspired me. Although I conclude my writing with deep respect for Sarah, it is still Molly—midwife, miner's daughter, wife, mother, spinner of webs, teller of tall tales, stretcher of blankets—who most fascinates me. As feminists we write our subjects consciously, yet their impact on us remains less visible. Molly challenged me, in a different way than could any scholar, to attempt to understand a culture vastly different from my own and to venture into new intellectual territory—the politics of folk song. She compelled me to listen to diverse voices, perspectives, grapple with predicaments of representation and appropriation. An informant from the hereafter, Aunt Molly Jackson became mirror, accuser, cumbersome presence, looking over my shoulder, nudging from behind. Sometimes I felt angry at her bold-faced arrogance, then enormous empathy for her and personally attacked when I saw evidence of others' mocking or exploitation. The writing seemed to drag on and compete with other interests, but Molly beseeched me to complete her story. I began singing her songs as part of my academic conference papers, hoping that performance would reduce the gulf, connect me and others to an Appalachian mountain woman who died in 1960 at the age of eighty, the year that I, at twenty-one, graduated from Brooklyn College.

In *A Thrice-Told Tale,* Marjorie Wolf reflects on ethnographic practice and scholarly privilege:

> The anthropologist listens to as many voices as she can and then chooses among them when she passes their opinions on to members of another culture. The choice is not arbitrary, but then neither is the testimony. However, no matter what format the anthropologist/reporter/writer uses, she eventually takes the responsibility for putting down the words, for converting their possibly fleeting opinions into a text. I see no way to avoid this exercise of power and at least some of the stylistic requirements used to legitimate that text if the practice of ethnography is to continue.[3]

The lives of Molly and Sarah were theirs—but my own rendering of them leaves its stamp on the experiences, and the way readers will know them. Despite our postmodern attempts to "collaborate" with our subject, creating space for polyphonies and partialities, we remain empowered authors.

In these last pages, I want to revisit some issues surrounding two illusive concepts: truth and responsibility. Archie Green, senior folklorist and labor historian, remains enamored with younger Sarah, who never wavered through cultural-political storms and romantic revisionings. The essence of Sarah's radicalism lies, for Green, in her purity of style, integrated personality, synthesis of divergent positions—traditionalism, resistance, autonomy. Archie Green's Sarah was "incapable of dissimulation, exaggeration, or self-pity," with a "truth" that emerges from the preservation of her cultural legacy.[4] Sarah's resistance, for him, is embodied in her tradition. Less impressed with Molly, Green described the older Appalachian woman a few years before her death as "profane," "eager to talk," "filled with self-aggrandizement."

Green wasn't alone in his preference for the younger sister. The secretary who typed some transcriptions at my university told me how Sarah's voice and stories touched her, how she empathized with her misfortunes. Molly usually elicited different responses—amusement, appreciation of her theatricality, surprise at her conceit.

Images of Sarah's dignity and Molly's arrogance survived after their deaths. Sarah insisted on her integrity and centeredness, in contrast and perhaps *to* contrast herself to Molly. "I never wanted to change . . . anybody that ever know'd me in our life, if they hear my voice in the mountains of Kentucky in the darkest night they know it's me."[5]

But each woman kept referring to how the truth emanated from the depths of her soul. Molly's interpretive renderings didn't seem to shake her ardent belief in her facts, which were always, to her eyes, in service of a larger good. The Garland sisters thus continually competed with each other as *the* paramount truth teller.

Molly insisted that *others* and not *she* altered tradition. She balked when she thought that her songs were being tampered with, oblivious to her own modifications. Sarah remarked that Molly told stories so many times she believed them herself.[6] But while Sarah's truths continue to define her, Molly's truths fell by collectors' and folklorists' waysides, unvalidated, discredited. How do I, as writer of their stories, know who to believe? Does the truth of one mean the lies of another? We know that everyone remembers selectively, fictionalizes, informants and writers alike; as scholarly gatekeepers, we and our editors (not our informants) have the final say in published words. The questions then become: Why do people tell the stories that they do? How do they arrive at the truths they tell? Who are their (our) audiences for the stories, and what stake do they (we) have in the kinds of stories being told? Although Molly emerges as an egotistical and often unlikable woman, her truths came from deep within her—rooted in her perceptions of herself as witness, crusader, savior, visionary, witness. Defining herself by mission and struggle, she distorted details for the interest of important messages for future generations.

While I was wrestling with the issue of truth telling, a session on Latin American women's testimonials at the 1993 American Anthropological Association meetings in Washington, D.C., revealed some insights and led me to the literature. Remarkable parallels seemed to exist between Molly's stories and women's testimonials. The *testimonio,* as a form of subordinate survivor story, began to emerge during the 1970s and 1980s from the mouths of indigenous, radicalized men and women. These testimonials, in the recovering of women's history, join feminist revisions in several ways: breaking silences, raising consciousness, and merging personal and political concerns.[7] Rigoberta Menchú's *I, Rigoberta Menchú* (1984), Domitila

Barrios de Chungara's *Let Me Speak!* (1978), and Elvia Alvarado and Medea Benjamin's *Don't Be Afraid Gringo* (1987)—all translated into English—are three exemplars of books by Latin American women who wanted the world to know about the injustices, tortures, disappearances in their countries— they tell their stories for political reasons. Early family relationships, particularly experiences as girls and women, become crucial hinges for their political commitment and activism. Rather than rooting narratives in political party or movement, women's testimonials begin from personal history.[8] Testimonial differs significantly, however, from autobiography: one voice speaks for the collective truth. It isn't just the story of one, but of a whole community. One woman becomes every woman. Distinctions between feminism and female consciousness mute in this context.

Central to testimonial as political process are issues of collaboration and audience. Middle-class women, same sex intermediaries, become "silent" collaborators who translate, filter, negotiate the tellings. In the same way, middle-class consumers comprise the audience for whom authenticity lies in the witnesses' backgrounds and political ideologies, rather than in the particular details of their stories.

Testimonial literature's authenticity emerges from the witness who needs to urgently communicate, summoning truth to contradict official history. Truths may thus take other forms and meanings, serving the collective good. Anthropologist Lynn Stephen, collaborating with Salvadorean activist Maria Theresa Tula, suggests, "the true value of testimonials is a complex one . . . they contain within their text survival strategies that may conflict with readers' notions of wanting to know 'the whole truth.' . . . Rather than judge the contents against the supposedly objective record of journalists and social scientists, they should be valued for the vision and experience they represent."[9] Omissions and secrets become intentional choices, part of the purpose for telling the story.

Guatemalan activist Rigoberta Menchú's particular truths, as Molly's, were challenged, but the atrocities and losses she and others experienced have been validated.[10] Although Mother Jones ranked the dramatic over the factual, her stories were, for the most part, confirmed. We never doubt that Aunt Molly clutched dying babies in her arms, nursed injured and demoralized men, or aided haggard despairing mothers as they scavenged morsels for their children. Particular embellishments paled in comparison with the importance of garnering attention, performances geared to co-opting empathy and aid from the advantaged. Mission (aside from self-interest) drove Molly, as other testifiers, to speak for a plural subject. She produced songs, as Sarah produced songs, like Rigoberta and Maria's stories—to be heard, not necessarily *by* their communities, but *in the service* of their communities Although Molly's initial crusade was the Harlan coal miners, she shifted, when coal struggles were no longer in the limelight, to a more generalized cause: the oppression of marginal workers. In this light, the reasons for her particular castings, as those of other testifiers, become clearer. But we academics, collaborators, collectors, writers—the crucial "others" for the testifiers—fashion their realities for *our* audiences and purposes.

Although Molly's, as Sarah's, repertoire ranged widely from traditional ballads, religious songs, to bawdy songs, the particular composition that catapulted Molly out of Kentucky and into the public radical arena was a political ballad, "Ragged Hungry Blues"—an ideal testimonial offering a universal theme of oppression. Molly's songs fit with northern radical conceptions of people's music and were perceived, like testimonials today, as useful organizing devices to gain middle-class support. Although the Communists failed to win the strike in Harlan County, the ideology transferred successfully to New York City, where the songs served up powerful, concrete images, allowing city folk to connect with the miners and contribute money to ease their misfortunes.

Molly's scorn for the excesses of the rich parallels that of Rigoberta Menchú's. Remember the evening at Margaret Vance's house in Washington, D.C., when Molly was offered the evening gown; and the rage she felt toward Lord Morley's insensitive wife with her jangling diamonds: both stories serve as moralistic fables. Molly emphasizes willingness to do physical battle, perceiving herself as voice of the collective oppressed. Through stories of difference she delivers her message—that she couldn't be co-opted, knew her sense of place. Her power sprang from her "realness," as a coal miner's wife who understood exploitation from the inside.

As one of the marginal poor in New York, empowered by her contrast to soft-cushioned audiences, Molly felt entitled to tell her history. The Kentucky coal miner's wife-midwife-union organizer-songwriter's tellings became the stuff of authenticity. She survived the bloody and bludgeoned Harlan and Bell County during the late 1920s: this was enough. Molly's songs were of people oppressed, their attempts to triumph over evil.

Molly, like Domitila Barrios and Rigoberta Menchú, had contact with the organized left; but Domitila, like Molly, asserted that human needs and not official politics spurred her activism. In Domitila's words: "I don't owe my consciousness and my preparation to anything but the cries, the suffering, and the experiences of the people."[11] Molly would scoff in her usual way and say something like this: "If red is to be upset about hunger than I'm the reddest red you'd ever meet."

Molly, like Rigoberta, traveled away from home in order to appeal to urban audiences who could lend assistance. Rigoberta, like Molly, was subject to insinuations and accusations of sexual availability. Molly, in common with other women survivors, used personal and family experience as a basis for political insight. Most important, maternalist strategies generate the power behind their revolutionary tellings and actions. One Salvadoran witness says "'Having children is the most beautiful and most revolutionary experience there is. . . . As a mother, I can't just watch out for one child, there are millions of children in the country. . . . Maternity has a historical dimension and not just an individual one.'"[12] Rigoberta, although not a wife or mother, considers herself (not unlike Molly) as mother of all, "fighting for a people and for many children who hadn't anything to eat."[13]

But there are differences. Molly's personal triumphs seemed to take precedence over community, whereas in Latin American women's testimonials the collective seems to dampen the individual author's identity. To what extent can we attribute this to translators, collaborators, timing, diverse political contexts and strategies? Authorship of testimonial, despite the apparent plural voice, becomes problematic. Sternbach points to a dilemma: when we admire heroism, whose is it—the testifier, the intermediary, the collective?[14]

Molly, unlike the other witnesses whose testimonies emerge victoriously today in a politically supportive environment, lost sympathy when political winds blew cold and when folklorists like Mary Elizabeth Barnicle and Alan Lomax rejected her accounts as inaccurate or inflated. Molly, unlike Maria Theresa Tula, was never inspired or encouraged by a feminist movement, but by a radicalized urban left, whose gender interests were still unformed. It is interesting to imagine how Molly would be received today at feminist anthropology meetings. As a woman representing the rural poor telling of her own life experiences, would she not be taken seriously? Or would her haughty manner put listeners off? Unlike other survivors who produced written works during their lifetimes, Molly, as we know, sought her collaborator in vain. Had I known Molly in the flesh before 1960 would I, too, have shelved her story? But today, buttressed by feminist and postmodern vision, I vault at the challenge.

What about tradition? Roger Abrahams, writing of traditional singer, Granny Almeida Riddle, suggests that individuality and creativity are expressed through repertoire choice and preference, and understanding of community values.[15] As creator of new songs and not merely a singer of old, Molly would defy these constraints. But Molly's "realness" as a mountain woman allowed her the right to alter traditional songs and to criticize outsiders, who lacked such privilege. She thought of (not real) singers like Burl Ives as "material thiefs" because he "rearranged them around 'til they don't make no sense."

In an exchange in Sacramento with Archie Green in the late 1950s, we can see Molly expressing this sense of prerogative:

> A: A folk song is this, that the people makes up them songs out of their own lives about their sweethearts and about their wives and about the way they live . . . then they [others] change them around and I think it's very wrong, simply because on the account of ancestors, the tradition of our ancestors. I think they should be left just like our ancestors compose them. . . . Then if these young peoples growing up, if they want their rock and roll and their jitterbug stuff, let them compose it themselves. . . . That's the way I feel about it and I don't hestitate to tell nobody.
>
> Q: Aunt Molly, if you knew someone that knew part of the song and they really wanted to sing it and they couldn't, I mean someone that knew part of the song and they wanted to sing it and they couldn't remember the whole thing and they just sort of filled in the parts they didn't remember in order to make it make sense.
>
> A: But these people in New York, in the West here, well all around, they tried to fill in and they don't know what they're talking about. Like Old Burl Ives took that song and had it "On Top of Ol' Smokey" when I know as well as I'm a standing here that there's no such a place as "On Top of Ol' Smokey" because "Ol' Smokey" is a valley three miles and a half from the county seat of Knox County [in Kentucky]. . . . It is really Down in Ol Smokey, all covered with snow, I lost loving Nancy by courtin' too slow.

Ives's version, Molly claims, is a mixture of this song and one she wrote about advice to young women about getting married that he heard her sing at a party.[16]

The further dissimilarity between Molly's testimonial and those today is, of course, the most obvious. While joint participation between testifier and translator (collaborator) generally involves ongoing negotiations with the journalist or academic who produces written work, Molly cannot negotiate with me in person. The problems I face in telling the Garland sisters' lives also differ from those of living collaborators. While I don't have to struggle in the flesh with Molly or Sarah, I think about the Garland sisters' family, the trust they showed me in sharing information and photographs for my book, their claim on the images of the two women, and on the family's history. What responsibilities do I have in not revealing certain parts of the story that may be hurtful to their public image? How do I deal with disagreements they may have with the way I represent the Garlands? How do I treat material that may be sensitive and problematic for scholars whose letters I have come across, or who have shared stories with me? Anthropologists frequently encounter dilemmas in the field, conflict between close relationships and the consequences of writing about living persons' lives. This becomes a particular dilemma for feminists who become personally involved with many of their informants and choose not to violate confidences even if their resulting ethnographies suffer.[17]

I return briefly to Portelli, whose interest in oral history's partiality, artificiality, variation, rather than "objectivity" or detachment, parallels my own feminist thinking about material. As in testimonial, the narrators of oral history strive to make sense of the past and set it in context: "the most precious information may be in what the informants *hide,* and in the fact that they *do* hide it, rather than in what they *tell.*" Portelli, too, would see Molly as a narrator, whose consciousness arrests at climactic moments of personal experience, a resistance fighter who becomes "wholly absorbed by the totality of the historical event of which [she was a] part, and [whose] account assumes the cadences and wording of *epic*" (italics in original).[18] My fascination with Molly as an oral informant is *not* in her specific truths, but in the *variations* in her tales, her *artifice,* her *partialness.* John Greenway, without benefit of postmodern constructions, understood Molly well. His insightful appreciation of her in her memorial issue of the *Kentucky Folklore Record,* 1961, bears repeating. The "good informant is above all things else an imaginative creator who molds the traditional material inherited by his group into a unique expression of the best things in himself and his people, and in so doing is *willing to sacrifice a small fact for a greater truth*" (italics mine). Despite Greenway's disappointments with Molly, he concluded that she was a "great informant."[19] Clearly, scholars, collectors, journalists have spurred Molly to recount her life, spin the webs that intrigued them. Her inconsistencies with dates, times, accounts may make the resulting story more complete, even plausible because remembrances don't come neatly packaged. My attempts to recount it, taking responsibility for it, become the essence of what Portelli would call radical history.

My story of Aunt Molly Jackson and her sister, Sarah, Appalachian women, led me to questions about how and why history gets told, its cultural/political production. With respect for the role of tradition as resistance to mass culture, I am more interested in the process of and reasons for its construction rather than the end product. The Garland sisters' repertoires and song careers shifted between traditional and composed. Both learned Appalachian repertoire as young children, later writing resistance texts geared to political moments. The time frames, as we know, and reasons for each of their shifts differ. Sarah altered her Appalachian repertoire with resistance texts after she moved to New York, while Molly penned new words (or so she reports) at much earlier junctures in her life. In the early 1930s, radicals inspired Molly's texts, while later in the decade Barnicle and Lomax culled both sisters' traditional songs. By the end of the 1930s, the wider appreciation for people's music in urban areas resulted in homogenization, when, according to Archie Green, Sarah's "hootenanny friends had begun to flatten folk style on the pop culture anvil."[20] When Archie Green met Molly in the 1950s he urged her to tap her traditional inventory, and in the 1960s asked Sarah to do the same.

The powerful centrality enjoyed by Aunt Molly, as both political missionary and traditional exponent, receded sharply by the late 1930s. With memories of Harlan faded, radical unionism pushed aside by nationalist solidarity, and the economic surge generated by President Roosevelt's war-related programs, Molly's ideological stance shifted. So strongly associated with labor militancy from the Kentucky coalfield days, she outlived her usefulness as symbol in the altered political times.

Mary Elizabeth Barnicle used Molly primarily as a cultural source of Appalachian life, midwifery experiences, and ghost tales, which she carefully recorded for her intended book. But as we know, the English professor's faith in Molly's reliability gradually declined, so that ultimately she deserted the project, along with detailed notes on mountain lore (now in archive). When she no longer trusted Molly's tellings, and was unable to distinguish "true" information from her informant's "inventions," Barnicle threw in the towel. Years later, Archie Green persistently pumped old crotchety Molly for her knowledge of traditional song, leading her back to her sources, trying to wring sense out of her inconsistencies. Frustrated by her continually changing accounts, he turned to Sarah as a more "reliable source."

By the time Sarah moved north, the National Miners Union had slipped into oblivion. Further from the ideological battles that defined Molly's relationships, the younger sister sought refuge in her roots. She came to value, first through Barnicle, then through Archie Green and Ellen Stekert, her Appalachianality. Sarah concluded that mountain people were more content than those in the city: "They never had a big lot of things and they don't really want them because of what you never had."[21] When Green visited Sarah in Detroit in 1963 he was determined to immortalize her extensive repertoire of traditional, labor, and sacred songs. His and Stekert's passionate interest in traditional song inevitably must have inspired Sarah's thinking of herself in these terms. They also arranged gigs for Sarah's return in the early and middle 1960s—Newport, University of Chicago, Carnegie Hall. In the early 1970s, Sarah performed at the Mariposa Folk Festival in Toronto. Appearing on festival stages as a "traditional" singer, Sarah's composed resistance repertoire didn't conflict with this definition.

Political ideologies and folklore scholars thus shaped both sister's repertoires and self-definitions. Both women felt let down when trusted friends like Alan Lomax didn't pay for their songs, or misrepresented ways they would be used. Sarah, in her interviews, revealed a sophistication regarding her feelings of exploitation by others. Although Molly too felt exploited and very bitter, I believe she never became as cynical as Sarah, who by the 1960s had gained perspective on her past. Molly's focus remained more local, personal, and narrowly ideological. Sarah's ironically broadened with exposure, as she felt the impact of folk music's commercialization and early second-wave feminist interest in her songs. Her resistance, if not radicalism, expressed itself more subtly than Molly's.

The Appalachian songmakers, both resistant women, pursued different avenues to self-fulfillment. Molly hoped to change the world and be acknowledged for her triumphs. Sarah wanted to preserve the traditions that identified her. "Liar" and "Truthteller": both told a kind of truth, but arrived at their versions for diverse reasons. One moving beyond traditional song and image, the other embracing it, both had repertoires expressing a politic. Although she later denied it, Aunt Molly banked her fortunes on the radicals who showed interest in her as archetype. Sarah rejected assimilation, co-optation, but sang with a bite and an anti-establishment vision. Both women understood exploitation, both witnessed and testified, felt connected to, responsible for others' lives as wives and mothers.

How do I want Molly and Sarah to be remembered? As women who understood the political significance of personal experience. As mothers who saw organizing potential in maternalist discourse. As singers confident that songs could vault chasms of gender, class, and region, and reach into souls. These Appalachian women, in different ways, tried to make a difference. With issues of identity at the core of contemporary conflicts over citizenship, territory, and cultural dominance, their stories are as timeless as the reasons for telling them.

PROFESSOR ROMALIS, known as "Shelly" (with scattered papers, tape recorder and laptop on her desk, eyeglasses poised on her nose, bookshelves in the background): Aunt Molly, how do you feel about me writing about your life?

AUNT MOLLY JACKSON (a wizened almost eighty, faded flowered dress, in a straight-backed chair, corn cob pipe clamped between her yellowed teeth, legs apart, and an air of impatience): Well, it took you long enough! You played that Archie Green's tapes so many times, you'll wear 'em out! I hope you'll tell the truth about my life, and not be like them others who lied to me and mommicked my words.

SHELLY (with appeasing tone): I'm trying, Aunt Molly, to tell the truth but you probably won't be happy with my version either. Did you know that I've been singing "Ragged Hungry Blues" and "Only a Miner" in some of my conference papers?

MOLLY (belligerently perched on the edge of her chair, annoyed with me): Hmmff! What do you know about the songs I learned from a time I was a baby? How can you sing about coal miners, coming from that cushy house in Brooklyn, and now with that fancy university job . . . you never laid eyes on the poverty and suffering that I did . . . !

(Then with a smirk): My "Blues" sure got them writers where they sit! I can see Dreiser now starin' at me. . . . (a snort and shift in topic): When I think about all them bloody capitalist material thiefs that stole my songs—you're probably one of them too. I hope you know it was *me,* not that mewly mouthed Sarah, that wrote "Dreadful Memories" and that it was *me* and not Jim Garland, that wrote the song about poor Harry Simms.

(Then puffing up): Oh, I could open my mouth and sing for years and not do the same song twicet [*sic*].

(Finally, backing off a bit): Well, I hope you write the book . . . not like that Lomax, and Barnicle and Earl Robinson who promised me and let me down. But you be careful now of not talking high falootin' language. At least some people will know how them coal bosses made us suffer. All I can say is I hope they'll finally know the truth!

Notes

AMJ   Aunt Molly Jackson

BCP   Barnicle-Cadle Papers, Schlesinger Library, Radcliffe College, Cambridge, Massachusetts

Green tape   Tape-recorded interviews conducted by Archie Green with AMJ at Sacramento, California, 1957–59: FT 2828–FT 2841, FT 4288–FT 4290, FT 4296–FT 4298, FT 4292–FT 4294 (John Greenway); with SOG at Detroit, Michigan: FT 2780 (Jan. 2, 1964), FT 2781 (Jan. 3, 1964, with Dolores Pascal), FT 2782 (Jan. 3, 1964, with Ellen Stekert and Oscar Paskal), FT 2783–FT 2785 (Mar. 3, 1964, with Ellen Stekert); all tapes on deposit at the Southern Folklife Collection, Wilson Library, University of North Carolina at Chapel Hill

Greenway tape   Tape-recorded interviews conducted by John Greenway with AMJ sometime before 1961 (FT 4291, FT 4295), on deposit in the Green collection at the Southern Folklike Collection, Wilson Library, University of North Carolina at Chapel Hill

SOG   Sarah Ogan Gunning

Stekert tape   Tape-recorded interviews conducted by Ellen Stekert with SOG at Detroit, Michigan: FT 2786–FT 2787 (June 2, 1964), FT 2788–FT 2789 (Nov. 6, 1964 and Dec. 3, 1964), FT 2790–FT 2791 (Dec. 20, 1964), FT 2792–FT 2793 (Apr. 19, 1968); all tapes on deposit at the Southern Folklife Collection, Wilson Library, University of North Carolina at Chapel Hill

Introduction

1. Denisoff, *Great Day Coming,* 68.
2. Greenway, "Aunt Molly Jackson as an Informant," 146.
3. Kohli, "Biography," 70–71.

4. See Clifford and Marcus, *Writing Culture.*

5. Polier and Roseberry, "Tristes Tropes."

6. Portelli, *Death of Luigi Trastulli,* 49.

7. Ibid., 50–51.

8. Moore, *Feminism and Anthropology,* 6.

9. See Caplan, "Engendering Knowledge"; di Leonardo, *Gender at the Crossroads of Knowledge;* and Ginsburg and Tsing, *Uncertain Terms.*

10. See Behar, *Translated Woman;* Behar and Gordon, *Women Writing Culture;* and Wolf, *Thrice-Told Tale.*

11. Joan Scott, *Gender and the Politics of History.*

12. Portelli, *Death of Luigi Trastulli,* 51.

13. Popular Memory Group, "Popular Memory," 243.

14. Langness and Frank, *Lives,* 93.

15. See Whisnant, *All That Is Native and Fine,* for a sophisticated analysis.

16. See Eller, *Miners, Millhands, and Mountaineers.*

17. Garland, *Welcome the Traveler Home,* 65.

18. Geiger, "Women's Life Histories."

19. For example: Kaplan, "Female Consciousness and Collective Action"; Romalis, "Carrying Greenham Home."

20. James Scott, *Weapons of the Weak.*

21. Archie Green, interviews and discussions with the author, in person and by phone, 1989–95. All subsequent unattributed Archie Green quotes in the text are from these interviews and discussions.

22. Greenway, *American Folksongs of Protest,* 8.

23. For example, Torgovnick, *Gone Primitive.*

24. Popular Memory Group, "Popular Memory," 243.

25. Handler and Linnekin, "Tradition, Genuine or Spurious," 281.

Chapter 1: "Hard Times in Coleman's Mines"

The chapter title comes from one of Aunt Molly Jackson's songs (though Jim Garland also claims to have written the song).

1. Raitz and Ulack, *Appalachia, a Regional Geography,* 19–22.

2. Coles, *Migrants, Sharecroppers, Mountaineers,* 277.

3. Shapiro, *Appalachia on Our Mind.*

4. Whisnant, *All That Is Native and Fine.*

5. Sharp, *English Folksongs;* Malone, *Southern Music, American Music,* 31–32.

6. Batteau, *Invention of Appalachia.*

7. Cunningham, *Apples on the Flood.*

8. Shifflet, *Coal Towns,* 15–16.

9. See McCauley, *Appalachian Mountain Religion,* for an extensive analysis.

10. Mary Elizabeth Barnicle-Cadle, handwritten notes for a class on "American Folklore" taught at New York University, Nov. 12, 1935, BCP.

11. AMJ, untitled autobiographical notes, typescript, Sept. 5, 1945[?], 16, BCP.

12. Ibid., 6.

13. Garland, *Welcome the Traveler Home,* 24.

14. Eller, *Miners, Millhands, and Mountaineers,* 64.

15. Ross, *Machine Age in the Hills,* 50.

16. Korson, *Coal Dust on the Fiddle,* 32.

17. Thomas, *Ballad Makin' in the Mountains of Kentucky,* 153.

18. Eller, *Miners, Millhands, and Mountaineers,* 162.

19. Keely, "Successful Wives in Coal Camps," 591.

20. Shifflet, *Coal Towns,* 85.

21. Garland, *Welcome the Traveler Home,* 65.

22. Kirchwey, "Miners' Wives in the Coal Strike," 83.

23. Ibid., 89.

24. Greenway, *American Folksongs of Protest,* 255.

25. Mary Elizabeth Barnicle-Cadle, "Early Marriage and Child Bearing," hand-written notes, n.d., BCP.

26. Shifflet, *Coal Towns,* 48.

27. Corbin, *Life, Work, and Rebellion,* 38.

28. Portelli, *Death of Luigi Trastulli,* 201.

29. Ibid., 205.

30. Garland, *Welcome the Traveler Home,* 53.

31. Mary Elizabeth Barnicle-Cadle, "AMJ (Alan's Note)," handwritten notes, n.d., BCP.

32. Korson, *Coal Dust on the Fiddle,* 17.

33. Malone, *Southern Music, American Music,* 58–59.

34. Garland, *Welcome the Traveler Home,* 79.

35. Ibid., 101.

36. Gaventa, *Power and Powerlessness,* 93.

Chapter 2: "I Am a Union Woman"

The chapter title comes from one of Aunt Molly Jackson's songs.

1. Dos Passos, "Harlan," 63.

2. Ibid.

3. Ross, *Machine Age in the Hills,* 169–70.

4. Garland, *Welcome the Traveler Home,* 142.

5. Draper, "Communists and Miners," 375.

6. Ross, *Machine Age in the Hills,* 175.

7. Garland, *Welcome the Traveler Home,* 145.

8. Draper, "Communists and Miners," 391.

9. Garland, *Welcome the Traveler Home,* 147.

10. Tillman Cadle, interview with the author, Dec. 6–7, 1989, Rich Gap, Tenn.

11. Garland, *Welcome the Traveler Home,* 130.

12. Ibid., 149.

13. AMJ, Green tape FT 2841.

14. Garland, *Welcome the Traveler Home,* 169–71.

15. Ibid., 171.

16. Swanberg, *Dreiser,* 384.

17. Dos Passos, "The Miners Speak for Themselves," 153–54.

18. Dos Passos, "Free Speech Speakin's," 279–83.

19. Quoted in National Committee, "Aunt Molly Jackson's Kentucky Miners' Wives Ragged Hungry Blues," v–vii.

20. Garland, *Welcome the Traveler Home,* 149–50.

21. Hevener, *Which Side Are You On?* 65.

22. Crawford, "What Have We to Lose," 8.

23. Swanberg, *Dreiser,* 386.

24. Gaventa, *Power and Powerlessness,* 114.

25. Johnson, "Starvation and the 'Reds' in Kentucky," 141.

26. Gaventa, *Power and Powerlessness,* 108, quoting from the *Middlesboro News,* Feb. 12, 1932.

27. Ibid., 110. This summary appeared in the *Middlesboro Daily News,* Nov. 18, 1931.

28. Garland, *Welcome the Traveler Home,* 149.

29. Draper, "Communists and Miners," 385–86.

30. Dos Passos, "Harlan," 67.

31. Portelli, *Death of Luigi Trastulli,* 223.

32. Gaventa, *Power and Powerlessness,* 113.

33. Portelli, *Death of Luigi Trastulli,* 224. Although this quote isn't attributed directly to Molly, the content strongly suggests that it is hers. But according to the text, the quote came from a miner.

34. AMJ, Green tape FT 4289.

35. Cadle interview. Subsequent citations in this chapter appear in the text.

36. Garland, *Welcome the Traveler Home,* 152.

37. Ibid., 152–53.

38. Ibid., 153.

39. Ibid., 143

40. Portelli, *Death of Luigi Trastulli,* 216–38.

41. Ross, *Machine Age in the Hills,* 183.

42. Quoted in Portelli, *Death of Luigi Trastulli,* 232.

43. Quoted in Draper, "Communists and Miners," 386.

44. Ross, *Machine Age in the Hills,* 185.

45. Portelli, *Death of Luigi Trastulli,* 235.

46. Quotes from Draper, "Communists and Miners," 387.

47. Tippett, *When Southern Labor Stirs,* 32.

48. Draper, "Communists and Miners," 387.

49. Crawford, "What Have We to Lose?" 8.

50. Anderson quoted in National Committee, "I Want to Be Counted," 303.

51. Ibid., 306–7.

52. Dos Passos, "Harlan," 64.

53. Ibid., 66.

54. Dos Passos, "Free Speech Speakin's," 288.

55. Dos Passos, "Harlan," 62.

56. AMJ, "I Am from Kentucky Born."

Chapter 3: "I Was Born and Raised in Old Kentucky"

The chapter title comes from one of Aunt Molly Jackson's songs.

1. AMJ, "The Story of My Life by Aunt Molly Jackson, Herself: Chapter One," typescript, n.d., 3–4, BCP.

2. Ibid.

3. AMJ, Green tape FT 4288.

4. AMJ, Greenway tape FT 4295.

5. AMJ, "Story of My Life," 4–5.

6. Garland, *Welcome the Traveler Home,* 41.

7. Greenway, *American Folksongs of Protest,* 254.

8. Ibid., 254–55.

9. AMJ, "Story of My Life," 6.

10. Ibid., 5.

11. AMJ, "By Aunt Molly—Monday, Oct. 8, 1945," typescript, n.p., BCP.

12. AMJ, "Story of My Life," 4. Elsewhere, Molly gives the date as December 16.

13. AMJ, untitled autobiographical notes, 3.

14. AMJ, "By Aunt Molly."

15. Garland, *Welcome the Traveler Home,* 44.

16. Ibid., 62.

17. AMJ, "Story of My Life," 8.

18. AMJ, Green tape FT 4288.

19. AMJ, "By Aunt Molly."

20. Ibid.

21. Ibid.

22. Ibid.

23. Ibid.

24. Greenway, *American Folksongs of Protest,* 255.

25. AMJ, "By Aunt Molly."

26. Although Molly always referred to Jim Stewart as her first husband, Jim Garland claims she married John Mills before him. AMJ, Green tape FT 2838; Garland, *Welcome the Traveler Home,* 45.

27. AMJ, "By Aunt Molly."

28. Ibid.

29. Mary Elizabeth Barnicle-Cadle, "Notes on Aunt Molly Jackson: Dictation Taken December 1 and 2nd, pp. 1–35 (1935?)," typescript, 6, BCP.

30. Ibid., 7.

31. AMJ, "By Aunt Molly."

32. AMJ, untitled autobiographical notes, 2.

33. Ibid., 3

34. Ibid.

35. Garland, *Welcome the Traveler Home,* 63.

36. AMJ, Green tape FT 4292.

37. Ibid.

38. Mary Elizabeth Barnicle-Cadle, "Education," handwritten ms., n.d., BCP.

39. Barnicle-Cadle, "Notes on Aunt Molly Jackson," 38.

40. AMJ, "By Aunt Molly."

41. Valentine Ackland, "Aunt Mollie [*sic*] Jackson—Revolutionary," typescript of interview for *The Daily Worker,* n.d., BCP.

42. AMJ, "By Aunt Molly."

43. AMJ, Green tape FT 2839.

44. Garland, *Welcome the Traveler Home,* 33.

45. Barnicle-Cadle,"Notes on Aunt Molly Jackson," 24–25.

46. Ibid., 25, 27.

47. Ibid., 18.

48. Ibid., 33–35.

49. Ibid., 30–32.

50. Greenway, *American Folksongs of Protest,* 258.

51. AMJ, untitled autobiographical notes, 1.

52. Mary Elizabeth Barnicle-Cadle, "Aunt Molly Jackson," typescript, n.d., 3, BCP.

53. AMJ, untitled autobiographical notes, 5.

54. Ibid.

55. Ibid., 6.

56. Ibid., 8.

57. Ibid., 9.

58. Ibid., 10.

59. AMJ, Green tape FT 2838.

60. Garland, *Welcome the Traveler Home,* 64.

61. Greenway, "Aunt Molly Jackson and Robin Hood," 23–24.

62. AMJ, Green tape FT 2839.

63. Ibid.

64. Green, *Only a Miner,* 82.

65. AMJ, Green tape FT 2838.

66. Greenway, *American Folksongs of Protest,* 258.

67. AMJ, Green tape FT 2838.

68. Mary Elizabeth Barnicle-Cadle, handwritten notes dated Nov. 30, 1937, 17–18, BCP.

69. Green, "Ben Robertson Meets Aunt Molly," 136.

70. Garland, *Welcome the Traveler Home,* 64.

71. Greenway, *American Folksongs of Protest,* 259.

72. Garland, *Welcome the Traveler Home,* 64.

73. AMJ, Green tape FT 4289.

74. Tosches, "Interview with Al Dexter," 5.

75. Garland, *Welcome the Traveler Home,* 147.

76. Ackland, "Aunt Mollie [*sic*] Jackson," 4.

77. Ibid., 3–4.

78. Ibid., 4.

79. AMJ, "By Aunt Molly."

80. AMJ, Green tape 4290.

81. AMJ, "By Aunt Molly."

82. Garland, *Welcome the Traveler Home,* 130.

83. Dos Passos, "Free Speech Speakin's," 278.
84. National Committee, "Aunt Molly Jackson's Kentucky Miners' Wives Ragged Hungry Blues," v–vii.

Chapter 4: "Christmas Eve on the East Side"

The chapter title comes from one of Aunt Molly Jackson's songs.

1. Green, "Ben Robertson Meets Aunt Molly," 134.
2. Ibid., 136.
3. Ibid., 134.
4. Greenway, *American Folksongs of Protest,* 259–60; second verse from AMJ, Green tape FT 4289.
5. Catalog number 15731-D, Matrix number W152040 and W152041.
6. Garland, *Welcome the Traveler Home,* 171.
7. AMJ, Green tape FT 4289.
8. Federal Writers' Project, *Guide to 1930s New York,* 108.
9. Garland, *Welcome the Traveler Home,* 171.
10. Note in the author's possession.
11. Greenway, *American Folksongs of Protest,* 260.
12. Garland, *Welcome the Traveler Home,* 182.
13. Ibid., 63.
14. Greenway, Recording Notes: "The Songs and Stories of Aunt Molly Jackson," 2.
15. Denning, *Cultural Front,* 4.
16. Klein, *Woody Guthrie,* 146.
17. Howe, "New York in the Thirties," 242.
18. Henrietta Yurchenco, interview with the author, May 18–19, 1990, New York, N.Y.
19. Ackland, "Aunt Mollie [*sic*] Jackson," 6.
20. Ibid.
21. AMJ, "By Aunt Molly."
22. Greenway, *American Folksongs of Protest,* 260.
23. Barnicle-Cadle, "Miscellaneous Selection of Songs," typescript, n.d., BCP.
24. Greenway, *American Folksongs of Protest,* 265.
25. Reuss, "American Folklore and Left-Wing Politics," 56–57.
26. Gordon, *Mark the Music,* 99.
27. Reuss, "Roots of American Left-Wing Interest in Folksong," 270.
28. Quoted in Dunaway, "Charles Seeger and Carl Sands," 165.
29. Reuss, "American Folklore and Left-Wing Politics," 89.
30. Ibid., 64.
31. Reuss, "Folk Music and Social Conscience," 236.
32. Seeger, "Folkness of the Non-Folk vs. the Non-Folkness of the Folk," 4.
33. Seeger, *Incompleat Folksinger,* 558.
34. Dunaway, *How Can I Keep from Singing,* 57.
35. Pete Seeger, telephone interview with the author, Nov. 22, 1989.

36. Barnicle-Cadle, "American Folklore" course notes, Nov. 12, 1935.
37. Cadle interview.
38. Smyth, "Album Notes."
39. Garland, *Welcome the Traveler Home,* 183.
40. Lomax, "Aunt Molly Jackson," 131.
41. Alan Lomax, telephone interview with the author, Nov. 19, 1990.
42. Greenway, "Aunt Molly Jackson and Robin Hood," 25.
43. AMJ, Green tape FT 4289.
44. AMJ, "Listen and I'll Tell You," taped interview with Alice McLerran (including songs), 1959–60, Sacramento, Calif., copy in author's possession.
45. Ibid., "Come Listen."
46. AMJ, Green tape FT 4293.
47. Wolfe and Lornell, *Life and Legend of Leadbelly,* 204.
48. AMJ, Green tape FT 4290.
49. Klein, *Woody Guthrie,* 164–65.
50. Wolfe and Lornell, *Life and Legend of Leadbelly,* 217.
51. Guthrie, "Hell Busts Loose in Kentucky," 139.
52. Ibid., 139.
53. Garland, *Welcome the Traveler Home,* 182.
54. AMJ, interview with Fred Romanowski, 1938, transcript in BCP.
55. Cadle interview.
56. Wolfe and Lornell, *Life and Legend of Leadbelly,* 217.
57. Garland, *Welcome the Traveler Home,* 183–84.
58. Cadle interview.
59. Hazel Garland, interview with the author, January 19, 1990, Bellevue, Wash.
60. Cadle interview.
61. Yurchenco interview.
62. Denisoff, *Great Day Coming,* 68.
63. Klein, *Woody Guthrie,* 148.
64. Reuss, "American Folklore and Left-Wing Politics," 184.
65. AMJ, Green tape FT 2839.
66. AMJ, "By Aunt Molly."
67. Green, *Only a Miner,* 83.
68. Greenway, "Aunt Molly Jackson and Robin Hood," 24.
69. Greenway, "Aunt Molly Jackson as an Informant," 141.
70. Baggelaar and Milton, *Folk Music,* 199.
71. AMJ, untitled autobiographical notes, 12.
72. Greenway, "Great Rebel Passes On," 31.
73. Alice McLerran, personal communication, March 30, 1992.

Chapter 5: "Girl of Constant Sorrow"

The chapter title comes from one of Sarah Ogan Gunning's songs.

1. Cantwell, "When We Were Good," 190.
2. SOG, "My Name Is Sarah Ogan Gunning," 15.

3. SOG, Stekert tape FT 2787.
4. SOG, "My Name Is Sarah Ogan Gunning," 15.
5. SOG, Green tape FT 2780.
6. SOG, Green tape FT 2785.
7. SOG, Stekert tape FT 2788.
8. SOG, Green tape FT 2782.
9. Ibid.
10. SOG, "My Name Is Sarah Ogan Gunning," 16.
11. SOG, Green tape FT 2782.
12. Ibid.
13. Ibid.
14. Green, Notes to *Girl of Constant Sorrow*, 7–8.
15. SOG, Green tape FT 2781.
16. SOG, Green tape FT 2785.
17. SOG, Green tape FT 2782.
18. Ibid.
19. SOG, "My Name Is Sarah Ogan Gunning," 15.
20. Guthrie, "Story of Sara Ogan," 154–55.
21. Green, "Folklorist's Creed and Folksinger's Gift," 42.
22. SOG, Stekert tape FT 2786.
23. SOG, "My Name Is Sarah Ogan Gunning," 16.
24. Ibid., 17.
25. SOG, Green tape FT 2782.
26. SOG, Green tape FT 2785.
27. SOG, Stekert tape FT 2788.
28. Ibid.
29. SOG, Green tape FT 2782.
30. SOG, Stekert tape FT 2788.
31. SOG, Green tape FT 2782.
32. Ibid.
33. Ibid.
34. Ibid.
35. Smyth, "Album Notes."
36. SOG, Green tape FT 2785.
37. Ibid.
38. SOG, Stekert tape FT 2791.
39. SOG, Green tape FT 2785.
40. SOG, Green tape FT 2782.
41. SOG, Stekert tape FT 2789.
42. SOG, Green tape FT 2782.
43. Ibid.
44. SOG, Green tape FT 2785.
45. Stekert, "Cents and Nonsense in the Urban Folksong Movement," 91 n. 10.
46. Green, Notes to *Girl of Constant Sorrow*, 12–14.
47. SOG, Green tape FT 2785.
48. SOG, Green tape FT 2782.

49. Ibid.
50. SOG, Green tape FT 2785.
51. SOG, Green tape FT 2782.
52. Ibid.
53. Green, "Folklorist's Creed and Folksinger's Gift," 44.
54. SOG, Stekert tape FT 2789.
55. Ibid.
56. SOG, "My Name Is Sarah Ogan Gunning," 16.

Chapter 6: "White Pilgrims in the Foreign Heathen Country"

The chapter title combines two traditional songs: "The White Pilgrim" and "In the Foreign Heathen Country."

1. Cohen, "Overview, John Cohen I," 26.
2. Neil Rosenberg, "Introduction," 2.
3. Denisoff, *Great Day Coming,* 68–76.
4. Seeger, *Incompleat Folksinger,* 557–58.
5. Denisoff, *Great Day Coming,* 74.
6. Seeger, *Incompleat Folksinger,* 15.
7. Cantwell, *When We Were Good,* 141.
8. Ibid., 145; see also chap. 4.
9. Ibid.
10. Seeger, *Incompleat Folksinger,* 20–21.
11. Ibid., 22.
12. Dunaway, *How Can I Keep from Singing,* 151; see also chap. 7.
13. Cantwell, *When We Were Good,* 290.
14. De Turk and Poulin, *American Folk Scene,* 21–23.
15. Neil Rosenberg, "Introduction," 2.
16. Rodnitsky, "Evolution of the American Protest Song," 37.
17. Cantwell, *Ethnomimesis,* 234–35.
18. Cantwell, "When We Were Good," 176.
19. See Kirshenblatt-Gimblett, "Mistaken Dichotomies"; O'Brien and Roseberry, *Golden Ages, Dark Ages.*
20. Green, *Only a Miner,* 5.
21. Garland, *Welcome the Traveler Home,* 14.
22. Green, "Hillbilly Music," 223.
23. Malone, *Southern Music, American Music,* 63.
24. AMJ, Green tape FT 2838.
25. Greenway, *American Folksongs of Protest,* 8.
26. Dunaway, "Music and Politics in the United States," 269.
27. Greenway, *American Folksongs of Protest,* 10.
28. Denisoff, *Sing a Song of Social Significance,* 5–7.
29. Rodnitsky, "Evolution of the American Protest Song," 37.
30. Reuss, "American Folklore and Left-Wing Politics," 36.
31. Reuss, "Roots of American Left-Wing Interest in Folksong," 269–70.

32. Charles Seeger, quoted in Reuss, "Folk Music and Social Conscience," 228.

33. Reuss, "Roots of American Left-Wing Interest in Folksong," 271.

34. Williams, "Radicalism and Professionalism in Folklore Studies," 218.

35. Lieberman, *"My Song Is My Weapon,"* 37–39.

36. Reuss, "American Folklore and Left-Wing Politics," 105–6.

37. Reuss, "Folk Music and Social Conscience," 232; see also Green, "Resettlement Administration Song Sheet," and Warren-Findley, "Passports to Change."

38. Reuss, "Folk Music and Social Conscience," 236.

39. Green, "Charles Louis Seeger," 397.

40. Siegmeister, *Music Lover's Handbook,* 773.

41. Earl Robinson, interview with the author, June 10, 1990, Seattle, Wash.

42. Klein, *Woody Guthrie,* 148, 149.

43. Lieberman, *"My Song Is My Weapon,"* 34–36.

44. Cantwell, *When We Were Good,* 146.

45. Reuss, *American Folklore and Left-Wing Politics,* 172.

46. Denisoff, *Great Day Coming,* 23–25.

47. Filene, "Our Singing Country," 610.

48. SOG, Stekert tape FT 2789.

49. Neil Rosenberg, "Introduction," 12–14.

50. Seeger, "Record Review" (1948), 218.

51. Stekert, "Cents and Nonsense in the Urban Folksong Movement," 87.

52. Ibid., 91 n. 6.

53. Seeger, "Folkness of the Non-Folk vs. the Non-Folkness of the Folk," 4.

54. AMJ, Green tape FT 4289.

55. AMJ, Green tape FT 2839.

56. Seeger, "Record Review" (1948), 216.

57. Seeger, "Record Review" (1949), 68–69.

58. Seeger, "Record Review" (1948), 216.

59. AMJ, Green tape FT 4289.

60. AMJ, Green tape FT 4290.

61. Benford, "Folklorists and Us."

62. Davis, "Music from the Left," 8–9.

63. Phone interview, June 19, 1991.

64. Lemisch, "I Dreamed I Saw MTV."

65. Cohen, "Overview, John Cohen I," 29.

66. Botkin, "Folksong Revival," 99–100.

67. Hazel Dickens, interview with the author, May 20, 1990, New York, N.Y.

68. Posen, "On Folk Festivals and Kitchens."

Chapter 7: "Dreadful Memories"

The chapter title comes from a song for which Molly Jackson and Sarah Ogan Gunning both claimed authorship.

1. Clifford and Marcus, *Writing Culture.*

2. Rosaldo and Lamphere, *Women, Culture, and Society.*

3. Etienne and Leacock, *Women and Colonization.*

4. See Ardener, *Perceiving Women.*

5. Kadar, "Coming to Terms," 5–12.

6. See for example, Joan Scott, *Gender and the Politics of History;* and di Leonardo, *Gender at the Crossroads of Knowledge.*

7. Hall, "Disorderly Women," 355.

8. James Scott, *Weapons of the Weak.*

9. Abu Lughod, "Romance of Resistance."

10. Kaplan, "Female Consciousness and Collective Action," 545.

11. See Romalis, "Carrying Greenham Home"; Romalis, "From Kitchen to Global Politics."

12. Van Allen, "Sitting on a Man."

13. Romalis and Romalis, "Sexism, Racism, and Technological Change."

14. Femenia, "Argentina's Mothers of Plaza De Mayo."

15. Harriet Rosenberg, "From Trash to Treasure."

16. See Hall, Korstad, and Leloudis, "Cotton Mill People," for an extensive analysis.

17. Hall, "Disorderly Women."

18. Haessly, "'Mill Mother's Lament,'" 74.

19. Larkin, "Ella May's Songs," 383.

20. Ibid., 382.

21. Ibid., 385.

22. Ibid., 382.

23. Haessly, "'Mill Mother's Lament,'" 21–22.

24. Hall, "Disorderly Women," 356.

25. Haessly, "'Mill Mother's Lament,'" 29.

26. Garland, *Welcome the Traveler Home,* 64–65.

27. Foner, *Women and the American Labor Movement,* 246.

28. Hall, "Disorderly Women," 366–67.

29. Long, *Mother Jones, Woman Organizer,* 2.

30. Green, *Only a Miner,* 246.

31. Ibid., 261.

32. Gilbert, *Ronnie Gilbert on Mother Jones,* 12.

33. Green, *Only a Miner,* 247.

34. Ibid., 270.

35. Jones, *Autobiography of Mother Jones,* 32.

36. Ibid., 34.

37. Ibid., 90–91.

38. Ibid.; quotes from 145–47.

39. Ibid., 72.

40. Ibid., 203.

41. Gilbert, *Ronnie Gilbert on Mother Jones,* 10.

42. Long, "Women of the Colorado Fuel and Iron Strike," 63–64.

43. Lasky, "'Where I Was a Person,'" 183.

44. Gilbert, *Ronnie Gilbert on Mother Jones,* 17.

45. Kirchwey, "Miners' Wives in the Coal Strike," 89.

46. Foner, *Women and the American Labor Movement,* 247–48.

47. Long, "Women of the Colorado Fuel and Iron Strike," 81.

48. Wiley, "Songs of the Gastonia Textile Strike of 1929," 95.

49. Greenway, *American Folksongs of Protest,* 166.

50. See Yurchenco, "Trouble in the Mines."

51. Greenway, *American Folksongs of Protest,* 266–67.

52. AMJ, Green tape FT 2838.

53. Green, *Only a Miner,* 80.

54. Greenway, *American Folksongs of Protest,* 274–75.

55. SOG, Green tape FT 2781.

Reflections

The subtitle slightly alters the title of a traditional song, "Don't You Be a Grievin' after Me."

1. Reuss, "American Folklore and Left-Wing Politics," 184–85.

2. Berkinow, *World Split Open,* 305–30.

3. Wolf, *Thrice-Told Tale,* 11.

4. Green, "Folklorist's Creed and Folksinger's Gift," 42.

5. SOG, Green tape FT 2782.

6. SOG, Stekert tape FT 2791.

7. Sternbach, "Re-membering the Dead," 92–93.

8. Stephen, "On the Politics and Practice of Testimonial Literature," 69.

9. Ibid., 71–72.

10. Zimmerman, "*Testimonio* in Guatemala," 32.

11. Barrios de Chungara, *Let Me Speak!* 163.

12. Sternbach, "Re-membering the Dead," 97.

13. Menchú, *I, Rigoberta Menchú,* 224.

14. Sternbach, "Re-membering the Dead," 94–95.

15. Abrahams, "Creativity, Individuality, and the Traditional Singer," 12.

16. AMJ, Green tape FT 4289.

17. Stacey, "Can There Be a Feminist Ethnography?"; Diane Wolf, *Feminist Dilemmas in Fieldwork.*

18. Portelli, *Death of Luigi Trastulli,* 53.

19. Greenway, "Aunt Molly Jackson as an Informant," 141.

20. Green, "Folklorist's Creed and Folksinger's Gift," 43.

21. SOG, Stekert tape FT 2793.

Bibliography

Abrahams, Roger D. "Creativity, Individuality, and the Traditional Singer." *Studies in the Literary Imagination* 3.1 (April 1970): 5–34.

Abu Lughod, Lila. "The Romance of Resistance: Tracing Transformations of Power through Bedouin Women." *American Ethnologist* 17.1 (1990): 41–55.

Alvarado, Elvia, and Medea Benjamin, trans. and eds. *Don't Be Afraid Gringo: A Honduran Woman Speaks from the Heart—The Story of Elvia Alvarado.* San Francisco: Institute for Food and Development Policy, 1987.

Anderson, Sherwood. "I Want to Be Counted." In *Harlan Miners Speak: Report on Terrorism in the Kentucky Coal Fields.* National Committee for the Defense of Political Prisoners. 298–312. 1932; rpt., New York: Da Capo Press, 1970.

Ardener, Shirley, ed. *Perceiving Women.* London: J. M. Dent and Sons, 1975.

Baggelaar, Kristin, and Donald Milton. *Folk Music: More Than a Song.* New York: Crowell, 1976.

Barrios de Chungara, Domitila. *Let Me Speak!: Testimony of Domitila, a Woman of the Bolivian Mines.* Trans. Victoria Ortiz. New York: Monthly Review Press, 1978.

Batteau, Allen W. *The Invention of Appalachia.* Tucson: University of Arizona Press, 1990.

Behar, Ruth. *Translated Woman.* Boston: Beacon Press, 1993.

———, and Deborah Gordon, eds. *Women Writing Culture.* Berkeley: University of California Press, 1995.

Benford, Mac. "Folklorists and Us: An Account of Our Curious and Changing Relationship (with More Personal Reminiscences)." *Old Time Herald* 1.7 (Feb–April 1989): 22–27.

Berkinow, Louise, ed. *The World Split Open: Four Centuries of Women Poets in England and America, 1552–1950.* New York: Vintage Press, 1974.

Botkin, Benjamin. "The Folksong Revival: Cult or Culture?" In *The American Folk Scene.* Ed. David A. De Turk and A. Poulin Jr. 95–100. New York: Dell, 1967.

Cantwell, Robert. *Ethnomimesis: Folklife and the Representation of Culture.* Chapel Hill: University of North Carolina Press, 1993.

———. "When We Were Good: The Folk Revival." In *Folk Roots, New Roots: Folklore in American Life*. Ed. Jane C. Becker and Barbara Franco. 167–93. Lexington, Mass.: Museum of Our National Heritage, 1988.

———. *When We Were Good: The Folk Revival*. Cambridge, Mass.: Harvard University Press, 1996.

Caplan, Patricia. "Engendering Knowledge." *Anthropology Today* 4.5 (1988): 8–12 and 4.6 (1988): 14–17.

Clifford, James, and George Marcus, eds. *Writing Culture: The Poetics and Politics of Ethnography*. Berkeley: University of California Press, 1986.

Cohen, John. "Overview, John Cohen I." In *"Wasn't That a Time!": Firsthand Accounts of the Folk Music Revival*. Ed. Ronald D. Cohen. 25–56. Metuchen, N.J.: Scarecrow Press, 1995.

Cohen, Ronald D., ed. *"Wasn't That a Time!": Firsthand Accounts of the Folk Music Revival*. Metuchen, N.J.: Scarecrow Press, 1995.

Coles, Robert. *Migrants, Sharecroppers, Mountaineers*. Vol. 2: *Children of Crisis*. Boston: Little, Brown, 1971.

Corbin, David Alan. *Life, Work, and Rebellion in the Coal Fields: The Southern West Virginia Miners, 1880-1922*. Urbana: University of Illinois Press, 1981.

Crawford, Bruce. "What Have We to Lose?: The Story of Harlan, Kentucky." In *The National Miners Union, Harlan and Bell Kentucky, 1931-32*. Compilation from the *Labor Defender* and *Labor Age*. Huntington, W.Va.: Appalachian Movement Press, 1972.

Cunningham, Rodger. *Apples on the Flood: The Southern Mountain Experience*. Knoxville: University of Tennessee Press, 1987.

Davis, Ron. "Music from the Left." *Rethinking Marxism* 1.4 (Winter 1988): 7–25.

Denisoff, R. Serge. *Great Day Coming: Folk Music and the American Left*. Urbana: University of Illinois Press, 1971.

———. *Sing a Song of Social Significance*. Bowling Green, Ohio: Bowling Green University Popular Press, 1972.

Denning, Michael. *The Cultural Front: The Laboring of American Culture in the Twentieth Century*. London: Verso, 1996.

De Turk, David A., and A. Poulin Jr., eds. *The American Folk Scene*. New York: Dell, 1967.

di Leonardo, Micaela, ed. *Gender at the Crossroads of Knowledge: Feminist Anthropology in the Post-Modern Era*. Berkeley: University of California Press, 1991.

Dos Passos, John. "The Free Speech Speakin's." In *Harlan Miners Speak: Report on Terrorism in the Kentucky Coal Fields*. National Committee for the Defense of Political Prisoners. 277–97. 1932; rpt., New York: Da Capo Press, 1970.

———. "The Miners Speak for Themselves." In *Harlan Miners Speak: Report on Terrorism in the Kentucky Coal Fields*. National Committee for the Defense of Political Prisoners. 91–228. 1932; rpt., New York: Da Capo Press, 1970.

———. "Harlan: Working under the Gun." In *The New Republic*, Dec. 2, 1931, 62–67.

Draper, Theodore. "Communists and Miners, 1928–1933." *Dissent* 19.2 (Spring 1972): 371–92.

Dreiser, Theodore. "Introduction." In *Harlan Miners Speak: Report on Terrorism in the Kentucky Coal Fields.* National Committee for the Defense of Political Prisoners. 3–16. 1932; rpt., New York: Da Capo Press, 1970.

Dunaway, David. "Charles Seeger and Carl Sands: The Composers' Collective Years." *Ethnomusicology* 24 (1980): 159–68.

———. *How Can I Keep from Singing: Pete Seeger.* 1981; rpt., New York: Da Capo Press, 1990.

———. "Music and Politics in the United States." *Folk Music Journal* 5.3 (1987): 268–94.

Eller, Ronald D. "Industrialization and Social Change in Appalachia, 1880–1930: A Look at the Static Image." In *Colonialism in Modern America: The Appalachian Case.* Ed. Helen Matthews Lewis, Linda Johnson, and Donald Askins. 35–46. Boone, N.C.: Appalachian Consortium, 1978.

———. *Miners, Millhands, and Mountaineers: Industrialization of the Appalachian South, 1880–1930.* Knoxville: University of Tennessee Press, 1982.

Etienne, Mona, and Eleanor Leacock. *Women and Colonization.* New York: Praeger, 1980.

Federal Writers' Project. *Guide to 1930s New York.* 1939; rpt., New York: Random House, 1982.

Femenia, Nora Amalia. "Argentina's Mothers of Plaza De Mayo: The Mourning Process from Junta to Democracy." *Feminist Studies* 13.1 (Spring 1987): 9–18.

Filene, Benjamin. "'Our Singing Country': John and Alan Lomax, Leadbelly, and the Construction of an American Past." *American Quarterly* 43.4 (Dec. 1991): 602–24.

Foner, Philip S. *Women and the American Labor Movement: From World War I to the Present.* New York: Free Press, 1980.

Garland, Jim. "Biography." Album notes to *Silver Dagger.* Recording by Sarah Ogan Gunning. Rounder 0051. 1976.

———. *Welcome the Traveler Home: Jim Garland's Story of the Kentucky Mountains.* Ed. Julia S. Ardery. Lexington: University Press of Kentucky, 1983.

Gaventa, John. *Power and Powerlessness: Quiescence and Rebellion in an Appalachian Valley.* Urbana: University of Illinois Press, 1982.

Geiger, Susan. "Women's Life Histories: Method and Content." *Signs* 11.2 (1986): 334–51.

Gilbert, Ronnie. *Ronnie Gilbert on Mother Jones: Face to Face with the Most Dangerous Woman in America.* Berkeley: Conari Press, 1993.

Ginsburg, Faye, and Anna Lowenhaupt Tsing, eds. *Uncertain Terms: Negotiating Gender in American Culture.* Boston: Beacon Press, 1990.

Gordon, Eric A. *Mark the Music: The Life and Work of Marc Blitzstein.* New York: St. Martin's Press, 1989.

Green, Archie. "Aunt Molly Jackson: A Bio-Bibliography." Ms. Archie Green Papers. Southern Folklife Collection, University of North Carolina at Chapel Hill. 1964.

———. "Ben Robertson Meets Aunt Molly." *Kentucky Folklore Record* 7.4 (Oct.–Dec. 1961): 133–39.

———. "Charles Louis Seeger (1886–1979)." *Journal of American Folklore* 92 (Oct.–Dec. 1979): 391–99.

———. "A Folklorist's Creed and Folksinger's Gift." *Appalachian Journal* 7.1–2 (Autumn–Winter 1979–80): 37–45.

———. "Hillbilly Music: Source and Symbol." *Journal of American Folklore* 78 (July–Sept. 1965): 204–28.

———. Notes to *Girl of Constant Sorrow*. Recorded by Sarah Ogan Gunning. Folk-Legacy Records FSA-26. 1965.

———. *Only a Miner: Studies in Recorded Coal-Mining Songs*. Urbana: University of Illinois Press, 1972.

———. "A Resettlement Administration Song Sheet." *JEMF Quarterly* 11.2 (Summer 1975): 80–87.

———, ed. *Aunt Molly Jackson Memorial Issue*. Special issue of *Kentucky Folklore Record* 7.4 (Oct.–Dec. 1961).

Greenway, John. *American Folksongs of Protest*. Philadelphia: University of Pennsylvania Press, 1953.

———. "Aunt Molly Jackson and Robin Hood: A Study in Folk Re-creation." *Journal of American Folklore* 69 (1956): 23–38.

———. "Aunt Molly Jackson as an Informant." *Kentucky Folklore Record* 7.4 (Oct.–Dec. 1961): 141–46.

———. "A Great Rebel Passes On." *Sing Out!* 10 (Dec.–Jan. 1960–61): 31–32.

———. "The Songs and Stories of Aunt Molly Jackson." Folkways Records FH 5457, 1961.

Gunning, Sarah Ogan. "My Name Is Sarah Ogan Gunning. . . ." *Sing Out!* 25.2 (July–Aug. 1976): 15–17.

Guthrie, Woody. "Hell Busts Loose in Kentucky." In *Hard Hitting Songs for Hard-Hit People*. Ed. Alan Lomax, Woody Guthrie, and Pete Seeger. 139–40. New York: Oak, 1967.

———. "The Story of Sara Ogan." In *Hard Hitting Songs for Hard-Hit People*. Ed. Alan Lomax, Woody Guthrie, and Pete Seeger. 154–55. New York: Oak, 1967.

Haessly, Jo Lynn. "'Mill Mother's Lament': Ella May, Working Women's Militancy, and the 1929 Gaston County Strikes." Master's thesis. University of North Carolina, Chapel Hill, 1987.

Hall, Jacquelyn Dowd. "Disorderly Women: Gender and Labor Militancy in the Appalachian South." *Journal of American History* 73.1–2 (Sept. 1986): 354–82.

———, Robert Korstad, and James Leloudis. "Cotton Mill People: Work, Community, and Protest in the Textile South, 1880–1940." *American Historical Review* 91.2 (Apr. 1986): 245–86.

Handler, Richard, and Jocelyn Linnekin. "Tradition, Genuine or Spurious." *Journal of American Folklore* 97 (1984): 273–90.

Hevener, John. *Which Side Are You On?: The Harlan County Coal Miners, 1931–39*. Urbana: University of Illinois Press, 1978.

Howe, Irving. "New York in the Thirties: Some Fragments of Memory." *Dissent* 8.3 (Summer 1961): 241–50.

Jackson, Molly. "I Am from Kentucky Born." Pamphlet reproduced from the *Labour Defender, The National Miners Union, Harlan and Bell Kentucky, 1931–32*. Huntington, W.Va.: Appalachian Movement Press, June 1972.

Johnson, Oakley. "Starvation and the 'Reds' in Kentucky." *The Nation,* Feb. 3, 1932, 141–43.

Jones, Mother. *Autobiography of Mother Jones.* Ed. Mary Field Parton. 1925; rpt., New York: Arno and the New York Times, 1969.

Kadar, Marlene. "Coming to Terms: Life Writing—From Genre to Critical Practice." In *Essays on Life Writing: From Genre to Critical Practice.* Ed. Marlene Kadar. 5–16. Toronto: University of Toronto Press, 1992.

Kaplan, Temma. "Female Consciousness and Collective Action: The Case of Barcelona, 1910–1918." *Signs* 7.3 (1982): 545–66.

Keely, Josiah. "Successful Wives in Coal Camps." *Coal Age,* Apr. 7, 1917, 591–92.

Kirchwey, Freda. "Miners' Wives in the Coal Strike." *Century* 105 (Nov. 1922): 83–90.

Kirshenblatt-Gimblett, Barbara. "Mistaken Dichotomies." *Journal of American Folklore* 101 (April–June 1988): 140–55.

Klein, Joe. *Woody Guthrie: A Life.* New York: Knopf, 1980.

Kohli, Martin. "Biography: Account, Text, Method." In *Biography and Society: The Life History Approach in the Social Sciences.* Ed. Daniel Bertaux. 61–75. Beverly Hills, Calif.: Sage, 1981.

Korson, George. *Coal Dust on the Fiddle: Songs and Stories of the Bituminous Industry.* Philadelphia: University of Pennsylvania Press, 1943.

Langness L. L., and Gelya Frank. *Lives: An Anthropological Approach to Biography.* Novato, Calif.: Chandler and Sharp, 1981.

Larkin, Margaret. "Ella May's Songs." *The Nation,* Oct. 9, 1929, 382–83.

———. "Revolutionary Music." *New Masses* 8 (Feb. 27, 1933): 27.

Lasky, Marjorie Penn. "'Where I Was a Person': The Ladies' Auxiliary in the 1934 Minneapolis Teamsters' Strikes." In *Women, Work, and Protest: A Century of U.S. Women's Labor History.* Ed. Ruth Milkman. 181–205. Boston: Routledge and Kegan Paul, 1985.

Lemisch, Jessie. "I Dreamed I Saw MTV Last Night." *The Nation,* Oct. 18, 1986, 372–76; response letters, Dec. 13, 1986.

Lieberman, Robbie. *"My Song Is My Weapon": People's Songs, American Communism, and the Politics of Culture, 1930–50.* 1989; rpt., Urbana: University of Illinois Press, 1995.

Lomax, Alan. "Aunt Molly Jackson: An Appreciation." *Kentucky Folklore Record* 7.4 (Oct.–Dec. 1961): 131–32.

———, Woody Guthrie, and Pete Seeger, eds. *Hard Hitting Songs for Hard-Hit People.* New York: Oak, 1967.

Long, Priscilla. *Mother Jones, Woman Organizer: And Her Relations with Miner's Wives, Working Women, and the Suffrage Movement.* 1–40. N.p.: Red Sun Press, 1976.

———. "The Women of the Colorado Fuel and Iron Strike, 1913–14." In *Women, Work, and Protest: A Century of U.S. Women's Labor History.* Ed. Ruth Milkman. 62–85. Boston: Routledge and Kegan Paul, 1985.

Malone, Bill C. *Country Music, U.S.A.* Austin: University of Texas Press, 1968.

———. *Southern Music, American Music.* Lexington: University Press of Kentucky, 1979.

McCulloh, Judy. "Writing for the World." *Journal of American Folklore* 101 (July–Sept. 1988): 293–301.

McCauley, Deborah Vansau. *Appalachian Mountain Religion: A History.* Urbana: University of Illinois Press, 1995.

Menchú, Rigoberta. *I, Rigoberta Menchú: An Indian Woman in Guatemala*. Ed. Elizabeth Burgos-Debray. Trans. Ann Wright. London: Verso, 1984.

Moore, Henrietta L. *Feminism and Anthropology*. Minneapolis: University of Minnesota Press, 1988.

National Committee for the Defense of Political Prisoners. *Harlan Miners Speak: Report on Terrorism in the Kentucky Coal Fields*. 1932; rpt., New York: Da Capo Press, 1970.

O'Brien, Jan, and William Roseberry. *Golden Ages, Dark Ages: Imagining the Past in Anthropology and History*. Berkeley: University of California Press, 1991.

Polier, Nicole, and William Roseberry. "Tristes Tropes: Post-Modern Anthropologists Encounter the Other and Discover Themselves." *Economy and Society* 18.2 (May 1989): 245–64.

Popular Memory Group. "Popular Memory: Theory, Politics, Method." In *Making Histories: Studies in History-Writing and Politics*. Ed. Richard Johnson et al. 205–52. London: Hutchinson, 1982.

Portelli, Alessandro. *The Death of Luigi Trastulli and Other Stories: Form and Meaning in Oral History*. Albany: State University of New York Press, 1991.

Posen, I. Sheldon. "On Folk Festivals and Kitchens: Questions of Authenticity in the Folksong Revival." In *Transforming Tradition: Folk Music Revivals Examined*. Ed. Neil V. Rosenberg. 127–36. Urbana: University of Illinois Press, 1993.

Raitz, Karl, and Richard Ulack. *Appalachia, a Regional Geography: Land, People, and Development*. Boulder, Colo.: Westview Press, 1984.

Reuss, Richard A. "American Folklore and Left-Wing Politics, 1927–1957." Ph.D. diss. Indiana University, 1971.

———. "Folk Music and Social Conscience: The Musical Odyssey of Charles Seeger." *Western Folklore* 38.4 (Oct. 1979): 221–38.

———. "The Roots of American Left-Wing Interest in Folksong." *Labor History* 12.2 (Spring 1971): 259–79.

Rodnitzky, Jerome. "The Evolution of the American Protest Song." *Journal of Popular Culture* 3.1 (Summer 1969): 35–45.

Romalis, Shelly. "Carrying Greenham Home: The Women's Peace Support Network." *Atlantis* 12.2 (Spring 1987): 90–98.

———. "From Kitchen to Global Politics: The Women of Greenham Common." In *Up and Doing: Canadian Women and Peace*. Ed. Janice Williamson and Deborah Gorham. 170–74. Toronto: Women's Press, 1989.

———, and Coleman Romalis. "Sexism, Racism, and Technological Change: Two Cases of Minority Protest." *International Journal of Women's Studies* 6.3 (May–June 1983): 270–87.

Rosaldo, Michelle, and Louise Lamphere, eds. *Women, Culture, and Society*. Stanford: Stanford University Press, 1974.

Rosenberg, Harriet. "From Trash to Treasure: Housewife Activists and the Environmental Justice Movement." In *Articulating Hidden Histories: Exploring the Influence of Eric R. Wolf*. Ed. Jane Schneider and Rayna Rapp. 190–204. Berkeley: University of California Press, 1995.

Rosenberg, Neil V. "Introduction." In *Transforming Tradition: Folk Music Revivals Examined*. Ed. Neil V. Rosenberg. 1–25. Urbana: University of Illinois Press, 1993.

Ross, Malcolm. *Machine Age in the Hills.* New York: MacMillan, 1933.

Scott, James C. *Weapons of the Weak: Everyday Forms of Peasant Resistance.* New Haven, Conn.: Yale University Press, 1985.

Scott, Joan Wallach. *Gender and the Politics of History.* New York: Columbia University Press, 1988.

Seeger, Charles. "The Folkness of the Non-Folk vs. the Non-Folkness of the Folk." In *Folklore and Society: Essays in Honor of Benjamin A. Botkin.* Ed. Bruce Jackson. 1–9. Hatboro, Pa.: Folklore Associates, 1966.

———. "Record Review." *Journal of American Folklore* 61 (Apr.–June 1948): 215–18.

———. "Record Review." *Journal of American Folklore* 62 (Jan.–Mar. 1949): 68–70.

———. *Studies in Musicology, 1935–1975.* Berkeley: University of California Press, 1977.

Seeger, Pete. *The Incompleat Folksinger.* Ed. Jo Metcalf Schwartz. 1972; rpt., Lincoln: University of Nebraska Press, 1992.

Shapiro, Henry D. *Appalachia on Our Mind: The Southern Mountains and Mountaineers in the American Consciousness, 1870–1920.* Chapel Hill: University of North Carolina Press, 1978.

Sharp, Cecil. *English Folksongs from the Southern Appalachians.* 2 vols. London: Oxford University Press, 1966.

Shifflett, Crandall A. *Coal Towns: Life, Work, and Culture in Company Towns of Southern Appalachia, 1880–1960.* Knoxville: University of Tennessee Press, 1991.

Siegmeister, Elie, ed. *The Music Lover's Handbook.* New York: William Morrow, 1943.

Smyth, Willie. "Album Notes: TFS 108—*It's Just the Same Today.*" Barnicle-Cadle Field Recordings from Eastern Tennessee and Kentucky, 1938–49. Tennessee Folklore Society, 1986.

Stacey, Judith. "Can There Be a Feminist Ethnography?" *Women's Studies International Forum* 11.1 (1988): 21–27.

Stekert, Ellen. "Cents and Nonsense in the Urban Folksong Movement, 1930–66." In *Transforming Tradition: Folk Music Revivals Examined.* Ed. Neil V. Rosenberg. 84–106. Urbana: University of Illinois Press, 1993.

Stephen, Lynn. "On the Politics and Practice of Testimonial Literature: The Story of Maria Teresa Tula and the CO-MADRES of El Salvador." *Latino American Journal* 4.1 (Jan. 1993): 55–78.

Sternbach, Nancy Saporta. "Re-membering the Dead: Latin American Women's 'Testimonial' Discourse." *Latin American Perspectives* 18.3 (Summer 1991): 91–102.

Swanberg, W. A. *Dreiser.* New York: Charles Scribner's Sons, 1965.

Thomas, Jeanette. *Ballad Makin' in the Mountains of Kentucky.* New York: Henry Holt, 1939.

Tippett, Tom. *When Southern Labor Stirs.* New York: Jonathan Cape and Harrison Smith, 1931.

Torgovnick, Marianna. *Gone Primitive: Savage Intellects, Modern Lives.* Chicago: University of Chicago Press, 1990.

Tosches, Nick. "Interview with Al Dexter." *Old Time Music* 22 (1976): 4–8.

Van Allen, Judith. "Sitting on a Man: Colonialism and the Lost Political Institutions of Igbo Women." *Canadian Journal of African Studies* 6.2 (1972): 165–81.

Warren-Findley, Janelle. "Passports to Change: The Resettlement Administration Folk Song Sheet Program, 1936–1937." *Prospects: An Annual of American Cultural Studies*, 10th ed. Ed. Jack Salmon. 197–241. Cambridge, U.K.: Cambridge University Press, 1986.

Whisnant, David E. *All That Is Native and Fine: The Politics of Culture in an American Region.* Chapel Hill: University of North Carolina Press, 1983.

Wiley, Stephen R. "Songs of the Gastonia Textile Strike of 1929: Models of and for Southern Working-Class Woman's Militancy." *North Carolina Folklore Journal* 30.2 (Fall–Winter 1982): 87–98.

Williams, John Alexander. "Radicalism and Professionalism in Folklore Studies: A Comparative Perspective." *Journal of the Folklore Institute* 11.3 (Mar. 1975): 211–34.

Wolf, Diane L., ed. *Feminist Dilemmas in Fieldwork.* Boulder, Colo.: Westview Press, 1996.

Wolf, Margery. *A Thrice-Told Tale: Feminism, Postmodernism, and Ethnographic Responsibility.* Stanford: Stanford University Press, 1992.

Wolfe, Charles, and Kip Lornell. *The Life and Legend of Leadbelly.* New York: HarperCollins, 1992.

Yurchenco, Henrietta. "Trouble in the Mines: A History in Song and Story by Women of Appalachia." *American Music* 9.2 (Summer 1991): 209–24.

Zimmerman, Marc. "*Testimonio* in Guatemala: Payeras, Rigoberta, and Beyond." *Latin American Perspectives* 18.4 (Fall 1991): 22–47.

Index

SHELLY ROMALIS is an associate professor of anthropology at York University in Toronto, Canada. At one time she was simultaneously the director of York's Graduate Program in Interdisciplinary Studies, organizer of the Woods Music and Dance Society, a founding member of the Folk Alliance, a singer, and a fiddle player.

Music in American Life

Only a Miner: Studies in Recorded Coal-Mining Songs   *Archie Green*
Great Day Coming: Folk Music and the American Left   *R. Serge Denisoff*
John Philip Sousa: A Descriptive Catalog of His Works   *Paul E. Bierley*
The Hell-Bound Train: A Cowboy Songbook   *Glenn Ohrlin*
Oh, Didn't He Ramble: The Life Story of Lee Collins, as Told to Mary
    Collins   *Edited by Frank J. Gillis and John W. Miner*
American Labor Songs of the Nineteenth Century   *Philip S. Foner*
Stars of Country Music: Uncle Dave Macon to Johnny Rodriguez   *Edited by*
    Bill C. Malone and Judith McCulloh
Git Along, Little Dogies: Songs and Songmakers of the American West
    John I. White
A Texas-Mexican *Cancionero:* Folksongs of the Lower Border   *Américo Paredes*
San Antonio Rose: The Life and Music of Bob Wills   *Charles R. Townsend*
Early Downhome Blues: A Musical and Cultural Analysis   *Jeff Todd Titon*
An Ives Celebration: Papers and Panels of the Charles Ives Centennial Festival-
    Conference   *Edited by H. Wiley Hitchcock and Vivian Perlis*
Sinful Tunes and Spirituals: Black Folk Music to the Civil War   *Dena J. Epstein*
Joe Scott, the Woodsman-Songmaker   *Edward D. Ives*
Jimmie Rodgers: The Life and Times of America's Blue Yodeler   *Nolan Porterfield*
Early American Music Engraving and Printing: A History of Music Publishing in
    America from 1787 to 1825, with Commentary on Earlier and Later Practices
    Richard J. Wolfe
Sing a Sad Song: The Life of Hank Williams   *Roger M. Williams*
Long Steel Rail: The Railroad in American Folksong   *Norm Cohen*
Resources of American Music History: A Directory of Source Materials from
    Colonial Times to World War II   *D. W. Krummel, Jean Geil, Doris J. Dyen,*
    and Deane L. Root
Tenement Songs: The Popular Music of the Jewish Immigrants   *Mark Slobin*
Ozark Folksongs   *Vance Randolph; edited and abridged by Norm Cohen*
Oscar Sonneck and American Music   *Edited by William Lichtenwanger*
Bluegrass Breakdown: The Making of the Old Southern Sound   *Robert Cantwell*
Bluegrass: A History   *Neil V. Rosenberg*
Music at the White House: A History of the American Spirit   *Elise K. Kirk*
Red River Blues: The Blues Tradition in the Southeast   *Bruce Bastin*
Good Friends and Bad Enemies: Robert Winslow Gordon and the Study of
    American Folksong   *Debora Kodish*
Fiddlin' Georgia Crazy: Fiddlin' John Carson, His Real World, and the World of
    His Songs   *Gene Wiggins*
America's Music: From the Pilgrims to the Present (rev. 3d ed.)
    Gilbert Chase
Secular Music in Colonial Annapolis: The Tuesday Club, 1745–56
    John Barry Talley
Bibliographical Handbook of American Music   *D. W. Krummel*
Goin' to Kansas City   *Nathan W. Pearson, Jr.*